FAMILY SHIFTS
Families, Policies, and Gender Equality

Margrit Eichler

OXFORD UNIVERSITY PRESS
Toronto New York Oxford

Oxford University Press
70 Wynford Drive, Don Mills, Ontario M3C 1J9
http://www.oupcan.com

Oxford New York
Athens Auckland Bangkok Calcutta
Cape Town Chennai Dar es Salaam Delhi
Florence Hong Kong Istanbul Karachi
Kuala Lumpur Madrid Melbourne
Mexico City Mumbai Nairobi Paris
Singapore Taipei Tokyo Toronto Warsaw

and associated companies in
Berlin Ibadan

Oxford is a trademark of Oxford University Press

Canadian Cataloguing in Publication Data

Eichler, Margrit, 1942–
    Family shifts : families, policies, and gender equality

Includes bibliographical references and index.
ISBN 0-19-541250-8

1. Family. 2. Family policy. 3. Sex role. I. Title.

HQ734.E32 1996   306.85   C96-932002-7

Design: Max Gabriel Izod

This book is printed on permanent (acid-free) paper ∞.
Printed in Canada

Contents

Acknowledgements

The first incarnation of this book was a technical report prepared for the Department of Justice entitled 'Fractured Families: Families and Policies under Gender Equality'. It was funded by the Law Reform Fund, Department of Justice Canada. The views expressed herein are solely mine and do not necessarily represent those of the Department of Justice.

Some of the people at the Department of Justice were most helpful at various stages in the preparation of this book. Doug Williams conceived of the project, initiated it, and helped set parameters for the content. Lisa Hitch was a dream come true as a reviewer: she read the chapters and provided helpful comments. Jessica Kerr was my all-around helper: she did innumerable things, from sending me materials to finding other people who might help, straightening out legal references, holding my hand over the telephone on various issues, and occasionally gently prodding me. I am extremely grateful for the support I received. Jim Sturrock provided some unpublished figures related to support payments. Several assistants provided invaluable and competent help: Lianne Carley, Rebecca Chernecki, Doreen Fumia, Sherilyn MacGregor, and Margaret Malone.

Several others helped with specific issues: Riva Lieflander helped me locate materials about spousal violence and sexual abuse; Helene Moussa provided voluminous information about refugees; Ruth Roach Pierson provided several historical references, lent me her materials, and advised on a number of historical issues; and Justice Marvin Zuker provided some advice and materials on family law. Suzanne Peters allowed me to examine her materials on family policy and photocopy all those that were relevant. Yevgenia Issraelyan found and translated statistics on Russian life expectancy data for me.

In particular, I wish to thank Meg Luxton. A year ago I pondered about how to integrate helping relationships among kin, given that I had not found suitable empirical materials on that issue. I shared my concern with Meg, who suggested that I use a case-study approach and then offered a case-study that I was welcome to use—truly a generous offer. Robert Glossop read the entire manuscript and made several incisive and helpful suggestions.

Finally, the folks at Oxford University Press were lovely to work with. Euan White was my first and ongoing contact. Valerie Ahwee, as developmental editor, did a lot to straighten out my convoluted Germanic sentences; wherever they remain convoluted, it is at my insistence.

Introduction: Family Shifts

Families are groups with a shifting composition. This was so in the past and is so now. New members join through birth, marriage, or by moving in together. Others leave through death, desertion, separation, divorce, or by moving out. The fact that people come and go and that both those who stay and those who leave have to adjust to changing circumstances is therefore not new.

Nevertheless, there is a new type of movement shaking families today. It is a tectonic shift. The very ground on which families are built has shifted. This underground shift creates a general instability. We do not recognize the ground any longer. As a consequence, it may be difficult to assess exactly where we are because the landscape has altered. As we see new landmarks, we try to describe them, but the ground keeps shifting.

One such shift has been the introduction of gender equality as a legal and moral principle. Families used to be firmly premised on the notion of gender differentiation. Now we are faced with the legal and moral request for gender equality. It necessitates a rethinking and re-evaluation of what being a spouse, a parent, and a child is all about. What can my partner, my child, or my parent reasonably expect from me? What can I reasonably expect from her or him?

Technology has completely altered the way we experience pregnancy and birth. No longer do the old rules apply. Postmenopausal women have given birth to the genetic children of their own child. The first child generated without viable sperm has been born.[1] Children are generated from the genetic materials of dead parents.[2]

Regardless of how they are generated, many families fracture. Many fathers (and some mothers) do not live with their biological children. Hence more and more children will experience a complex form of parenting—living with one parent, while having sporadic (if any) contact with the other biological parent. They may be parented by a stepfather, who may have one or more biological children with whom he does not play an active father role often enough.

Our conceptual apparatus has not kept pace with these developments. There are now a multitude of familial relationships for which we have not yet evolved the language to describe appropriately. This may have serious policy consequences. For instance, we tend to include under the term 'family' spousal relationships, child-parent relationships, sibling relationships, and more extended familial relationships. One assumption used to be that spousal and parental relationships involved the same adults, yet this is no longer the case for an increasing proportion of people. They are neither married, nor do they live with the biological parent of their children, and they may be married to someone else. If these relationships are simply identified as 'family', without recognizing the fundamentally different relationships involved, it will lead to muddled thinking and inappropriate policies.[3]

Our policies have become so complicated that the definition of spouse in the 1994 income tax guide takes up a good portion of a page! Twenty years earlier, the term was not defined at all because it was considered obvious. This is simply one indication that we no longer know what the terms husband and wife, father and mother actually mean. Do spouses include common-law and same-sex spouses? Is the second husband of the woman who brought the children into the union the father of those children, or is it the biological father, with whom the children have no contact, or are both men fathers? Is neither one a father? Is a mother the woman who gave birth to a child, the one from whose egg the child was generated, or the one who is raising it? Are none, one, or all of them a mother to the same child?

There have been a number of highly publicized cases relating to family status in the highest courts in the country, such as the right of lesbian and gay lovers to be recognized as family members,[4] the status of common-law spouses,[5] the taxation of child-support payments,[6] the right to deduct child-care expenses as a business expense,[7] and others.

Policies have to evolve as circumstances change. At present, there seems to be a general agreement that policies and reality are out of sync, but there is no agreement as to how to get them into sync again.[8] Public opinion is divided as to what are appropriate responses. Some argue that we should support families wherever there are familial relations, regardless of the biological, marital, or type of sexual relationship involved. Others argue that this is precisely where the problems started and that we must protect the nuclear family against the demands of alternative types of families to be treated on an equal footing.

The debate about family values, family policy, and family needs is intersected by a debate about gender equality. About 100 years ago, families were based on gender inequality: the wife and mother was responsible for house and children, the husband and father for the economic well-being of the family. The wife was legally, socially, politically, and economically her husband's dependant, not his equal. Today we have an official commitment to gender equality, but families continue to be major vehicles for maintaining gender inequality. One American review of family policy concluded that 'many of the problems that child and family policies are meant to address arise from gender inequality.'[9] Is it possible to have strong and well-functioning families while practising gender equality? What policies are needed to support this goal? Do we know what gender equality means?

Families are the crucibles in which our personalities are formed, and, as such, are crucial to us as individuals. They are equally important for society. If families, as the major caring units, fall apart, society will ultimately fall apart. On the other hand, this is only half the picture. The other half is that society provides the context within which families can prosper—or fail to prosper. If society is under great strain, the strain will be evident in the way families function. This is a particularly serious problem in the 1990s in central and eastern Europe, a region that has undergone tremendous political, social, and economic changes since the late 1980s with the collapse of the Soviet Union. Wherever war and civil strife are tearing apart the social fabric, all other problems are exacerbated.[10] In North America, unemployment results in greatly increased economic, social, and emotional strain within families. The social security net is being dismantled just when families need it the most. Feelings of insecurity are transmitted from the adults to children.[11]

Young people graduating from school (at whatever level) find few jobs, and of those that are available, more and more are only temporary. We are suffering from a surplus of labour power, with devastating effects on those who are not able to find a 'good' job.[12] To make things worse, as the need for social assistance becomes greater, existing benefits are withdrawn. Programs that assisted families are being eliminated. There is a debate about whether this pulling back of the safety net is necessary or not, but it is happening.[13] Just by walking down the street we can see people who have fallen through the holes in the net—and the holes are becoming larger.

The National Forum on Family Security recently put forward the following contentions:

- Quantum shifts, and not tinkering with public perspectives and policy changes, are required to address issues of family security.

- There is a challenge to find a new balance between individual and collective responsibilities to ensure the economic and social security of families and their individual members. There is a need to address the proper balance between public and private approaches.

- The shared commitment to a collective responsibility for ensuring that families are economically capable of raising the next generation of citizens is eroding, and the individualization and privatization of risk is neither in the best interest of individuals and society nor morally acceptable.[14]

I will pick up these contentions in this book, which examines the role that conceptions of the family play in the public policy process. All of us have contact with members of families on an ongoing basis (whether our own or other people's families), and therefore we tend to be aware that major shifts have occurred in familial relationships. Families are, however, at least partially shaped by the policies that affect them. In turn, the policies are shaped by what our politicians, policy makers, and (increasingly) judges think families are or should be. If their thinking is not informed by what is actually happening within families, their policies will not meet our collective needs.

I shall look at how families and family policies have evolved during this century. This involves describing a moving target—the *definition* of what a family is has changed as well.[15] Who gets included in or excluded from families therefore changes over time. Common-law couples and lesbian and gay families are prime examples of such shifts.

In Chapter 1, I will present eight questions that address policies. From the answers to these questions, I will construct two models of families that have underlain past and present policies. I will argue that we have moved from the patriarchal model of the family to the individual responsibility model of the family, and use the federal income tax guide as an example of this shift.

In Chapter 2 I will look at the general social, economic, and legal trends that have affected families in the past decades. These tend to be similar in all highly industrialized countries, suggesting that the changes we are currently experiencing are not due to some peculiar national characteristic but to underlying factors that are shared among otherwise very diverse nations.

In chapters 3 and 4 I will look closely at what has happened with spousal and parental roles. How do we determine whether someone is a spouse or not? It is not easy when neither legal marriage nor a person's sex provides a clear indication of spousal status. Also, how do we know whether someone is a parent or not when there are multiple parenting figures (a biological father or mother, one or more stepfathers or stepmothers) or too few (no parenting father, although the biological father is alive)? How do we determine who is a mother with the splitting of gestational and genetic motherhood?

Having looked at some of the trends and the ensuing uncertainties, in Chapter 5 I turn to the model of the family that underlies most current policies: the individual responsibility model. Close examination suggests that it does not work now and cannot work in principle the way it is supposed to work. And here we take a deep breath. That our policies need to be changed is certainly not a new conclusion. The question is in which direction should we turn?

In Chapter 6 I look at three different conceptions, ranging from a return to the patriarchal family (the stance that underlies most political 'family-value' movements today), the individual responsibility model, and a suggestion for the abolition of the family. None of them seems to overcome the current problems.

Chapter 7 presents an alternative model, the social responsibility model of the family, and outlines some of the policy consequences such a model would entail. Chapter 8 subjects this model to a test by applying it to several current issues, as identified in recent Supreme Court decisions or through an ongoing policy debate.

My conclusions are quite clear: If we want to have strong families, gender equality, and a healthy society, we need to make it possible for people to care for inevitable dependants—that is, children and adults who are unable to look after themselves—by supporting them in this task morally, economically, and socially. Unfortunately, we are faced with a political climate in which the opposite is currently being practised—we are making the task harder and sometimes impossible. This is a short-sighted approach for which we will all have to pay the price in the future. We are rich enough to take a more positive route. One such route is suggested in this book.

From the Patriarchal Model to the Individual Responsibility Model of the Family

INTRODUCTION

Family policies are not a clear set of policies since they include all those that affect families. This includes social welfare legislation, policies concerning social services (such as day care), income tax regulations, provisions in civil and criminal codes that determine who is responsible for certain types of dependants, family law, regulations concerning most social benefits, custody decisions, and many other social tools. These and other policies together constitute what we tend to call 'family policy', although not all of them are always considered.

If one broadly outlines policy changes that have occurred over the past 100 years or so, focusing on the current situation, one needs a way to integrate such disparate information to analyse shifts. I am using three models of the family to serve this function. These models are ideal types[1] in Max Weber's sense of the word—that is, they do not reflect reality perfectly, but measure the degree to which a given policy actually does (or does not) conform to a particular model.[2] In order to create these models, I applied eight questions to various policies:

1. What is the underlying ideology concerning gender equality?[3]

2. What are the assumptions about the legal status of marriage?

3. What are the assumptions about household/family memberships' incongruence/congruence?

4. What is seen as the appropriate unit of administration?

5. What are the assumptions concerning economic responsibility/dependency?

6. What are the assumptions about care and service provision for family members in need of care?

7. What is seen as the appropriate private-public division of responsibilities?

8. What are the assumptions regarding heterosexuality/homosexuality?

I then construct two models of the family based on past and present policies, and one model that outlines desirable (rather than existing) policies. I am not suggesting that policy makers ever got together and decided to adopted any of the models presented here. Policy making is a process that is much too messy for such a rational approach. However, I am suggesting that there are common notions that inform policy makers, and that these notions change over time. Working with these models is simply a way of bringing some order into what is otherwise a hopelessly confusing situation.

The first model is the *patriarchal model* of the family. It is descriptive of the broad outlines of policies that were in vogue until about 1970, after which legislative action and policy making moved us away from the patriarchal model to what I call the *individual responsibility model* of the family. This second model is still operating to a large degree, although it is out of sync, I will argue. The way it answers the eight questions applied to this model are not in accord with the lived reality of many families. I will then develop a third model of the family, *the social responsibility model*, which is grounded in the contemporary empirical reality of families.

The models serve three purposes. First, they allow us to describe disparate policies across very different times in a manner that makes them comparable. Second, they allow us to compare policies with what is actually happening within families and to evaluate these policies. Third, they provide a basis for developing alternative policies. I also use the terms patriarchal and individual responsibility 'family' to characterize families that evolved in response to these policies. Before dealing with the models, however, it is important to recognize an important problem: biases within the literature that deals with families.

SEVEN BIASES IN THE FAMILY LITERATURE

Statements about the family are fraught with judgements. Religions take a definite stance about what are 'good' or 'bad' families, public morality is associated with sexual behaviour that is (or is supposed to be) regulated through families, and all of us have personal feelings about families that stem from our own personal experiences, good or bad, but rarely indifferent. Families are idealized in popular culture, advertising, and marketing; family ideology is used as a political tool; and sometimes families are condemned as the cradle of oppression and everything that is wrong in society. The scholarly literature shows some of these same divisions. It is therefore helpful to have a perspective that enables us to discern various problems as they creep up from behind in scholarly literature as in the popular media.

We can identify seven different biases within the relevant literature. During the 1980s and particularly in the early 1990s, there was some critical literature that tried to avoid some or all of these biases. (And of course there have always been some writers who have successfully avoided the problems.) Nevertheless, having an idea of the biases and therefore a set of concepts that allow us to identify these problems allow us to weigh the evidence in a more reflective manner. The seven biases are the monolithic, conservative, sexist, ageist, microstructural, racist, and heterosexist biases.[4]

The *monolithic bias* is a tendency to treat the family as a monolithic structure by emphasizing uniformity of experience and universality of structure and functions over diversity of experiences, structures, and functions. The *assumption* of uniformity leads to a data collection process that greatly underrepresents the actual diversity. For instance, when Statistics Canada did not collect information on common-law couples, we did not know how many actually existed and therefore could not argue that this was a socially important subform of the family. We still do not know how many couples do not reside together for most of the time, since the census continues to assume that couples have one residence. Nor do we know how many same sex-couples there are or how many biological parents do not live with their biological children, and so on.

Another manifestation of the monolithic bias is confusing a particular *structure* with the fulfilment of certain *functions*. This happens if someone argues that any particular type of family (defined by its composition, e.g., two heterosexual adults and their biological or adopted children) is the single 'best' family form to deal with whatever problems have been identified, rather than examining which types of structures may most effectively handle the identified problems. The non-monolithic way of addressing the question of the 'best' family form is to specify the desired features. For example, I would list genuine love and caring, emotional support from each family member to each member, and the ability to meet the diverse needs of each family member (residential, social, economic, sexual, procreational, etc.). Where these functions are met, we have a well-functioning family, regardless of its structure.

The *conservative bias* consists of a romantic view of the nuclear family in the past and present, while ignoring the ugly aspects of familial relationships (such as wife battering, incest, other types of abuse), which were and continue to be prevalent within this type of family. There is a simultaneous denigration of other family forms.[5]

The *sexist bias* is expressed in many ways, the most important of which is the treatment of the family as the smallest unit of analysis in cases when we are really dealing with individuals within the family. For instance, the sexist bias is present in analyses or policy statements that charge 'the family' with a particular task (such as raising its children, caring for the elderly, etc.) without considering who is actually doing this work (usually women) and how the assignment of such tasks differentially affects women and men.[6] A particularly drastic expression of the sexist bias occurs when there is an assumption that there is a 'natural' division of functions between the sexes.[7]

The *ageist bias* exists when familial interactions are primarily or exclusively considered from the perspective of middle-aged adults, while the perspectives of children, as well as those of the elderly, are largely or entirely ignored.[8]

The *microstructural bias* is a tendency to treat families as encapsulated units. Behaviours are then explained by simply looking at what happens within the unit rather than by trying to understand how familial behaviours are partially affected by extraneous factors. The microstructural bias used to be expressed in a neglect of family policy. This has changed. There is now much literature on various aspects of family policy. However, there are still expressions of this bias to the degree that individuals within families are blamed (there seems to be no celebration of strengths!) without any regard to external circumstances. An example is when people express a concern about 'fostering dependence' among families who receive social assistance without considering the availability or non-availability of jobs, day care, and other infrastructural supports that are necessary if one is to get off welfare.

The *racist bias* devalues families of culturally or ethnically non-dominant groups that tend to be racialized. A particularly tragic example of this in Canadian history has been the treatment of Aboriginal families. Children were put into residential schools and thus alienated from their families and their culture, including their language. If there were family problems, the children were put up for adoption, usually by White couples in Canada and the United States, rather than for custom adoption within the band.[9]

The *heterosexist bias* is treating the heterosexual family as 'natural', thereby denying family status to lesbian and gay families.[10] This includes a postulate that the ability to parent is related to one's sexual orientation.[11]

THREE MODELS OF THE FAMILY

The Patriarchal Model of the Family

Around the turn of the century, the head of the household—that is, the husband in a husband-wife marriage—was the undisputed master of the household, legally, socially, and economically. Legally, the wife was to a large degree subsumed under her husband: she took his name upon marriage, his domicile was her domicile, she had no property rights, she could not conduct business independent from him, etc. Women did not have equal rights (women gained the vote only after the First World

War). A woman could become a head of household only when there was no adult male present. All of this had some bizarre implications.

For instance, the fact that a married woman could not establish her own domicile meant that if her husband deserted her without leaving an address, she could not sue for divorce because one could only sue for divorce in the province of one's domicile—and her domicile was with him! If he moved to another province without her consent and she wanted to divorce him, the woman would have to move to his new province of residence in order to establish a domicile. In practice, this could make divorce impossible for her, given the economic implications of such a move.

The world was quite distinctly divided into masculine and feminine spheres. Science and religion buttressed this world view, which pervaded every aspect of society, but was most strongly expressed within the family. Laws and policies enforced adherence to this model. This was true, to a greater or lesser degree in Euro-America.[12]

With respect to assumptions concerning the legal status of marriage, the clear expectation was that a woman and a man would legally marry in order to be recognized as a couple. This affected not only them but also their children: 'children born out of wedlock' were illegitimate and had a different—a much lower—legal status than did children born in wedlock.[13] People we would today consider spouses in common-law relationships had little protection with respect to inheritance or support in the case of separation. They were considered legal and economic strangers.

There was almost no divorce (there was a total of eleven divorces registered in Canada in 1900).[14] The actual number of marital separations was considerably higher—husbands could desert their families (leave without a forwarding address), or they could leave with a forwarding address. This is sometimes identified as a 'migratory divorce'.[15] Sometimes a man's arrival in Canada was a migratory divorce if he had a wife in England, or Australia, or elsewhere. In such cases, neither husband nor wife could legally remarry, although some did so nevertheless, but if they were found out, they could be imprisoned for bigamy. This meant that in effect family and household members were considered largely identical, if we exclude boarders and servants from our equation.

Life expectancy was significantly lower. In 1931, the life expectancy for a boy at birth was sixty years, whereas in 1993 it was seventy-five years. The life expectancy for a girl at birth was sixty-two years in 1931, and about eighty-one years in 1993.[16] Given the significantly lower life expectancies at the beginning of this century, women and men were often widowed while still actively parenting, whereas today the number of such parents has become statistically insignificant.[17]

In the case of remarriage after widowhood, the new spouse would become the step-parent of any dependent children, with all the rights and responsibilities of a biological parent. However, in the case of remarriage after divorce, this is less likely to be the case if the other parent is still alive and at least potentially available for active parenting, albeit at a distance.

Various policies that supported families treated the family as an administrative unit. For instance, a wife could not receive public assistance if her husband was alive and had some money, even if he did not live with her and did not provide her with financial aid. This was connected to the strong gender-differentiation of tasks, with the husband responsible for the economic well-being of his wife and children, and the wife responsible for the personal care of her husband and their children and all the housework. Consequently, wives and children were treated as economic dependants of the husband/father. This served as a justification for blatant sex discrimination against women: women in the labour force often lost their jobs upon marriage, people were paid on the basis of their sex, rather than on the basis of the work they performed,[18] many jobs were simply barred to women, and higher education was reserved largely for men. Indeed, women were regarded non-persons for many purposes (they were declared persons only in 1929 with the famous *Persons* case).[19]

In terms of social policy, the subsidiarity principle reigned. This principle assigned the responsibility for a person's well-being first to his or her family; if the family was unable to cope, responsibility was assigned to the next higher level, and so on. In practice, this meant that fathers/husbands were responsible for the economic well-being not only of themselves but also of their wives and dependent children. (Of course, many children worked for pay at the beginning of the twentieth century and thus contributed to the economic survival of the family.) Nevertheless, the responsibility was vested in the fathers. As this was the case, families with an able-bodied father/husband were not entitled to economic help, even if the father neglected to discharge his duties.[20]

The obverse applied to care for children: the mother was responsible for them unless she was proven to be an unfit mother. If it was known that she committed adultery, she would be regarded as an unfit mother, in which case the father retained sole custody. A double standard was rampant: even if the husband was adulterous, that did not make him an unfit father.[21] His adequacy as a parent was measured in economic terms, while hers was measured in moral, sexual, and social terms.

It is important to realize that while public assistance was seen as legitimate in principle when one of the spouses was absent or incapacitated, this did not necessarily imply that it was forthcoming. For instance, in 1937 the Montreal Unemployment Relief Commission decided to make the following classes of women ineligible for relief: 'those whose husbands were being held in provincial institutions, those whose husbands had deserted them, and those separated from their husbands where alimony had been awarded (the husband's failure to meet his payments was immaterial). Unmarried mothers were also cut from the rolls at the same time.'[22] Such women and children were doubly trapped: they were forced into economic dependency on one man, but when the man failed to support them, no one else took over his role.

Homosexuality was considered an illness. It was not a sexual orientation that could be proudly affirmed or even cautiously acknowledged in most social circles. It was therefore regarded either as irrelevant to policies affecting families (since it did not lead to family formation) or as diametrically opposed to family values.

To put these broad sketches into the form of principles, then, the patriarchal family is premised on the following eight principles:

1. The ideology with respect to gender is premised on the notion of separate spheres, which in turn results in gender inequality.

2. Legal marriage is the basic constituent of a family. Non-legal unions do not generate the same rights and responsibilities as legal marriages do. Children of a non-legal union are considered illegitimate, with no legal claims on their fathers.

3. At the nuclear level, household and family memberships are treated as congruous.[23] Hence, a spouse is equated with a parent.

4. The family household is treated as the unit of administration.

5. The husband is responsible for the economic well-being of the family household. The wife and children are treated as economic dependants of the husband, whether or not they actually contribute to the household through paid or unpaid labour.

6. The wife/mother is seen as responsible for providing care and services to family members in need of care.

7. The public has no responsibility for the economic well-being of a family if there is a husband/father present, and no responsibility for care provision if there is a wife/mother present. However, if one of the spouses is missing or incapacitated, and if there are children, public assistance is seen as legitimate (although not always rendered).

8. Homosexuality is seen as an illness or a crime, and partners within same-sex couples are not publicly recognized as having any social, economic, or legal obligations towards each other. The issue is seen as irrelevant for family policy, since same-sex couples are regarded as antithetical to the nuclear family.

The Individual Responsibility Model of the Family

Since the turn of this century, families and society have undergone several major upheavals, including several wars, a great depression, and a modern recession, which is, to all intents and purposes, another great depression. Family structures have evolved substantially, as will be discussed in Chapter 2. Consequently, policies have evolved as well.

The greatest change has taken place at the ideological level. From being a society that was premised on gender differentiation, we have become one that prides itself on being committed to equal treatment of individuals, regardless of gender distinctions. This is best exemplified by the incorporation of this principle in the *Canadian Charter of Rights and Freedoms*. This single change—itself the result of many smaller changes— turns families upside down, or rather right side up. Of course, it does not mean that we have achieved gender equality in any substantive sense. Indeed, many critics have argued that the introduction of formal equality—treating people equally despite continuing actual inequalities—has actually reinforced existing inequalities.[24] It has, however, had a great effect on family law. The privileged status of the legally married couple has been largely eroded through the inroads made by spouses in common-law relationships and, lately, same-sex couples. The concept of illegitimacy has been abolished for all intents and purposes.

However, most policies still consider household and family memberships at the nuclear level as congruous, although often they no longer are. This will be discussed in later chapters. As a consequence, family households are for many (although not all) purposes still considered the basic unit of administration, leading to a number of unanticipated and unintended problems.

Husbands and wives are now assigned the same economic functions in family law. They are both considered responsible for their own economic well-being, as well as that of their spouse and children. Wives are no longer conceptualized as dependants but as equal to their husbands, and children are regarded, at least in law, as the dependants of both parents.[25] In the economic, social, and political reality, this is not always so, as we will see in chapters 2 and 3. Fathers and mothers are legally assumed to be equally responsible for the care of their children, although in practice this is not the case, as we will see in Chapter 4.

The recent trend in family law towards assuming equal economic and care responsibilities of wives and husbands, mothers and fathers stems directly from the assumption of gender equality. This has a paradoxical effect: since *both* parents are assumed capable of fulfilling the care and provider functions, it follows that *either* parent is capable of doing both, and from this the conclusion is drawn that *one* parent should be able to do both. In contrast, under the patriarchal model, only one parent was assumed to fulfil *either* the economic *or* the care function. Under the individual responsibility model of the family, the ideological ground is therefore prepared for an erosion of public entitlements for substantial numbers of families, particularly lone-parent families, because of the lack of recognition that one parent needs extra support in the absence of the second parent. Such a redefinition of social responsibilities is, moreover, not gender neutral. There are many more female-led, lone-parent households than there are male-led ones. I say households rather than families because in most instances, the second parents are still alive. However, because of the tendency to treat household and family memberships as congruent, the non-resident parent (usually a father) is treated as a non-parent in many policies. Finally, same-sex couples are well on their way to being recognized as members of a familial grouping.

Overall, we can identify the following principles as underlying the *individual responsibility* model of the family:

1. The ideology is one of gender equality.

2. Legal marriages are no longer the sole basic constituent unit of a family. Instead, functioning relationships are recognized as creating this basic unit. Consequently, common-law partners are held responsible for each other's economic support, both during the union and after the union has broken up. There is no legal distinction between legitimate and illegitimate children.

3. At the nuclear level, household and family memberships are mostly treated as congruous. This being so, a spouse is equated with a parent. Conversely, an external parent is largely treated as a non-parent.

4. The family household is treated as the normal unit of administration (with a few exceptions).

5. Husband and wife are equally responsible for the economic well-being of themselves, each other, and any dependent children. Children are considered economic dependants of both their parents, and spouses are considered economically interdependent rather than one as the dependant and the other as the head of the household.

6. Fathers and mothers are equally responsible for providing care and services to family members in need of care.

7. The public has no responsibility for the economic well-being of a family or for the provision of care if there is either a husband/father or wife/mother. It will provide *temporary* help if one of them is absent or incapacitated, but the basic assumption is that

a parent is responsible for both the economic well-being and care of dependent children.

8. Same-sex couples are starting to be recognized as a valid family form.[26]

In the following chapters I will demonstrate that the individual responsibility model of the family is as inadequate as the patriarchal model, in principle as well as in practice, as a basis on which to formulate family policy. The problems described are experienced in Canada and in highly industrialized countries in general. In spite of varying family legislation, social,[27] economic, and legal[28] trends are similar crossnationally in highly industrialized countries, and they are at least partially related to the adoption of some version of the individual responsibility model.[29]

However, before proceeding with this critique, it is important to point out the advantages of the individual responsibility model over the old patriarchal model, since there is a strong and vocal minority that clamours for a return to the patriarchal model of the family. The individual responsibility model of the family *is* based on the notion of gender equality, whereas the patriarchal model is based on male dominance and female dependency, with the attendant double standard and the difficulties in leaving a marriage even if it is brutalizing for the woman and/or children, or sometimes the man. The individual responsibility model is also in principle able to accommodate common-law and same-sex couples, although it has done so very imperfectly.

The longing for a return to the patriarchal model is based on a nostalgic view of that type of family life. That model is unrealistic and actively harmful: by putting forward an idealized version of the family that does not correspond to the actual range of families in existence today (or, for that matter, in the past), and by pressuring for policies that will privilege this one family type over other family types, the patriarchal model actually exacerbates the situations of families who already have problems. Its proponents usually have a conservative bias in ignoring problems of violence and domination. They endow a certain structure with the inherent capacity to function well, despite much evidence to the contrary.

An adequate model of the family should lead to policies that address the needs of *all* families. A good test is to ask what policies a particular model would lead to for lone-parent families and first families in which one ex-partner has remarried. If the model cannot adequately serve these two very common types of families, it is certainly not appropriate for present times.

For instance, declaring that a family consists of 'a married man and woman living together with their dependent children'[30] thereby declares the *first* family of this man (if he is divorced and has a child from the first marriage) as a non-family. It justifies and legitimizes a tax and social policy system that in many instances condemns his children with his first wife to poverty with its many social disadvantages. In the case of a lesbian couple with children, the virulent homophobia that accompanies the patriarchal model of the family poisons the atmosphere for children and adults living in such families. Finally, it continues to restrict familial relationships to couples and parents, thereby ignoring that other groupings may also carry out familial functions.[31]

The Social Responsibility Model

An alternative to both the patriarchal and the individual responsibility models of the family is the social responsibility model. It will be sketched here only briefly since Chapter 7 will develop this model fully. It has the following features:

1. There is an ideological commitment to minimizing stratification on the basis of sex.

2. Functioning relationships constitute a family unit. Legal marriage is present but not privileged over the other relationships.

3. At the nuclear level, household and family memberships *may* be but are not *assumed* to be congruous. Therefore, spousehood is not automatically identified with parenthood, and parenthood is not automatically identified with spousehood.

4. The individual is the unit of administration (with a few exceptions).

5. All dependency relations are socially recognized regardless of whether they are between kin or non-kin. Adult members of an interdependent unit are responsible for their own and each other's economic well-being. Fathers and mothers are both responsible for their children's economic well-being, whether or not they live with them.

6. Mothers and fathers are both responsible for providing care for their children. Parents retain parental responsibilities—which are not tied to parental rights—even if they do not live with their children.

7. The public shares the responsibility with both parents for the care of dependent children. If one parent is genuinely absent or unable to contribute his or her share, society will pay the cost of his or her contribution. The cost of care for inevitably dependent adults is a public responsibility (while the delivery of the care may be rendered by a family member).

8. There is no distinction between same-sex or opposite-sex couples in terms of their treatment by the state.

The multiple issues regarding any of these aspects are dealt with in Chapter 7. However, there is one conceptual issue that is basic to understanding all three models. It will therefore be dealt with here.

THE FAULTY DEFINITION OF 'PRODUCTIVE' VERSUS 'UNPRODUCTIVE' LABOUR

In traditional economic terms, all activities that generate money are considered 'work' and are hence 'productive', while activities that do *not* involve the exchange of money are regarded neither as work nor as productive. For instance, the *International Encyclopedia of the Social Sciences* defines work as follows:

> In every culture, most persons are engaged, a good part of their lives, in activities that may be considered as work. But such activities may or may not qualify them for inclusion in what may be regarded technically as part of the working force. For example, in the United States the services performed by housewives, although highly desirable from a societal point of view, are not regarded as economic. Housewives are therefore excluded from what is measured as the working force ... Moreover, their inclusion in the working force, for purposes of economic analysis, would not help policy makers to solve the significant economic problems of American society.[32]

This understanding underlay the designation of a housewife who was raising children as her husband's economic dependant in the patriarchal model of the family. It also applied if she worked without pay on the family farm or in the family business. The fact that she worked without pay disqualified her activities from being defined as work (and that disqualified her from earning an interest in the family farm or business). Under this system, the same activity counts as either work or non-work, as a productive or non-productive activity, depending on who does it and whether or not it is paid for. If a babysitter, nanny, or day-care worker looks after a family's children, an activity for which she is paid, this counts as productive work. If the mother or another family member engages in the same activity, it does not count as work or as a productive activity.[33] The same applies to other tasks done at home: preparation of food, cleaning of premises and clothes, personal care for household members, yard work, shopping, etc.

The division of tasks into work and non-work is therefore largely independent of *what* is actually done; it depends on *who* is doing it and *under what conditions* it is being done. There are many critiques of this approach,[34] and as a consequence Statistics Canada has engaged in a number of calculations to estimate the value of these unpaid work activities. The latest estimate[35] is that Canada's GDP in 1992 would have increased by 41.4 per cent[36] had we included unpaid housework.[37] This translates into an annual replacement cost of $16,580 for women and $9,960 for men, and into 59.7 per cent of personal disposable income. Of this work, 65.9 per cent was performed by women.[38] This is important because of its policy implications. We have already mentioned one: the historical designation of the housewife as her husband's economic dependant in the patriarchal family.

In the individual responsibility model of the family, the economic contribution a spouse can make through unpaid work is specifically acknowledged.[39] This entitles her (or him) to a share in the family business assets upon dissolution of the union. In that sense, some progress has been made. However, there is a serious problem because while we recognize the private value of unpaid work, we do not recognize its public value. If a child is not cared for by its parents, the state will take over this responsibility by providing the care or by paying for it. Hence, care services for people who are unable to care for themselves are not only of private value but also of public value.[40] Family law, then, recognizes in some form the value of unpaid work, but the rest of society does not. This is the core of the problem.

It becomes evident that we do not regard unpaid work as 'real' work because it is not included in our computations in various policies, such as those regarding employment. Why, for instance, is road construction seen as a form of job creation, while the creation of day-care centres is regarded as an expense we cannot afford? Why is the one seen as improving our infrastructure and the other is not? Are roads more important than children? Since we do not see unpaid work as real work, we also do not provide the fringe benefits that accompany 'real' work, such as unemployment insurance, paid holidays, maternity leaves, and very few pension entitlements.[41]

However, there is a caveat to be made before we argue for the wholehearted incorporation of all unpaid labour (which would go beyond housework and include voluntary labour performed inside and outside private homes). One of the attributes of paid work is that we are taxed on the earnings. If we have accurate measurements of the dollar value of unpaid work, conceivably an effort could be made to tax such work.[42] This would, in effect, penalize effective home workers and encourage them to lie or to reduce their productive work—neither of which would be a socially desirable consequence.

On the other hand, failing to generate and publicize knowledge about the value of unpaid work continues to downplay the vital contribution this type of work makes to the well-being of individual families and of the country as a whole. We therefore need to find a way in which this work is counted, acknowledged, and taken into account when policies are formulated without creating disincentives for people to perform it.

FROM A PATRIARCHAL TO AN INDIVIDUAL RESPONSIBILITY MODEL: FEDERAL INCOME TAX PROVISIONS FROM 1970–1994.

I have postulated that we have experienced a broad shift from a patriarchal to an individual responsibility model of the family. If this is indeed the case, such a shift should be manifested in many policies, including income tax. 'There has been tremendous resistance to seeing the Income Tax Act[43] for what it is: a social policy document, influenced by notions of just distribution and ideologically specified understandings of ideal forms of social ordering. Instead, the ITA is often viewed as a politically and morally neutral document, structured by dictates of financial accounting, economic theory and tax principles that permit no political shades or shaping.'[44]

This is a profound misunderstanding. For one thing, there is no such thing as a neutral policy. It may be neutral with respect to a particular issue, but it cannot be neutral in general, or else it is not a policy. The purpose of policies is to achieve particular effects. Income tax is our way of redistributing income by taking money from tax-paying citizens and using it for a variety of goals (run the government; build and maintain streets, hospitals, and other capital ventures; fund schools, medical systems, defence, etc.). On the other hand, the income tax system is used to transfer money from one set of people to another set of people via direct payments (welfare, veterans' allowances, spouses' allowances, child tax credits, survivors' pensions, etc.) or via deductions. It is the *one* policy instrument that affects all members of a society, either directly or indirectly. It is therefore a particularly important one to examine. I will address the eight questions identified earlier to selected aspects of the federal income tax guides for the quarter century that encompasses the shift from a patriarchal to an individual responsibility model of the family, namely from 1970 to 1994.[45]

1. What Is the Ideology Concerning Gender Equality?

From 1970 to 1984, Canada underwent a drastic change from a widespread assumption of separate spheres and hence gender inequality to one of gender equality. In income tax, this shift is best shown in the way in which the child-care deduction is handled. In 1972, 'The child care expenses … can only be those incurred to permit the mother, or in some cases the father, to work. Babysitting expenses for other purposes are not eligible. A father who was separated must have a written agreement of separation. He becomes eligible to claim child care expenses the date the agreement is signed.' In 1976, the conditions under which child-care expenses can be claimed are *slightly* expanded 'to permit the mother, or in some cases the father, to work, to undertake an occupational training course if an adult training allowance was paid, or to carry out research if a grant was paid. Babysitting expenses for other purposes such as those paid in order to attend school or university will not normally qualify.' This formulation is clearly premised on the notion that taking care of children is a task that is the natural domain of women, to be undertaken by men only in exceptional cases. It led to some interesting discriminations. If in one couple the man was a student and the woman was working for pay 'to put hubby through', she could claim a portion of her child-care expenses. Another couple in exactly the same circumstances, except with the woman as student and the man as working for pay to put his wife through school, could not claim the equivalent portion of their child-care expenses.

By 1983, the Constitution had been repatriated, and the equality clause was to come into force in 1985. At that point, the situation changed drastically, so that the occupations of parents were treated equally. The phrasing shifted to a 'supporting person' (rather than spouse), thus treating the household as the administrative unit. Payments made to relatives could not be claimed. By contrast, the married or equivalent deduction was in principle available to either spouse from 1970 onwards, although in reality it was mostly men who would claim their wives as dependants, and single mothers who would claim their children as equivalent-to-married. Nevertheless, in principle the provision applied to both sexes.

2. What Are the Assumptions About the Legal Status of Marriage?

Tremendous changes took place in this area with respect to common-law relationships. In 1970, there was no definition of who is a spouse, nor was there a criterion that spouses had to be legally married—it was simply assumed that readers would understand that this was so. By 1974, this was spelled out: 'A person who is not legally married is not entitled to a deduction for married exemption or the equivalent to married exemption for a person to whom he is not related.' Two years later, matters are put even more forcefully and clearly: 'you may not claim a married exemption for a common-law spouse'. In order to generate such a clear statement, the challenge must have been made that common-law spouses should be able to claim the married exemption. This was not to be for quite some time. However, in 1982 common-law spouses were required to report alimony or separation allowances received from their former partners: 'Periodic maintenance payments received from a former common-law spouse under court order must ... be reported ...' In exchange, they may also deduct such payments if they are the payer rather than the recipient.

In 1983, the liability of common-law spouses expands further. With respect to the Child Tax Credit, which was by then in existence, the regulation specifies:

> *Other supporting person*: In 1983, the income of a person other than your spouse may have to be added to yours when calculating your claim. If at the end of the year you were living with, but not married to the other parent of an eligible child, the other parent's income must be entered ... This applies even if the other parent is not claiming a personal exemption for the child. In addition, the income of any person (other than yourself or your spouse) who is claiming a personal exemption for an eligible child must be included ... whether that person was living with you or not ...

In 1987, common-law partners could claim the child-care expenses for their own children or their partner's children: 'Common-law in 1987: If you lived common-law with an individual who had a child, include all payments made at any time in the year for children of whom you are the parent, or for whom you are claiming a personal exemption.' The special provisions are so complex, however, that several examples are included to provide further guidance.

Although the common-law spouse's income had to be reported for the purpose of establishing eligibility for the Child Tax Credit as of 1983, only in 1993 were common-law spouses recognized as equivalent to legal spouses for income tax purposes. In that year, the spousal amount was available to couples, whether legally married or living common law. In 1994, the term spouse, which was not defined at all in 1970 (presumably because it was taken to be self-evident) was defined as follows:

> *Spouse*: The term spouse used throughout this guide applies to a legally married spouse and a common-law spouse. A common-law spouse is a person of the opposite sex who, at that particular time, is living with you in a common-law relationship, and
>
> • is the natural or adoptive parent (legal or in fact) of your child; or
>
> • had been living with you in such a relationship for at least 12 continuous months, or had previously lived with you in such a relationship for at least twelve continuous months (when you calculate the 12 continuous months, include any period of separation of less than 90 days).
>
> Once either of these two situations applies, we consider you to have a common-law spouse, except for any period that you were separated for 90 days or more because of a breakdown in the relationship.

Example 1
On May 1, 1991, Susan and Serge, who have no children, began to live together in a common-law relationship. On July 15, 1992, they separated because of a breakdown in their relationship. On February 29, 1994, they began to live together again. We consider Susan and Serge to be spouses as of February 27, 1994, the date they reconciled. This is because they once lived together in a common-law relationship for 12 continuous months.

Example 2
David and Renata, who have no children, have been living together in a common-law relationship since April 13, 1993. However, for the months of July 1993 and October 1993 they lived apart because of a breakdown in their relationship. We consider David and Renata to be spouses as of April 13, 1994. When calculating the 12 continuous months requirement, they have to include the two months they lived apart because each period of separation was less than 90 days.

With this definition, we can conclude that the transition to including common-law spouses in the income tax has been made. Legal marriage no longer creates the constituent unit of a family for income tax purposes.

3. What Are the Assumptions About Household/Family Memberships' Incongruence/Congruence?

This is a somewhat more difficult question to answer. In one sense, the answer is clear. Upon dissolution of the union, the non-resident parent (usually the father) can deduct his support payments for his children (income tax does not distinguish whether the payments he makes are for his wife or for his children), while the coresident parent (usually the mother) must declare these payments as income. There was no change in this matter, except that payments from common-law spouses are now included, as noted earlier. In so far as a father who was living with his children would not be able to deduct payments he made on behalf of his children (except for claiming them as dependants if he is the higher income earner), the state now regards the mother and her children, living in one household, as the relevant unit. However, this will change as of 1997 (see Chapter 8). To the degree that payments are made and acknowledged at all, there is some recognition that there may be incongruence between household and family memberships. On the other hand, the very recognition of a common-law spouse (as well as a second legal spouse) as a 'supporting person' for income tax purposes makes it clear that the residence of an adult (of the opposite sex to the first adult) within a household establishes family relationships between the various household members for income tax purposes. By and large, then, household and family memberships are seen as congruent. There was no change on this issue, and indeed this is one of the characteristics that are shared by both the patriarchal and individual responsibility models of the family.

4. What Is Seen as the Appropriate Unit of Administration?

Canada is one of the countries that taxes earners as individuals rather than as members of a couple.[46] This was so in 1970 and is still mostly the case today, although to a much lesser degree. The major current child benefit, the Child Tax Benefit, is squarely based on the joint income of spouses. Canada has thus taken a significant step towards couple taxation.[47]

5. What Are the Assumptions Concerning Economic Responsibility/Dependency?

While the spousal exemption was in principle always available to either a husband or wife, both the language as well as the content of provisions are making it clear that now ex-wives carry parallel responsibilities for supporting ex-husbands (whether legal or common-law) as ex-husbands do for ex-wives. Examples are carefully sex neutral. However, income tax does not regulate who pays how much to whom on what basis; this is determined by the legal system. The major manifestations of a shift in assumptions can therefore *not* be found in income tax provisions but in family law and judicial settlements.

6. What Are the Assumptions About Care and Service Provision for Family Members in Need of Care?

We have already noted when considering the child-care deduction that child care used to be seen as the exclusive domain of women. Now it is regarded as the responsibility of either parent, in line with a shift to the individual responsibility model of the family.

7. What Is Seen as the Appropriate Private/Public Division of Responsibilities?

I have not summarized the monetary value of tax support that families receive in Canada for their dependent members (children as well as others). Nor is that a simple matter, since the combination of tax deductions, direct transfers, and use of family income as a basis for computing entitlements means that the value varies greatly depending on the particular family constellation involved.[48] However, international comparisons make it clear that Canada's support is rather meagre.[49] It is also quite clear that the *Income Tax Act* assumes that child care will be provided or paid for by parents. They are then able to recover a small amount of their expenses, provided they have enough income to profit from the available deduction.

There is a clear message that care provided by most relatives—even if paid for—is not eligible for even this partial reimbursement.[50] If there is a relevant adult assumed to be available within the household (e.g., because of unemployment), this person is assumed to render child care for free.

8. What Are the Assumptions Regarding Heterosexuality/Homosexuality?

At this point, the income tax does not recognize same-sex couples in principle.

CONCLUSION

Overall, the federal income tax demonstrates a clear shift from the patriarchal to the individual responsibility model of the family. Both mother and father are assumed to be able to render child care; both are assumed to be able to look after the economic well-being of themselves, their spouse, and their children; the ideology is one of gender equality; the household is for most purposes assumed to be the administrative unit of relevance; legal marriage is no longer seen as creating the constituent unit of a family, although this is only true with respect to common-law spouses, and not with respect to same-sex spouses; and the responsibility for the care of dependent family members lies with the family/household, not with the public. There are, of course, some contradictory elements in the overall scheme.

The single most striking feature, when looking over the tax guides in chronological order, is how complex they have become. They have at least quadrupled in size and offer extremely clumsy, lengthy, and awkward definitions of familial designations (such as 'spouse'). The sheer complexity suggests that the current approach has reached its limits.[51]

In the next chapter, I will examine the actual composition of families. This constitutes one (but not the only) important basis from which to critique the currently prevailing individual responsibility model of the family.

CHAPTER 2

Social, Economic, and Legal Trends Affecting Families

INTRODUCTION

The Who, What, and How of Family Formation

There is now a debate about the definition of the family among students of the family,[1] in law,[2] among politicians,[3] and among the general public.[4] These debates typically revolve around such issues as the proper treatment of common-law and legally married couples, whether lesbian and gay couples should be recognized as equivalent to common-law heterosexual couples, whether they should be recognized legally and economically as functioning coparents to their partners' children, whether lone-parent families are well-functioning families, and whether children are better off in traditional two-parent families; the entitlement of first families versus subsequent families with regard to support; whether or not the state should support families at all and, if so, the types of families it should support.[5] And here we have come full circle to the beginning of our questions. We can divide the debate roughly into two camps: the patriarchalists and the egalitarians.[6] This simplifies the situation somewhat as there are a number of people who would position themselves somewhere between these two polar opposites, but it serves as a convenient analytical ordering device.

Patriarchalists argue that the only 'real' family is a patriarchal nuclear family,[7] while egalitarians argue that all caring relationships should be recognized as family relationships.[8] Patriarchalists draw the line around families by asking *who* constitutes a family (if you are legally married, heterosexual, or have children, you are included); egalitarians draw the dividing line by asking *what* makes a family (if you assume familial responsibilities for other people, whether of the same sex or of the other sex, whether legally married or not, or if you play a parental role towards a child, whether biologically your own or someone else's, you are included; if you do not play such a role, you are excluded). Neither side asks *how* a family is made.

Yet in a long-term perspective, the 'how' is the incomparably more important question to address, due to the revolution (which has redefined not only how families are formed but what it means to be human) that has occurred via the new reproductive and genetic technologies.[9] I shall discuss this topic in Chapter 4. In this chapter, I shall deal with who and what constitutes a family.

Real Problems and False Solutions

Patriarchalists draw a rosy image of families as they used to be 'when the natural order still prevailed'. It exemplifies the conservative and sexist biases. The image is premised on a number of assumptions: that there are biological differences between the sexes, which result in a natural division of labour, which in turn is best served by what is called 'role complementarity' between wives and husbands (or 'two spheres' in the parlance prevalent at the turn of the century), which just happens to coincide with 'instrumental leadership of the husband' in the outside world and 'expressive leadership of the wife' in the home. These latter two types of leadership fit neatly into the view of the husband as the head of the household and the wife as his dependant. Around the turn of the century, this view of the family was the religious ideal, reflected in the state's multitude of laws and policies. The 1920s, with the first wave of feminism and the loss of many men during the First World War, put many of these precepts into question. However, the great depression and the subsequent Second World War, led to a secular reaffirmation of this religious ideal as the norm.

One major (although by no means the only) scientific reformulation of this old vision of the family was spearheaded by the sociologist Parsons and his colleagues in the middle of this century. Their interpretation of the appropriate male and female spousal roles dominated social science for several decades.[10] Men, as those with paid external jobs, were declared to be the instrumental leaders, and women, as housewives, were declared to be the expressive leaders of their families.

It is interesting to realize that this conceptualization of spousal roles emerged out of the study of small groups that consisted entirely of male undergraduate students. It was transferred to families by a leap of imagination that is still rather breathtaking. According to this school of thought, all small groups have an instrumental leader and an expressive leader. The family is a small group; ergo, it, too, must have an instrumental and an expressive leader.[11] Husbands and wives are thus assigned their proper places—a rather ironic inference to draw.

Patriarchalists today can therefore draw on a long history of religious and scientific thought to justify their stance. One modern reformulation, for instance, argues that the biological difference between the sexes requires that men be tamed by women, a feat that women achieve via the nuclear family. The family, then, is 'a means for taming male sexual and physical aggression.'[12]

In this nuclear family, there is a natural hierarchy in which the man is head of the household and family,[13] while his wife is his direct subordinate and the children are her subordinates, although they, too, fall under the ultimate authority of the paterfamilias.

In this family, everyone's needs are supposedly optimally looked after.

The man devotes his energies to supporting his wife and children by earning a 'family wage', and in return he is serviced by his wife, who is solely responsible for the emotional, physical, and other needs of the family. Children are cared for by the mother, who devotes her energies to raising them and looking after her husband. The wife and her children, in turn, are economically provided for by the husband and socially protected by him—and this is seen as the optimal set-up for children. How this looked in reality in nineteenth-century Montreal is described as follows:

> The complementary of the roles of husbands and wives, sons and daughters, should not blind us to their inequality. Power and rights were not evenly distributed within any families at this time. In working-class families wage dependency locked wives and children to husbands and fathers in a relationship that was at once mutual and complementary, yet hierarchical and dependent. Women were legally incapacitated upon marriage. This meant that most had no right to administer property or even their own wages. Nor could they usually appear in court without the husband's permission. The Civil Code proscribed the wife's submission to her husband, the obligation to live where he wished, and marital fidelity. Husbands were to provide according to their means. Their infidelity was sanctioned as long as a mistress was not brought into the family home. Married women's legal incapacities were reinforced by their unequal earning power in the marketplace and their circumscribed role in the wider economy.[14]

Any social policies that foster this version of the family are seen as friendly to the family, while any policies that are premised on a different version of reality—for instance, by including gender equality—are seen not only as despicable in and of themselves but as part of a 'war against the family'.[15]

Patriarchalists note that we are in a period of uncertainty and are experiencing serious social problems. They blame these problems on our deviation from the 'natural' form of the family. The family—and particularly women who are not willing to play their God- and nature-appointed roles as wives and mothers in the manner described earlier—are thus responsible for a whole slew of problems, which include economic problems (all these married women taking jobs away from married men), drug abuse, youth crime (the children are uncared for), etc. As its name suggests, the patriarchal vision is in line with the patriarchal model of the family.

By contrast, egalitarians question that families were ever such wonderful, smoothly functioning units as argued by the patriarchalists. Egalitarians start from a human rights perspective that assumes the human rights of women and men are equal, and that therefore we cannot premise families on an assumption of female subordination and male authority over women and children. Indeed, this is part of our Constitution in Canada, through the *Charter of Rights and Freedoms* (which is consequently bitterly attacked by patriarchalists, who rightfully regard it as incompatible with patriarchal family structures).

Egalitarians point to existing problems and suggest that we need to recognize and assist those people who carry out familial functions: that is, people who raise children, who live in supportive unions of adults, who provide intergenerational care for the elderly, who look after temporarily or chronically ill family members, etc. It is not important whether the adults involved are of the same sex or of different sexes, or even if there is a sexual relationship at all.[16] What matters is whether the union of adults is a mutually supportive one and whether any children or other dependants are well taken care of. In other words, the vital question is: Does this family constellation address the needs of all its members and is it beneficial for all participants? The family is thus conceptualized as a group of individuals who form an entity, but within which all members maintain their individual needs, rights, and responsibilities. In particular, there are no rights assigned to the unit itself apart from those connected to the people within the unit. Conservative thinkers often tend to argue for rights for the unit itself, such as the right to 'remain intact'. This is scary when some family members may be suffering *because* of their membership in this unit, as in the case of abuse.

If a family adequately meets the needs of all its members, it is worthy of support; if not, to support the unit as a legal fiction would be a violation of the human rights of members who would be forced to participate within it even though such participation is harmful to them.

We therefore have two starkly contrasting views of what constitutes 'good' families that result in diametrically opposed policy consequences. However, both versions of families are problematic. The patriarchal model, although fiercely defended by a minority,[17] is unacceptable to the majority of Canadians. It is also based on unconstitutional principles. The egalitarian model is the currently prevalent one (at least in rhetoric!), but there are obvious problems: we have many people who are uncared for; we have thousands of street kids who have no one to look after them; we have hundreds of thousands of overburdened mothers who are in the labour force and who are also solely or mostly responsible for child care, housework, and personal care of self and husband (if there is one), as well as sometimes an elderly or incapacitated relative.

Patriarchalists will point to these same problems and blame them on the demise of the patriarchal family. Egalitarians, by contrast, point to the lack of infrastructural supports, such as day care for children, home care for sick people, and so on. However, there is no clear concept as to what a family premised on *actual equality* of the sexes would look like, given that we have never collectively experienced such a thing. While Canada has made some significant strides towards gender equality, it is certainly not realized today.

Canada has conceptualized equality rights better on the individual level (via a human rights approach) than on the collective level. Consequently, people are put into a situation where they have to demonstrate that they have been personally harmed by a particular incident or set of circumstances. An alternative approach would have been to identify and systematically work on removing structural barriers towards equality.[18]

This has led to what I have called the individual responsibility model of the family. Families internationally are experiencing serious problems, which can be partially (not, of course, totally) blamed on policies that are premised on a model of the family based on individual rights rather than on an understanding of caring relationships. This book, then, is primarily a critique of the individual responsibility model of the family. Less effort will be devoted to critiquing the patriarchal model of the family, since the literature on this issue is voluminous.[19]

Part of the legacy of imperfect agreement on the definition of the family, and of an imperfectly overcome monolithic bias, is that we know a lot more about couples and families with dependent children than we know about alternative groupings. To this day we do not know how many same-sex couples there are in Canada, for instance.[20] Nor do we know how many biological parents do not live with their biological children, and how many biological children do not live with one or both of their biological parents, although the latter are alive and residing in Canada. This chapter is largely concerned with heterosexual couples and families with dependent children, since this is the way in which most of our statistics are collected. Other familial groupings will be considered in later chapters.

In the last half of the twentieth century, family structures *between* industrialized countries have converged,[21] while at the same time they have diverged *within* individual countries. This may be one of the reasons that legal trends have also converged,[22] and it is certainly a major reason why family policy has been the topic of much political debate and social experimentation since the early 1970s.[23]

At the simplest level, family structures are much more complicated than they used to be, not just in Canada but in highly industrialized countries in general. This is evident in the tax guides' elaborate definitions of who is eligible or liable for particular tax regulations where family status is involved.[24] It is a far cry from the early 1970s when it was assumed that everyone would know who and what a spouse is. As we have seen, today a lengthy definition of this term is considered necessary. As we will see in Chapter 3, spousal roles have been blurred from three different directions, and as we will see in Chapter 4, parental roles are even more unclear, muddled, and subject to competing claims and counterclaims. All of this is intricately connected with the changes that have been taking place in families in general, and are relevant when trying to determine what model of the family should be adopted for which policy purposes.

Convergence of Family Structures in Highly Industrialized Countries

Several observers of the family have noted that demographic patterns in highly industrialized countries are converging. The trends include the following:

1. The decline of fertility to below-replacement levels.

2. The postponement or avoidance of legal marriage and an increase in the prevalence of nonmarital cohabitation.

3. A sharp rise in the incidence of divorce, along with high rates of instability in nonmarital unions that do not lead to marriage.

4. A rise in the proportion of persons living in small households— one-or two-person households, single-parent families—with a concomitant decline in average household size. Associated trends are a decline in the frequency of non-nuclear relatives or non-relatives in family households.[25]

To this we can add the trend in increased union dissolutions where children are involved, as well as the formation of new unions leading to a pervasive discrepancy between being a spouse and being a biological parent.

Convergence in family structures does *not* imply sameness in outcomes. Because societies have different starting-points (for instance, in the prevalence of divorce), there continue to be significant differences in any one of the noted trends between countries. What it *does* imply is that the *trends* are going in the same direction.

From 1960 to 1991, all industrialized countries—without exception— have experienced a decreasing fertility rate. While the greatest decrease has been experienced by Canada (Canada's fertility rate in 1991 was only 47 per cent of what it was in 1960), this does not mean that Canada's fertility is the lowest. That position was held by Italy in 1991 with a fertility rate of 1.3, while Canada's fertility rate was 1.8—still below replacement levels—as were the fertility rates of twenty-three other countries.[26] Three other countries were at replacement level (a fertility rate of 2.1),[27] and only five countries were slightly above replacement levels.[28] At the same time, life expectancy has increased. Together, these trends mean that these industrialized societies are aging—there are fewer young children as compared to old people. Similarly, divorce has been increasing,[29] as has the ratio of children born to unmarried rather than married women.[30] Further, the labour force participation of women has greatly increased.

CANADIAN SOCIAL TRENDS

Canada, as one of the highly industrialized countries with a high standard of living, is not atypical in terms of its family structures. The problems and issues that Canada is facing are similar to those in other highly industrialized countries. Canada's families are substantially different today from what they were at the beginning of the twentieth century. One way in which this expresses itself is the nature of family disruption.

From Death to Divorce as Family Disrupter

Family disruption is by no means a new phenomenon. When life expectancy was lower, it used to be relatively common for children to lose a parent and for partners to lose a spouse to death. In that case, often the widow or the widower would remarry, and the new spouse/parent would become a full parent to any dependent children still living in the household. However, recent historical research has demonstrated that single parenthood has been an important subform of the family since the beginning of this century. In 1900, approximately 8.5 per cent of all children in the US lived with single parents; in 1960, this figure was 9.1 per cent. In 1900, approximately 14 per cent of children were living apart from one or both parents; in 1960, the comparable figure was 12.3 per cent. Since that time, there have been substantial increases in these figures, but it is important not to exaggerate the degree of homogeneity at the turn of the century.[31]

Today, widowhood is a relatively infrequent phenomenon in families with small children. The importance of this shift in family disruption can hardly be exaggerated.[32] When a spouse/parent dies and the remaining spouse/parent remarries, the new spouse/step-parent can take over the role of the departed spouse/parent, for better or worse. When a spouse/parent divorces, the new spouse cannot necessarily take over the parental role since there is still a second living parent around, even though the two parents are no longer married to each other. This leads to a completely different constellation.

Births to Unmarried Women

Another phenomenon that leads to a discrepancy between marital and parental roles is the increasing number of births to unmarried women in

Canada and other highly industrialized countries. The increase has been quite stunning and continuous: between 1931 and 1960, so-called 'out-of-wedlock' births accounted for about 4 per cent.[33] By 1974, 6 per cent of all births were to unmarried women; this figure rose to 27 per cent (more than one-quarter of all births) in 1991.[34] There are some strong regional differences hidden in this average number; in Quebec, for instance, the proportion of children born to unmarried women was 40.7 per cent in 1991.[35]

The vast majority of these births were to never-married women, then to divorced women, and the others were statistically insignificant.[36] It should be noted, however, that a fair number of these children may, in fact, be born into common-law unions.[37] While the census counts common-law couples as married, vital statistics count children born to women in common-law unions as born to unmarried women.[38]

Nevertheless, the result of these two trends—the divorce of parents who share children, and births to unmarried women—is that there is an increasing incongruence between household and family memberships. One of the effects of such incongruity, and the fact that it has been insufficiently assimilated into our consciousness, is that terms are used in an extremely slippery manner. For example, in a recent highly publicized court case, *Thibaudeau* v. *Canada*,[39] the judges refer to the father and mother as 'parents', the 'couple', the 'post-divorce "family unit"', the 'broken family', the 'family as a whole', and the 'separated' or 'divorced couple'. All of these concepts are used to refer to Ms Thibaudeau and Mr Chaine, a custodial mother and a non-custodial father. Are they a couple? Definitely not. The two parents are still parents to the children, but are definitely no longer a couple, nor do they belong to the same family. The *children* form a family both with their mother and with their father, and thus have a double family membership, but the ex-spouses are no longer members of each other's families.

Remarriage after Union Dissolution

Those who are divorced may be available for remarriage or a common-law relationship. In addition, there is a high proportion of women who give birth outside of marriage. If they form a family with a man other than the father of their children, we have blended families as a result. In 1990, there were 343,000 blended families in Canada, representing about 7 per cent of all families raising children.[40] We actually have to double these figures to get an appreciation of the real amount of discrepancy because for most[41] of the blended families, there is another person who is a biological parent but is not a part of the children's household and hence experiences a different type of discrepancy. In addition, these numbers only represent families in which there are dependent children present at the time the counting is done—they would be considerably higher if we were to count all families that have ever experienced an incongruence between household and family memberships.[42]

From Congruence to Incongruence
between Household and Family Memberships

The end result of the combined trends of divorce, births to unmarried women, and new union formation[43] is a considerable incongruence between household and family memberships. We do not know exactly how high the proportion is, but we do know that it is substantial.[44] The assumption of congruence between household and family membership characterizes both the patriarchal family model as well as the individual responsibility model. Both models assume that if people live in the same household, share the same kitchen, sleep together, and have the same front door, they are a family. They usually also tacitly assume that if people do *not* share the same household, they are *not* family members. The second assumption rather than the first is particularly problematic, although both complicate matters considerably.

Assuming congruence between family and household memberships is a highly consequential assumption to make, given that divorce and births to unmarried women are so frequent. In 1990, over 77,000[45] couples were divorced and around 50,000[46] children were involved.[47] In the vast majority of cases, divorce results in one parent living with some or all of the children.[48] What about the non-resident parent? If we assume that household membership and family membership are congruent, then by that logic the non-resident parent is no longer socially a parent. In fact, that seems to be the way in which many men behave. Although there are some lone-parent families that are headed by men rather than women, the overwhelming majority are headed by women. We will look at some of the specific forms of lone-parent families in Chapter 4. Here I am interested only in the incidence itself.

Changes in the Life Cycle of Families

Once upon a time (certainly around the beginning of the twentieth century and well into the 1960s) we thought we knew what the life cycle of a typical family looked like.[49] There were eight stages:

1. A nice young woman and man (both single and childless) met, courted, and married.

2. They started having children.

3. They constituted a family with preschool children.

4. They were a family with school children.

5. They were a family with teenagers.

6. They were a family that launched young adults. This stage started when the first child left and lasted until the last child left home.

7. We encounter the empty nest: the middle-aged parents live together until retirement.

8. We have the aging family: the couple live together from retirement onward until first one and then the other dies.[50]

Given such a nice, neat system, one could systematically discuss problems and issues to be solved that were typical to each stage. In stage 1, the couple had to create a common culture for themselves, which was facilitated by the fact that they were by themselves and did not yet have to care for small and demanding children. What happens when one of them brings a ready-made child with her? Also, how is this stage affected if the other has a child who visits periodically?

Spouses may each belong to two different sets of families, which are at different developmental stages: they may have a biological baby, a teenager who is the biological child of one of them living in the household, and a school child who visits periodically. What stage is this particular family in?

Recognizing that families go through various stages remains a helpful concept,[51] but assuming that there is a 'normal' cycle for the majority of families in Canada is inappropriate.[52] Instead, we have a multiplicity of cycles, some of which are exceedingly complex.[53]

Economic Trends

Family members have always been economically interconnected, albeit in different ways. There are inter- as well as intragenerational transfers that routinely take place within families. The major forms of intragenerational transfers concern those between wife and husband. One hundred years ago, we had a relatively strict division of labour by sex both within and outside of the family. Since women were completely responsible for all the household and caring work within the family (as well as for much of the so-called 'economically productive work'[54] such as unpaid farm work,[55] taking in boarders, etc.), there were few married women in the active labour force. This has changed dramatically.

The Increasing Labour Force Participation of Wives and Mothers

The labour force participation of wives and mothers has gone through three distinct stages during the last century. Around the turn of the century, it was rare for a married woman to be in the labour force, and since most mothers were also married, it was therefore also rare for a mother to be in the labour force.

This was not just a matter of personal choice. Married women were actively discriminated against. For instance, many women routinely lost their jobs upon marriage. It was legal and usual to pay women less money for doing the same work a man did, even within the same establishment. Women were effectively barred from many types of jobs. The birth rate was considerably higher than it is today, and there were almost no public nursery schools or kindergartens,[56] although many households employed servants, who were often female and hence women in the labour force. For middle- and upper-class women, it was generally socially unacceptable to be actively employed, although there were some notable exceptions.[57] The overall female participation rate was 14.4 per cent in 1901,[58] and women (of all marital statuses) made up only 13.4 per cent of the overall labour force.[59]

The war years, particularly the Second World War, represented a break in this pattern. Married women were actively recruited during the Second World War to work in various occupations to support the war effort. To facilitate their employment, the government extended special tax benefits and established day nurseries for children. After the end of the war, women were just as actively discouraged from continuing in paid employment: the favourable tax measures were revoked, and the day nurseries were closed.[60] Indeed, women were encouraged to go home and raise children as their patriotic duty. It was unpatriotic to keep a job that could be done by a returning veteran.

Disregarding these fluctuations, which were temporary, and looking only at the overall trend, we can note a steady increase in the participation of wives and mothers in the labour force. Ostry (1968) described the prevalent pattern for the middle of the century as one in which women would drop out of the labour force either upon marriage or upon the birth of their first child, and often return to the labour force after their last child had entered school. The average number of children per woman during that time was about three or four.[61]

In 1980, Canada crossed the threshold with respect to the labour force participation of married women, which still largely coincides with the labour force participation of mothers, since most women were married when they gave birth. In that year, for the first time there were more married women in the labour force than there were full-time housewives.[62]

Since then, the labour force participation of married women has continued to increase steadily. In 1992, 56 per cent of all married women were in the labour force, compared to 71 per cent of all married men.[63] We are rapidly approaching a time in which male and female labour force participation will likely be the same. The increase in labour force participation is particularly marked for married women with children. In 1992,

64 per cent of all married women with children under the age of sixteen were employed.[64] The norm today in Canada is that women (whether married or not, mothers or not) are active in the labour force. Full-time housewives have become the exception.

Continuing Economic Differences between Wives and Husbands

In spite of the great influx into the labour force, wives continue to be economically disadvantaged compared to husbands. This is the result of being female and married and/or a mother. Women as a group continue to have lower incomes than men. In addition, early marriage has been found to be just as detrimental economically as becoming a mother while still a teenager.[65]

Family life tends to have a negative effect on women's economic position *as individuals*. The vast majority of people will marry (most legally, some common law) at some point in their lives. For men, marriage often seems to set them more firmly on the path of uninterrupted earnings. For women, this is often the beginning of an interrupted pattern of labour force participation. If they move in with a man, they may have to give up a job and find another under conditions of limited geographical mobility. If such interruptions happen more than once, this may have a permanent negative effect on their earnings. As long as the couple stay together, this may not matter so much. Only when the union dissolves do the consequences of the interrupted pattern become apparent.

Even with an equal split of the assets, the single most important asset today are job-related benefits: earnings, pensions, and other benefits.[66] If family life is oriented around the husband, then his life path will be relatively smooth because the union dissolution will not require a fundamental economic reorientation for him. The opposite is the case for a wife who has oriented her paid and unpaid work around a husband, and who suddenly finds she is no longer part of a couple but is now on her own. This seems to suggest that economic differences between marital partners only become apparent after union dissolution, but there is evidence that even within an ongoing marriage wives tend to have less money at their disposal than their husbands do. This has been documented for Australia,[67] Canada,[68] and Great Britain.[69]

The Demise of the Concept of the Family Wage

The concept of the 'family wage' emerged in the nineteenth century; that is, the notion that a male industrial worker would be paid enough so that he could support a wife and dependent children on this wage. This ideal was never actually achieved by all workers. The concept arose when it was impossible for working-class families to maintain themselves on a family head's wages alone. Had they tried to do so,

... poverty, even starvation, would have been chronic. Men would not have arrived at work with the strength to labour for ten to eleven hours. Women would not have been sufficiently nourished to produce babies that could survive ... Families subsisted because men's wages were supplemented by those of other family members and because wives stretched wages by careful shopping and house-keeping and helped devise various other survival strategies.[70]

The 'ideal' of the family wage is not necessarily desirable since it is premised on the assumption of the wife and children's economic depen-dence on the male breadwinner, the staunch centrepiece of a patriarchal family. Indeed, when this 'ideal' became dominant, married women were denied the right to work for pay, especially when unemployment was high. During the depression, for instance, marriage bars for women were adopted in a number of fields.[71]

What is relevant in this context is that we can note a significant ero-sion of the family wage and, of course, pay disparity between women and men remains a fact of life, in spite of equal-pay legislation. Today, most husband-wife families need two incomes to make ends meet. While the real incomes of single-earner families increased modestly during the 1970s, the real incomes of such families actually fell during the 1980s.[72] In other words, most families need two income earners to maintain a sta-ble income. What happens if there is only one adult in a family who might potentially earn an income?

The Incidence of Poverty

Poverty has increased during the 1990s. In 1993, there were 4,775,000 people (or 17.4 per cent) living below the poverty line in Canada, com-pared to a poverty rate of 15.3 per cent in 1980. The poverty rate dropped to 13.6 per cent in 1989, and then started to increase again.[73] Poverty is not equally distributed by age. Children are overrepresented among the poor, as are women.[74] In 1993, 20.8 per cent of all children under eighteen were living in poverty. That amounts to 1.5 million chil-dren (1,415,000).[75]

The Economic and Social Situation of Lone-Parent Versus Husband-Wife Families

As a group, lone-parent families tend to be severely economically disad-vantaged when compared to husband-wife families.[76] In 1993, 59.6 per cent of all lone-parent families headed by a woman were poor, as com-pared to 12.5 per cent of husband-wife families with children under eigh-teen living at home.[77] The likelihood for a lone-parent family to be poor is therefore substantially greater than that of a husband-wife family with dependent children.[78] These families are *very* poor: their income equalled only 63.4 per cent of the poverty cut-offs in 1993; in other words, they had an income of $8,566 *below* the poverty line.[79] There is also a marked difference in the propensity to be poor depending on whether a lone-parent family is female- or male-headed. Not surprisingly, female-headed lone-parent families are much more likely to be poor than male-headed ones.[80]

Nonetheless, it is a fact that *there are more poor husband-wife families with children than lone-parent families.* In 1993, there were 375,000 husband-wife families with children who were poor compared to 323,000 female-headed lone-parent families who were poor.[81] Seen in a different way, 53 per cent of poor children lived in a husband-wife family, 42 per cent lived in a female-headed lone-parent family, and 5 per cent lived in other types of arrangements.[82] This seeming contradiction is due to different absolute numbers in each category of family. Since there are many more husband-wife families than lone-parent families, there are, in fact, more poor people living in husband-wife families than in lone-parent families. It is in the *proportion*, not in the absolute numbers, that women and children in lone-parent families are disadvantaged, particularly if the families are headed by women. This is important to keep in mind. Given that there are a substantial number of advocates who see the solution to the well-documented economic problems of lone-parent families as firmly attaching a male to each of these families,[83] it is important to remember that the numerically larger group of poor families already *do* include a male, but they are poor nonetheless.

The Economic Position of Young Versus Middle-aged Families

Taking a life cycle perspective of families in terms of the aging process rather than in terms of monolithic assumptions about uniform phases, and comparing families by the age of the primary earner, we find that Canadian families whose primary earner is under twenty-five had drastically lower family incomes between 1980 to 1992 than between 1965 to 1975. This is, to a somewhat lesser degree, also true for families whose primary earner is twenty-five to thirty-four.[84] Similarly, the distance to the median family income has increased substantially for families with a young primary earner between 1965 and 1991.[85] This is extremely worrying. The first years of a child's life are crucial to its development. If there is insufficient income for children, this is likely to have lasting negative effects throughout a lifetime.[86]

LEGAL TRENDS

Family law has undergone massive changes in the past century, but especially in the past quarter century. Divorce once required a private member's bill in some provinces, then was available only under strict conditions involving fault, and is now available on a unilateral basis after one year of living apart. Other aspects of family law have changed in similarly dramatic ways.

From Paternal Presumption over the Tender Years Doctrine to the Best Interest of the Child

During the eighteenth and nineteenth centuries, the common-law regime was premised on 'the rule of near-absolute paternal preference'.[87] The paternal presumption was gradually replaced by the tender years doctrine, which held that children of tender years (usually interpreted to mean below the age of seven) belonged with their mother, not with their father, in case of a custody conflict.[88] Although the two assumptions have opposite effects in terms of custody determination, both fit the patriarchal model of the family. The paternal presumption is premised on the father's overriding authority as opposed to that of the mother, but there was no assumption that the man would actually render the child care; for that purpose, there would be women other than the child's mother available, such as other female relatives or hired help.

The tender years doctrine, while reversing the custody patterns for young children, also fits the patriarchal model, but gives the mother exclusive responsibility for the care of young children. The tender years doctrine therefore represents the first step towards a gradual emancipation of mothers from patriarchal authority without challenging the patriarchal model of the family itself.

With the enactment of the *Divorce Act* in 1986,[89] the tender years doctrine was eliminated in favour of what is usually referred to as the best interests of the child standard, which is the *only* standard that may be applied.[90] However, in reality the *Divorce Act* applies a second standard, which might be called the two-parent standard. It directs judges to adhere to this second standard when making a custody determination:

(10) In making an order under this section, the court shall give effect to the principle that a child of the marriage should have as much contact with each spouse as is consistent with the best interests of the child and, for that purpose, shall take into consideration the willingness of the person for whom custody is sought to facilitate such contact.

Together these two principles signal a drastic turn towards the individual responsibility model of the family in custody determination, at least in theory if not in practice.

In so far as the *Divorce Act* is premised on an ideology of gender equality as exemplified by the gender-neutral identification of 'spouse' (interestingly, not 'parent'), and in so far as both spouses are held equally responsible for child care, this act is in accordance with an individual responsibility model of the family. However, in one way this act goes beyond the individual responsibility model, since household and family memberships are not treated as congruous—the non-resident parent is explicitly recognized as a parent. Is this a move towards the social responsibility model of the family? Not really. The recognition of the parent is oriented towards the *right* of the child to have as much contact with the other parent as is good for him or her. However, as Fineman has argued, the attribution of rights to the child is often identical with the non-custodial father's actual interests.[91] There is a less clear *obligation* for the non-custodial parent to treat the child fully as a dependent child for whom he shares responsibility, with all the financial and time commitments that this implies.[92]

The new directives of the *Divorce Act* concerning custody have had a measurable effect on custody decisions in Canada. Before 1986, the year the *Divorce Act* came into power, joint custody decisions were so rare that Statistics Canada did not even have a category for them. Since that year, joint custody awards have increased from 1.2 per cent in 1986 to 14.1 per cent in 1990.[93] It is interesting to note that most of the shift has occurred from 'no award' to 'joint custody'. The awards given to just mothers or fathers have declined less. This suggests that a minority of couples were willing to share custody in some way before joint custody awards were made more frequently. However, it is also important to realize that these figures tell us nothing about the degree of interaction that is actually taking place, nor are they reliable indicators of where children live. They are merely a record of judicial decisions. We do not know how this translates into actual parental behaviour, but all indications are that mothers continue to do most of the parenting, whether or not both parents have joint custody. This will be examined in detail in Chapter 4.

The Gradual Emancipation of Wives and Mothers

During this century, wives gradually changed their legal status from being their husbands' dependants to being their equal partners. This included, as milestones, the right to make contracts on their own behalf, the right to own and dispose of property, the right to keep their own name upon marriage, the determination of domicile on an equal basis for both wife and husband, etc. Legally, equality was supposed to be guaranteed with the implementation of section 15 of the *Charter of Rights and Freedoms* in 1985. However, socially, emotionally, and economically, this ideal has not yet been achieved, as we shall see in Chapter 3. Legally we have to deal with the paradox that because the law mandates legal equality, it presumes that equality exists despite socio-economic inequality. One area in which this paradox can be observed (there are many other examples) is in the area of family property.

Shifting Definitions of Family Property and Support

At the beginning of the twentieth century, women usually did not own any property. With some exceptions, their fathers, husbands, or brothers were supposed to act on their behalf with respect to property issues. In the case of divorce, alimony payments (from the husband to the wife) was contingent on who was found to be at fault for the divorce, and on the woman's continued sexual chastity *after* the divorce. A woman's adultery while married would automatically place her at fault, while sexual activity after divorce, if it became known, would endanger her alimony payments.

Legally, the wife was regarded as her husband's sexual property.[94] She was entitled to support, whether or not there had been a divorce, and she was expected to be supported by him beyond his death, through various dower rights and pension regulations, as long as she maintained her status as his sexual property, whether or not he actively took advantage of this. However, there was a twist to all this: a woman was entitled to be maintained by her husband after divorce in the style to which she was accustomed. Therefore, if her husband was rich, but had treated her in a miserly fashion during the marriage, he could continue to treat her in the same manner after the marriage was over. If, on the other hand, he had been a generous husband in meeting her needs and wishes, the wife could demand a greater sum upon the dissolution of her marriage. In other words, the wife's entitlement to what would now be called matrimonial property was at least partially dependent on her husband's spending patterns rather than on the actual amount of property available.

By and large the wife, in case of divorce, was not entitled to any of her husband's business assets. On the other hand, the wife often obtained the family home if she had dependent children.[95] Under current property regimes, the matrimonial home is often sold, given that it tends to be the largest financial asset to which the couple have a joint right. The result of this is that the partner with the better job and greater earning capacity (usually the husband) will be able to buy another house, while the partner with the lower-status job and lesser earning capacity will be unlikely to own another property unless she remarries a man who already owns a house or is able to purchase one.[96] We know that home-ownership is decisively affected by sex. In 1988, 32 per cent of all single mothers in Ontario, versus 69 per cent of all single fathers, lived in their own home.[97]

Today the law assumes that every marriage is an economic partnership in which both partners are equally entitled to the fruits of the work upon termination of the marriage.[98] This approach eliminates the dilemma of having predominantly middle-aged to aged male judges (who themselves grew up in an era of a firmly patriarchal family) decide on the respective contributions of wives and husbands to a marriage. However, the assumption of an equal contribution, while constituting important progress over the assumption of female dependency, is highly problematic. This will be discussed in detail in Chapter 5.

Looking at it from the male perspective, if the wife was a housewife, her contribution is implicitly valued more if her husband's income is high, and less if his income is low. If he was very successful economically (clearly not the norm), it may mean that an ex-wife cashes in on her ex-husband's economic success without having made a contribution to it, while the wife of a less economically successful man would receive less. Given, of course, that the spectacularly successful man can also afford this division of property (by definition), it is not a very worrisome scenario.

More troubling is the situation in which both spouses were in the labour force, and the wife earned a substantial income while doing all—or even most—of the housework and child care. This woman may have to share her property with her husband who earned less, while likely still retaining custody of their children.

While overall the income gap between women and men has not decreased in the past decade, the relative contribution that wives make to the family income has increased substantially. In 1967, 3.6 per cent of wives earned more than their husbands and 1.1 per cent were the sole earner in all husband-wife families. In 1992, by contrast, 14.2 per cent of wives earned more than their husbands, and an additional 5.1 per cent were the sole earner.[99] We shall consider the implications of this issue further in Chapter 5.

CONCLUSION

Overall, there has been a decisive shift from congruence to incongruence at the nuclear level in household and family memberships. Legally, husbands and wives are now considered co-owners of matrimonial property, but children are only incompletely factored into the equation. Legally, child care is seen as the joint responsibility of father and mother. In practice, this looks quite different, both while a union lasts and after it dissolves. We will now look at the actual development of spousal and parental roles in the twentieth century.

CHAPTER 3

The Blurring of Spousal Roles

INTRODUCTION

At the turn of the century, a married man had economic and legal responsibility for his wife, who was supposed to have sexual relations only with him, to bear and raise his children, and look after her husband's physical and social well-being. People generally knew (or thought they knew) who was and who was not married. Of course, even then things were never entirely this neat. Historically, Canada has had different versions of marriage, and it was not always clear who was and who was not free to marry or who was married to whom. Nevertheless, there is no doubt that in general, spousal roles are significantly more blurred today than they were earlier.

This blurring is due to several interrelated factors. For one, the status of being married or being not married is no longer as sharply differentiated as it used to be, either in terms of interactions between a couple, or in terms of rights and obligations. This is due to changing sexual mores and the prevalence of divorce. One of the interactions supposedly reserved for the wedding night was the beginning of sexual relations between the couple.[1] Today, pre- and non-marital sex, and occasionally postmarital sex, for both women and men, are socially openly acknowledged; a significant proportion of couples live together in a common-law relationship before they marry, and legal marriage (if it takes place) is only a step in a series of steps. At the other end, if a marriage ends in divorce, most likely one or both partners will remarry or live common law with someone else. The marriage tie is therefore no longer severed only by death but quite frequently by a *comparatively simple* legal act.[2]

Legal marriage between a woman and a man can therefore be seen as the centre-piece of a continuum of interactions that is preceded and followed by behaviour patterns similar to those in a legal marriage.[3] In addition, marriage as a union that is socially sanctioned and assumed to be permanent is no longer clearly reserved for heterosexual couples. While no country as yet allows marriage between same-sex partners, lesbian and gay domestic partnerships can now be registered in some international jurisdictions.[4] Some employers treat employees' same-sex partners like legal marriage partners with respect to eligibility for fringe benefits.

Given women's legal emancipation, which is most evident in the legal emancipation of wives, marriage (while still a major status change) no longer has the same profound legal, social, or economic consequences it once did. Lesbian and gay couples' advocacy for recognition as spouses has blurred the conception of spouses as husband (male) and wife (female).[5] Taking these various indicators together, there is no doubt that spousal roles today are significantly less sharply defined than they were at the turn of the century, in spite of the fact that they were never quite as clearly drawn even at that time as ideology would have us believe.

LEGAL MARRIAGES AND COMMON-LAW RELATIONSHIPS

Marital, Non-marital, and Quasi-marital Roles

Historically Canada has always had a diversity of marriage arrangements. The fur traders of the Hudson's Bay Company started contracting marriages *à la façon du pays* (or according to the custom of the country) from the late seventeenth century to the middle of the nineteenth century, at which time it was gradually replaced by church and civil weddings. While initially marriage according to the custom of the country was not seen as a permanent union, it became so over time, particularly as more and more male fur traders married the daughters of White male fur traders and their Native wives.

Marriage according to the custom of the country evolved from two different traditions, with very different attitudes towards marriage. Eventually, however, it took on all the elements of a 'civilized' marriage except for the blessing of the Church. Husbands would provide for their wives and children beyond their death, and the Hudson's Bay Company accepted some limited responsibility towards them as well. Indeed, in 1821 the Hudson's Bay Company introduced marriage contracts signed by both parties in the presence of witnesses, and in 1824 the Council of the Northern Department resolved: 'That no Officer or Servant in the company's service be hereafter allowed to take a woman without binding himself down to such reasonable provision for the maintenance of the woman and children as on a fair and equitable principle may be considered necessary not only during their residence in the country but after their departure hence.'[6] With the arrival of missionaries, marriage according to the custom of the country rapidly deteriorated. The Church worked to block the adaptive process with which newcomers to the country had been socialized to fur trade custom by reducing the status of Native women to that of mistresses or even prostitutes. It also introduced the Victorian double standard rampant in England at the time. As a consequence, 'the custom of the country' fell into disrepute in fur trade society by the mid-nineteenth century.[7] However, in an important legal case around that time, the *Connolly* case, in which the husband left his Native wife to marry a White cousin, the chief justice vindicated 'the custom of the country' by describing the twenty-eight-year union (from which at least six children were born) as one that 'would have been regarded as a valid marriage in the North West'. He concluded that 'There would be no law, no justice, no sense, no morality' in declaring such a union as concubinage and the offspring as bastards.[8]

In a legal marriage, once a couple signed all the relevant forms in the appropriate manner and consummated the marriage, they are married as far as the law is concerned, and their rights and responsibilities differ from those they each had just before they were married. The dividing line between being not married and being married is therefore usually assumed to be clean, unambiguous, and occupies little time: the marriage must be consummated to be legally valid if challenged, usually something in the order of one day and night.

This is not so with common-law relationships, which became legally recognized unions over time. While a legally married couple are not married one day before the wedding, but are on the next, the situation of a cohabiting couple changes gradually towards a more marriagelike state because of cohabitation. How long a common-law couple must cohabit to be recognized as common-law spouses varies. For the purpose of employment benefits, it may suffice for an employee to declare to her or his employer that a person is a common-law spouse. This may not entitle such a person to inherit in case the employee dies intestate, although it may be a factor taken into consideration if a case comes before the court. For income tax purposes, one year of continuous cohabitation is required.[9] For support purposes after union dissolution, recognition as common-law spouses varies from province to province and territory. The same couple that would be recognized as common-law spouses in some provinces might not be recognized as such elsewhere.

Divorce as a Mediator between Legal and Quasi-legal Marriages
Even legal marriages may not be as clear-cut as is often assumed. One of the functions of divorce is to free previously married people to marry again. The status of a marriage therefore depends on the status of a divorce in the case of previously married people. Canadians have used foreign divorces to a considerable extent to enable themselves to remarry. Bigamy, furthermore, was relatively easy to commit in a country as vast as Canada and with as high a degree of physical mobility as was possible in the early part of this century. Further, male immigrants who came across the ocean might 'forget' to mention to a potential new marriage partner that they already had a wife in the old country.

In general, the question of whether a relationship counts as a marriage or not is often particularly important after the union has dissolved. The law prescribes certain obligations in the case of a legal marriage or common-law relationship after the death of one partner or the dissolution of the union due to separation or divorce. Here the distinction between common-law relationships and legal marriages is even more blurred than at the start of a relationship or marriage. If a legally married couple separate but are not yet divorced, they are in a sort of limbo, neither fully married nor divorced. For example, Statistics Canada used to count separated couples as married. However, most of them no longer share a residence, nor do they exhibit some of the behaviour we associate with marriage: having a sexual relationship, offering mutual emotional support, and sharing a household. They may, however, continue to share dependent children during separation and after divorce, in which case there is likely some shared financial responsibility for those children, and today there may be joint custody.

Separated people cannot legally remarry another person, although they can move in with someone else. This may signal the beginning of a new relationship that may turn into either a common-law relationship before the old marriage is dissolved or a legal marriage after divorce has been granted. Common-law couples may share the same type of overlap between continuing shared responsibilities with an old partner while cohabiting with a new partner or living alone. Given the fuzziness of the marital status after separation but prior to divorce, and given that even after a divorce there will likely be some ongoing interaction with the previous marriage partner, particularly if there are children,[10] the simple prevalence of divorce blurs the distinction between the statuses of being married and being not married.

If we identify the various dimensions of familial interaction as coresidence, shared sexual relations, economic interdependence, shared procreation, shared socialization of any children, shared emotional ties, shared social networks, and shared household management, divorce would usually sever some but not all of these forms of interaction. In particular, some degree of economic interdependence is likely to continue, especially if there are children; shared procreation remains a fact due to past actions; shared socialization may or may not take place, and emotional ties (albeit often negative ones) may linger for a long time.[11] There may be ongoing interaction with in-laws and other members of the previously shared social network since the ex-in-laws of the divorced ex-spouse are the current relatives of the children.[12]

The status of being no longer married to a person with whom one has been married and with whom one has had children is therefore not comparable to that of a person to whom one has never been married, hence the use of the term 'ex': my ex-husband, my ex-wife. Divorce therefore creates a new marital status: that of ex-marriage partner, which stands somewhere between the marital status of being married and being single. One fuzzy category may create another fuzzy category. Before 1968, divorce was difficult to obtain in Canada. This led a substantial proportion of married people to end their legal marriage through various other means, ranging from formal judicial separations of bed and board over desertions to what has been called 'self-divorce'.

Judicial separations were the only *official* form of separation in Quebec, where divorce was not recognized.[13] However, they were difficult to obtain, and only a few people sought them. Having obtained them, the judicial separation still left the marriage tie unbroken, allowing the parties to reunite at will, in contrast to divorce, which 'ruptured the marriage tie so that it cannot be renewed'.[14]

Given this difficulty, some people turned to less formal means to leave an unsatisfactory marriage. Some men—and occasionally some women— simply deserted their spouse.[15] Such separated people might form common-law unions with others. In Montreal, court records show that some men who were still legally married set up house with a mistress, while others went further and married again by presenting themselves as widowed.[16] Of course, if they were found out, they were identified as bigamists and might be put into prison.

Another apparently frequently employed way of ending an unsatisfactory marriage was obtaining a foreign divorce, most often in the United States. While legally invalid in Canada, the same legal system effectively prevented enforcement of the law whenever people who had received foreign divorces remarried. Subsequent marriages were officially bigamous. Nevertheless, there was 'a certain amount of de facto tolerance of bigamy, both within local communities and among authorities.'[17] Foreign divorces heavily outnumbered Canadian divorces. In 1922, for instance, there were 543 divorces in all of Canada, while 1,368 divorces were granted in the United States to persons who had been married in Canada.[18] Foreign divorce was mostly a woman's device. Eighty-four per cent of the American divorces obtained by formal petition were obtained by wives, as were 66.7 per cent of those cited in informal petitions. Generally, 'Permeable and moving boundaries divided non-support, desertion, and separation.'[19] We can add that there were permeable boundaries between the status of being married legally, semilegally, and non-legally, but the boundaries were in no way as permeable as they are today.

The Gradual *Rapprochement* between Legal Marriages and Common-law Relationships

This brief sketch of marital relations in Canada shows that there have always been different forms of marriage, with varying degrees of religious, civil, and judicial involvement and sanctioning. The modern version of many of these older alternatives to fully legal marriages[20] are common-law relationships. One recent overview of common-law relationships concluded that 'With no clear standards in place, the law itself is unpredictable, and each case is evaluated in accordance with uncertain equitable principles, tempered by a healthy dose of judicial discretion. This process only promotes litigation in the long run ...'[21]

Deech has noted that cohabitation has gradually been accorded legal status in English law—in which she includes Canadian law—during the second half of this century. She deplores this tendency, and argues passionately that 'marriage should become more like cohabitation and not the other way round'.[22] She argues that given the strong pro-marriage factors pushing people to get married, it seems reasonable to assume that the majority of contemporary cohabitants have freely chosen not to marry.[23] 'There ought to be a corner of freedom for such couples to which they can escape and avoid family law.'[24] In particular, the law's tendency to impose the status and structure of traditional marriage on formerly cohabiting people just when they have ended the relationship means that 'the law is converting the relationship into marriage *ex post facto*'.[25]

What is the comparative status of common-law versus legal marriage in Canada today? Have common-law relationships become more like legal marriage, or vice versa? I shall look at five issues to answer this question: frequency, social acceptance, names, support obligations, and the status of children of the union.

Frequency. Just as there seems to be no good way to estimate the number of actual divorces before the times in which divorces became easier to obtain, so there seems to be no good way to establish the actual number of common-law marriages before these became more socially acceptable. It has never been a crime in Canada to take a different name, as long as it was not done for a fraudulent purpose. If, therefore, Bernard Brown and Wendy White were living together as a couple, and she called herself Wendy Brown, this was legally acceptable. Even close friends and neighbours, therefore, might not know whether a couple is legally married or living common law.

Since 1981, the Canadian census officially added common-law couples under married couples; an unknown number may have been counted all along under this heading. The increase in common-law couples since the 1980s has been remarkable. While in 1981 6 per cent of all couples were common-law couples, in 1991 10 per cent fell into this category.[26] There are marked differences between the provinces in the prevalence of this form of marriage. In 1991, Prince Edward Island had the lowest proportion of common-law couples (5.9 per cent of all couples), as compared to Quebec, which had 16.3 per cent.[27]

The increase may be more apparent than real, due to the increased social acceptance of such unions. As one report notes, 'people may be more willing to report living common law now than in the past because of decreased social stigma attached to this type of living arrangement.'[28] Nevertheless, an increasing proportion of couples living common law rather than in a legal marriage is part of an international trend.[29]

Social Acceptance. Social acceptance, in turn, is certainly facilitated by the growing number of married women who keep their own name. Common-law unions have gradually become eligible for a number of benefits (and obligations) previously restricted to legally married couples. For instance, as of 1975, common-law couples became eligible to receive the spouse's allowance.[30] Since 1978, common-law spouses incur a mutual support obligation in the case of union dissolution in Ontario. Other provinces have followed suit. In 1986, the Ontario legislature extended marriage benefits to cohabiting partners in over thirty statutes.[31] In 1995, common-law partners became eligible for insurance benefits in their capacity as spouse to the insured person.[32]

In terms of attitude, we have evidence from the United States that the normative acceptance of cohabitation increased greatly during the 1980s. Parental pressure to marry did not seem particularly salient in a national sample of cohabitants, nor was there any longer a clear notion that children should be born into a legal marriage.[33] The authors conclude:

> Attitudes concerning cohabitation and marriage suggest that while most expect to marry, normative pressures toward marriage are not very high. Indeed, one-fifth of cohabiting persons do not expect ever to marry (or marry again) ...
>
> Thus the picture that is emerging is that cohabitation is very much a family status, but one in which levels of certainty about the relationship are lower than in marriage ...[34]

Names. As mentioned earlier, Canada has always allowed considerable leeway with respect to names. This made it possible for common-law wives to take their husbands' last names, but it also made it possible for legally married wives to keep their own names, even after marriage, at least for professional purposes. Even decades ago, it was possible for a couple to be introduced in a social setting by two different last names.

The custom of keeping two different last names after marriage took a great swing upwards in the 1980s. Quebec led the way in 1981 by requiring wives to retain their maiden names. Couples may still end up with the same last name, but, at least in Quebec, the path of least resistance today is to have separate surnames. With the coming into force of section 15 of the *Charter of Rights and Freedoms*, the husband's/father's name is no longer privileged in law, even though it is still privileged in practice.

The symbolic importance of names can hardly be overestimated. By accepting her husband's last name, a wife (at the beginning of this century) was seen as being legally subsumed under her husband. This is particularly relevant in the case of divorce, in which a succession of wives might all be called Mrs John Smith. After divorce, a woman could either continue to use her former husband's last name, which symbolized a union that no longer existed, or to change her name once again (the first time being at marriage) and therefore probably lose some more distant friends and acquaintances who would no longer find her in the phonebook, on top of other associated inconveniences. The gradual emancipation of wives is fittingly symbolized by the right to retain their own name and the capacity to pass it on to their children.

At the same time, this constitutes a powerful symbolic *rapprochement* between common-law and legal marriages. If married people are introduced socially as Jane Doe and John Smith, this is a symbolic request to regard them not only as a couple but also as two individuals. In so far as people in common-law relationships are somewhat oriented towards maintaining people as individuals within a conjugal unit, we can note in this instance that legal marriage has become somewhat more like common-law marriage.

Support Obligations. It is otherwise with support obligations. Since the 1970s, we can note an increased tendency for the law to treat common-law couples similarly to legally married couples with respect to support obligations after a union ends. This is stipulated legally in several provincial family laws. Differences remain with regard to matrimonial property, but the tendency seems to be to assimilate common-law marriages with legal marriages.

The matter is not helped by the fact that provinces and territories vary in the duration of cohabitation required before they regard a couple as a common-law couple. A couple that would be considered as having a common-law relationship in Nova Scotia because they cohabited for one year would not be so considered in British Columbia (which requires two years), New Brunswick or Ontario (which require three years), or Manitoba (which requires five years of cohabitation).[35]

The Status of Children of the Union. 'Under common law, the illegitimate child of the union of an unmarried couple was legally considered to be in the sole custody of the mother and was, correspondingly, her responsibility alone to support.'[36] Around the turn of the century a wife who left a marriage to live in a common-law relationship with another man could expect to be declared an unfit mother and therefore to lose custody of her children. In the early 1970s, however, the focus of custody disputes veered away from a woman's sexual behaviour and towards the best interests of the child.[37] The concept of illegitimate children was gradually abandoned in law, and hence the status of children conceived in common-law unions compared to those conceived in legal unions has been equalized legally. Whether or not there are any social differences is unknown at this point.

There has been a marked *rapprochement* between legal marriages and common-law unions. In terms of social acceptance, support obligations, and the status of children of the union, common-law relationships have become more similar to legal marriages. With respect to names, legal marriages have become more similar to common-law unions. Regarding frequency, it is difficult to make clear judgements because earlier figures are none too reliable, but there seems to be a clear trend towards increased cohabitation. With increased frequency, we can also note a great variety in common-law relationships, as is true for legal marriages.[38]

HETEROSEXUAL AND HOMOSEXUAL UNIONS

Until fairly recently, certain homosexual acts, especially between men,[39] were illegal in Canada[40] and in many other Western countries. Gradually, homosexuality has become more socially acceptable, although homophobia remains strong. Even tragic deaths due to 'gay bashing' are not a thing of the past.

Despite the vigorous resistance of homophobic groups, a series of legal and policy changes have narrowed the gap between heterosexual and homosexual unions.[41] While not yet accorded the status of common-law relationships—in Ontario a law[42] expanding the definition of spouse to include same-sex partners was narrowly defeated in the summer of 1994—a partial recognition of same-sex unions has nevertheless occurred. This is an international trend. Many of the changes have taken place in the 1980s.[43] This is a far cry from what matters were like at the turn of the century.

Heterosexuality as the Only Legitimate Form of Sexuality

Until fairly recently, not only was heterosexuality the only accepted form of sexuality, but homosexuality led to a host of discriminations that were not prohibited. People could lose their jobs, divorced mothers could lose their children, and consenting adults could be prosecuted for sexual acts that happened in the privacy of their bedrooms.

There is no other form of cohabitation that challenges patriarchalists as homosexual families do.[44] The ideological underpinning of the patriarchal family is a division of labour by sex, which in turn is premised on the notion of a natural difference between the sexes.

If, however, two adults of the same sex are recognized as couples equivalent to heterosexual couples, the basis on which the patriarchal family rests topples. Sexuality, which in the patriarchal family is (supposedly) restricted to at least potentially procreative sex,[45] is definitely non-procreative in the case of same-sex couples.[46] In the Judaeo-Christian tradition, as in some other religious traditions, non-procreative sex is usually regarded as sinful. In law, as well, the *theoretical capacity* of heterosexual couples to procreate is cited in order to bar same-sex couples from benefits, even if these benefits (such as the spousal allowance) are granted to heterosexual couples who are beyond the procreative age and who may never have procreated together.[47]

The notion that marriage, as well as common-law relationships, involved one adult female and one adult male was such a given that it was not even always stipulated, just as one does not stipulate that people walk on their feet, rather than on their hands, to a given location. This taken-for-granted view had many social, economic, and political consequences. Homosexuals either did not publicly admit their sexual orientation, or they would face a potentially large number of discriminatory practices.

Since the early 1970s, with the advent of the gay liberation movement, this life at the social margins for gays and lesbians has been challenged—in some aspects successfully, in others not yet. The 1985 report of the Parliamentary Committee on Equality Rights, *Equality for All*, made the following statement with respect to discrimination on the basis of sexual orientation:

> We were shocked by a number of the experiences of unfair treatment related to us by homosexuals in different parts of the country. We heard about the harassment of and violence committed against homosexuals. We were told in graphic detail about physical abuse and psychological oppression suffered by homosexuals. In several cities, private social clubs serving a homosexual clientele were damaged and the members harassed. Hate propaganda directed at homosexuals has been found in some parts of Canada. We were told of the severe employment and housing problems suffered by homosexuals. Indeed, several witnesses appearing before us expressed some fear that their appearance before the Committee would jeopardize their jobs.[48]

Some of the issues that have been and continue to be fought about include:

(a) Overall Normalization of Social Relations. The goal is general social acceptance of homosexuality as a valid form of sexuality. This would have many ramifications: same-sex couples would be socially accepted in the same way in which heterosexual couples are accepted. Homosexuality used to be seen both as a mental illness as well as a criminal activity. The American Psychiatric Association removed homosexuality from its list of mental illnesses in 1974. In 1975, the American Psychological Association did likewise and adopted the following resolution:

Homosexuality *per se* implies no impairment in judgement, stability, reliability, or general social or vocational capabilities;

Further, the American Psychological Association urges all mental health professionals to take the lead in removing the stigma of mental illness that has long been associated with homosexual orientations.[49]

However, some US states still define homosexual acts as criminal, and these statutes are inconsistently enforced. For instance, the 1986 decision of the US Supreme Court in *Bowers* v. *Hardwick* upheld a decision by a lower court, which convicted a Georgian man for performing consensual homosexual acts in the privacy of his bedroom.[50] This contrasts with most European Community states, of which only Ireland still considers homosexual activity as criminal.[51]

'Coming out'—disclosing one's sexual identity—is fraught with problems. Its meaning has shifted over the years. While in the 1950s it meant entering the gay world, it now means disclosing one's lesbian or gay identity to others, including the straight world.[52] Some of the stories of gay people 'coming out' to their blood relatives are heart-wrenching, while others are heart-warming. Estimates as to the proportion of gays and lesbians who are accepted compared to those who are rejected by their families after 'coming out' are shaky at best.[53] Yet the need to maintain secrecy and to hide an important part of one's life take an enormous emotional toll, which may even result in suicide attempts.[54] It might save some adolescents from suicides or at least from severe mental and emotional problems if they realized that their feelings were one normal expression of sexuality, while at the same time perhaps reduce 'gay bashing' by others by introducing them to lesbians and gay men who are admirable individuals rather than unknown and slightly sinister abstractions. It is still seen as undesirable (and sometimes it is dangerous) for lesbian and gay couples to display affection in public, such as holding hands or kissing,[55] while certainly the former and often the latter is widely accepted for heterosexual couples. As one commentator simply states: 'homosexuality should be considered as part of someone's personality like blue eyes or left handedness.'[56]

(b) Access to Employment and the Associated Benefits that Heterosexual Couples Enjoy. As long as homosexual activity is defined as criminal (no longer the case in Canada, but still the case in about half of the US states), this may pose a risk of either obtaining (if out) or retaining (if found out) one's job. This is particularly so in the military and in jobs involving either high authority or involvement with children. In the US, part of Clinton's presidential campaign platform was to normalize homosexuality and allow homosexuals to serve openly in the army (presumably, there are many

homosexuals in the army who are not out). However, the resistance was so strong that so far this promise has not been fully met.[57]

Fringe benefits associated with employment, like employment discrimination, have become a legal battle field. There have been several law cases fought on various issues. Mossop sued the federal government because he was refused a day of bereavement leave when his long-term lover's father died and he wanted to attend his funeral.[58] Andrews wanted to obtain OHIP benefits for her lesbian lover and her lover's children through her job, a benefit that is extended to heterosexual spouses and their dependent children. Vogel tried to include his partner in his employee benefit plan.[59] While all three of these cases were ultimately lost, they are part of a string of cases that raised awareness of the issue and led to an increasing number of employers adding same-sex spouses to the list of family members who are eligible for their spouse's employment benefits.[60]

A very important type of employment benefit are pension entitlements. The *Leshner* case[61] involved a gay man in Ontario who wanted his partner included as his beneficiary in his employment pension plan. While the employer extended its family coverage to provide all benefits to same-sex spouses, the federal *Income Tax Act*, under which provincial pension plans are registered, does not allow for the inclusion of same-sex spouses. The Ontario Human Rights Board of Inquiry held in 1992 that the employer had to set up an equivalent pension plan for persons living in a conjugal homosexual relationship unless the *Income Tax Act* were amended within three years.

(c) Recognition as Family Members During Various Crises.[62] One of the famous cases in which a lesbian was denied the right to act for her long-time lover is the US case of Sharon Kowalski,[63] who was severely disabled after a car accident. The litigation involved a guardianship dispute between her parents and her lesbian lover, Karen Thompson. Thompson had to wait for eight years until Kowalski's parents had consigned Sharon to an institution before she was judicially recognized as the only person willing and able to help Sharon Kowalski live outside an institution.

Similar situations may occur when family members are given privileged access to people in intensive care. Lesbian and gay partners may find themselves excluded from access to the ill person, as well as from making decisions on his or her behalf. At funerals, gay and lesbian partners may find themselves pushed to the side, or even entirely excluded, depending on the wishes of other family members of the deceased. This makes mourning and coping with the death of a lover that much more difficult. This is an area in which some significant change has taken place, however.

In 1992, Ontario enacted Canada's first statute that enables same-sex partners to be 'next of kin' for consent to treatment purposes[64] if they had lived together for at least a year and had a relationship of primary importance in both persons' lives. While same-sex partners are not specifically mentioned, this definition does not exclude them.[65] However, employers are still not required to provide bereavement leave if a member of a gay or lesbian family dies.[66] Ironically, one recent study of twenty-eight lesbian couples *with children* found that 'couples feel more accepted as a family with their own families of origin and among their associates and friends than by the lesbian community.'[67]

(d) The Capacity to Inherit When a Long-Term Lover Dies. When a gay man or lesbian dies intestate, the long-term partner will find him- or herself excluded from inheriting, while other relatives (who may possibly have been hostile to the deceased's lifestyle) inherit. Even if the person died testate, the will must be carefully written if it leaves the bulk of the estate to a same-sex lover rather than to blood relatives.[68]

(e) The Capacity to Sponsor One's Homosexual Partner and Potentially His or Her Dependants as Family Members for Immigration Purposes. At present, Canada has a two- or arguably three-tiered system of immigration: people either immigrate as individuals, by meeting certain criteria, or as family members, by being sponsored by a citizen or immigrant who is in a position to do so. Third, a certain proportion arrive in Canada as refugees. People in the family category will be admitted even if they were inadmissible under the first category of immigrants. It is thus a highly consequential matter as to who is defined as a family member who can be sponsored.[69] At present, same-sex partners are excluded, although they can qualify under the humanitarian and compassionate provision.[70] By contrast, some European states,[71] Australia,[72] and New Zealand [73]allow same-sex sponsorship.

(f) Access to Housing on the Same Basis as a Heterosexual Couple or Family. Another famous US case is *Braschi* v. *Stahl Associates.*[74] In this case, Miguel Braschi lived with his lover, Leslie Blanchard, for approximately a decade in a rent-controlled Manhattan apartment. After the death of Blanchard, who had been the tenant on record, the owner of the building tried to evict Braschi. The case was fought (and eventually won) on the basis of whether or not Braschi was within the protected category of 'surviving spouse or some other member of the deceased tenant's family' and thus entitled to remain as a tenant in the rent-controlled apartment.

In general, there is at present little protection for homosexual couples who wish to rent an apartment together and to succeed to tenancy rights after the death of one of the partners.[75] In Canada, it depends on whether or not sexual orientation is a prohibited ground for discrimination under provincial human rights codes.[76]

(g) Custody of One's Children. 'Of all the cases which involve gay issues, those involving the custody of children of gay parents are the most numerous.'[77] Courts in the US use three approaches in determining custody involving gay and lesbian parents. The *per se* approach is premised on the rebuttable presumption that a gay or lesbian parent is unfit by virtue of his or her sexual orientation. The middle ground approach does not presume that the gay or lesbian parent is unfit *per se*, but assumes that a child will be harmed by exposure to the gay or lesbian parent's homosexuality. This results in restrictive behavioural guidelines if the gay or lesbian parent obtains custody. The third approach is the nexus approach, in which the court requires proof that the parent's homosexuality has or will adversely affect the child before it can deny custody to the gay or lesbian parent. In two out of the three prevailing approaches, then, the lesbian or gay parent is at fault simply because of her or his sexual orientation.[78] As a consequence, 'The odds are currently heavily skewed against gay parents in custody disputes.'[79]

(h) The Right to Adopt Children. Some lesbian and gay couples wish to adopt children. While it is difficult for anyone to find children available for adoption in Canada (the number of children available for adoption has steadily decreased over the past two decades),[80] it is particularly difficult for lesbian or gay couples.[81] If they are successful, most likely only one of the partners will be recognized as the legal parent. This is also the case when one of the two partners has a biological child. The homosexual partner will in most cases not be allowed to adopt as a coparent, and therefore will likely not receive custody in the case of the death of the natural parent. However, a 1995 landmark case[82] in Ontario may have changed this situation. In this case, the court considered four cases of lesbian couples jointly. In each case, one of the partners had given birth to a child conceived by artificial insemination, and the lesbian partner wanted to adopt the child as a parent. At issue, then, was

> ... whether there is a constitutionally valid reason why an application for adoption by a homosexual *couple*, living in a conjugal relationship, one of whom is the biological mother of the child, should not be accepted by the court and decided on the basis of what is in the best interests of the child (p. 4).

Justice James P. Nevins found that all the relationships in question were spousal relationships, since

Each of the couples have cohabited together continuously and exclusively for lengthy periods, ranging from six to thirteen years; their financial affairs are interconnected; they share household expenses, have joint bank accounts and in some cases they own property together in joint tenancy; they share the housekeeping burden to the extent they are able in light of their respective careers and employments; the individual partners share a committed sexual relationship. Most importantly, they all share equally the joys and burdens of child rearing (p. 5).

He concluded that the section of the *Child and Family Services Act*, which stipulates that spouses be of the opposite sex before they may apply for the adoption of a child, infringes the equality rights guaranteed under the *Canadian Charter of Rights and Freedoms* and that '"line" drawn by the legislation in this provision is irrational, not based on any compelling social interest, and is a completely unwarranted infringement of specifically protected *Charter* rights' (pp. 38–9). He finally concludes that the definition of 'spouse' as it appears in the *Child and Family Services Act* should be read and applied as if enacted in the following form: '"spouse" means the person to whom a person of the opposite sex is married or with whom a person of the same or opposite sex is living in a conjugal relationship outside of marriage' (p. 42; emphasized in the original). This is a definitive statement with respect to removing the line between opposite sex and same-sex spouses in this context.

(i) The Right to Be Supported by a Previous Lesbian or Gay Partner after the Union Has Dissolved. This is a problematic request, since the right to be supported[83] contains within it the responsibility of the other partner to provide support beyond the duration of the union. Opinions on this issue are sharply divided. On the one hand, some argue that same-sex unions should be given the same status as heterosexual common-law unions, in which the partners do incur a support obligation. On the other hand, there is a strong critique of this request, based on an overall critique of family relations as they currently exist.[84] Rather than arguing for recognition and integration into a system of the family that is inherently corrupt since it is based on property relations, and rather than fitting homosexual couples into the mode of heterosexual couples, lesbians should advocate 'the abolition of benefits based on family status, the reconsideration of what constitutes "benefits", or even the abolition of the category "family" itself'.[85]

(j) The Gradual Acceptance of Homosexual Unions as Familial Relationships. Since the 1970s, and particularly in the 1990s, there has been a growing recognition of homosexual relationships as family relationships.

Homosexuality is considered neither a mental illness nor a crime in Canada. While it is not an enumerated ground for discrimination under the *Charter of Rights and Freedoms*, it is an analogous ground.[86] It is a protected ground of discrimination in most but not all provinces.[87] Specifically, people can no longer be denied a job (including in the Canadian military) on the basis of their sexual orientation. Many employers[88] have voluntarily extended the same type of employment benefits to employees with same-sex partners as they do to employees with heterosexual partners.

The work of the gay liberation movement has borne fruit in the sense that gay men and lesbians are more socially visible, and higher visibility has led to some limited social acceptance. Several high-profile law cases have pushed the public debate towards considering gay and lesbian spouses and families as such, rather than restricting these terms to define heterosexual spouses and families. This is usually the basis on which such cases are fought—that family benefits (there is much less talk about family responsibilities) should be extended to lesbians and gay men.

Opposition to this assimilationist stance comes from two directions. On the one hand, there is a vocal homophobic opposition that fears the demise of the traditional family if rights are extended to same-sex couples. It is usually not explained why broadening the definition of the family would hurt those families currently included in it. However, there is also no consensus among lesbians and gay men as to whether this is the right path or not to pursue. The assimilationist position argues for having lesbian and gay families treated in the same way in which heterosexual families are treated. This may take the form of either fighting for the right to marry legally, and/or to have homosexual unions treated in the same way as heterosexual common-law unions.[89]

The tool to achieve this is to adopt a functional definition of the family in which same-sex unions and common-law unions would be evaluated in the same way, that is, by considering the various dimensions of familial interaction.[90] How long have the partners lived together? Are they economically interdependent? Are they mutually sexually involved? Have they represented themselves to the world as a couple? These are some of the questions that are posed in this context to recognize specific couples as equivalent or not equivalent to a common-law couple.

There are some authors and activists who reject this approach. Their argument is that 'The not-so-implicit message is that lesbian/gay relationships will be accorded the status of family only to the extent that they replicate the traditional husband-wife couple, a tradition based on property relations.'[91] This, in turn, reinforces the patriarchal definition of the family. 'The patriarchal link between marriage and women as property so devastatingly criticized by generations of feminist theorists is resuscitated and reified in familial functionalism.'[92]

This leaves us with a dilemma. Clearly, the current situation of lesbians and gays is inequitable and harmful not only to the people directly involved but to society as a whole.[93] To have one segment of society oppressed by the majority results in a direct diminishing of our collective human rights. However, are the issues identified in the previous section best solved by treating same-sex relations as equivalent to heterosexual unions, or would we all be better off by redefining family relations in such a way that they are changed for all, whether homosexual or heterosexual, depending on the purpose subserved by a particular definition? Do we need a sexualized couple at all in order to determine that family relations exist?[94] These questions will be addressed in Chapter 7.

WIVES AND HUSBANDS

Under the patriarchal model of the family, wives were responsible for all housework and other unpaid family work, for all service work for the household members (which might include a boarder), and for everything else that was needed to keep the family and the household on an even keel. To a large degree, unfortunately, this still describes today's reality, although at least at the normative level, it is now considered appropriate for men to 'help' with such matters, and there are a minuscule number of househusbands who—although statistically insignificant—at least demonstrate that alternative patterns are possible. While there have been considerable changes in wife-husband roles, there are also some continuities, particularly with respect to violence between the spouses. We will look at discontinuities as well as continuities.

From a Strict Division of Labour to Normative Ambiguity
The centrepiece of the patriarchal model of the family was the husband's role as economic provider for his wife and children. This was buttressed in law and in social policy by making it difficult to impossible for married women to participate in the paid labour force, thus reinforcing the wife and children's economic dependence on the male provider. The notion of economic dependence was also, of course, centrally premised on regarding the tasks of housewives as uneconomic. The entire infrastructure on which the official economic structure rested was thus made invisible and hence could be misdeclared as uneconomic. 'Out of sight, out of mind' describes the process well.

Division of labour by sex within the household was thus complemented by division of labour within society as a whole and vice versa. At the macro and micro levels, there were tasks seen as appropriate for one sex—*and hence as inappropriate for the other sex*—in a symmetrical manner. With the influx of wives and mothers into the paid labour force, this is no longer the case. One observer suggests that 'As a cultural ideal, the doctrine of separate spheres, in which adult women were expected to be full-time housewife-mothers while their husbands were the breadwinners, has virtually ended.'[95] I am not suggesting that the unequal division of labour as it existed at the turn of the century was ever a good thing, but at least in theory, there was the notion of complementarity and hence interdependence, although it took the form of female economic, social, political, and legal dependence in spite of the economically valuable contributions of women and girls. Today the division of labour is greatly out of kilter. Women have adopted most of the roles previously occupied by men, but men have not taken over half of the tasks previously done by women.

It is a well-documented fact that women all over the world do most of the unpaid housework and caring work, while at the same time doing a substantial portion of the paid work. This is already evident among adolescents: teenage girls do more of the housework and caring work than do teenage boys. The unequal division of labour continues through adulthood and into old age.[96] It applies to both married and cohabiting couples, although the gender differences are less for cohabiting couples.[97] There is unequal division of labour among couples married for the first time and among those in which one or both partners were previously married, although remarriage resulted in a *slightly* greater contribution by men.[98] There is a remarkable inelasticity in men's contributions to household tasks: 'no matter how much there is to do, men do the same amount'.[99]

Although there are some variations, the unequal division of labour is not affected by social class, urban-rural differences, the number of children present in a household,[100] whether or not the wife/mother is in the labour force (with the exception that there is some evidence suggesting that, paradoxically, men contribute more to household tasks when the wife works part time than when she works full time),[101] or how many resources women have as measured in employment, education, reproductive decision making, and family structure.[102] It includes instrumental housework as well as emotion work. Contrary to earlier expectations and predictions, 'with some qualifications, gender stereotyping of specific domestic tasks and unequal contributions between men and women *cannot* have shifted much in the last twenty years.'[103] As one researcher puts it, 'It is hard to resist the conclusion that women are being exploited, especially those who are themselves engaged in paid employment or who are married to men who have retired from paid employment.'[104]

There is thus a noticeable imbalance in the distribution of work between the sexes, which is expressed in terms such as 'the double day' (paid and unpaid work for the woman),[105] 'the second shift',[106] and other similar expressions. In crises, the fragility of women's expanded boundaries becomes particularly obvious.[107] One of the consequences of this unequal workload is that women experience significantly more interference from work to family than do men.[108]

There has, however, been a remarkable change at the normative level. When asked, most men today will admit that they *should* 'help' when the wife is in the paid labour force, and an impressive proportion of couples believe that household tasks and caring work should be shared equally between spouses.[109] While women are more committed to this belief than men, enough men proclaim their belief in equal sharing that the disparity between the norms they express and their actual behaviour is considerable.[110] Bittman and Lovejoy have described this discrepancy as 'pseudo-mutuality'.[111] 'Pseudo-mutuality is a false complementarity, where the emphasis is on the actor maintaining a sense of reciprocal fulfilment by denying or concealing evidence of non-mutuality. Pseudo-mutuality … is a characteristic "modern" form of the exercise of domestic power.'

The notion of 'helping' is itself an attempt to perpetuate the old division of labour, in which it was the wife/mother's responsibility to look after all household and family matters. 'Helping' requires that someone else take responsibility, decide what needs to be done, where, when, and how, plan for an orderly and rational way in which things get done—in short, assume the managerial tasks even when not executing all specific tasks. In the paid workforce, we tend to reward managers rather well for taking on just these types of functions. However, when dealing with housework and family care work, the managerial aspects tend to be forgotten.

Social expectations continue to be different for wives and husbands. Wives continue to be held disproportionately responsible for the well-being of all family members. In the case of conflicts between paid work and family requirements, often it is the woman who will stay home with a sick child, move when her husband receives a job offer elsewhere, look after a permanently disabled family member, etc.

Variations between couples with respect to status differentials between husband and wife are considerable. On the one hand, today there are still wives who are almost completely defined by their husband's status. One such example are military wives. They are ranked according to their husband's rank. Their own personal characteristics are not as important as their husband's rank in determining the social interaction between military wives: informal interaction between wives of officers and non-commissioned personnel is systematically discouraged.[112] The following quote from a non-commissioned army wife describes her first introduction into a mixed ranks' wives' club:

They had a wives' club for the members of the service battalion. And I'll never forget. I went to their first meeting. And I walked up and said, 'Hi, how are you?' and 'Where did you come from?' That type of thing. I walked up and talked to about six different people. Maybe I picked the wrong people, but every one of them within three questions asked me my husband's rank. Within three. One lady, it was the first question out of her mouth. Not even 'Hi—where are you coming from?' or 'How do you like it here?' It was, 'What rank is your husband?'[113]

Frequent moves make it all but impossible for the wives to pursue an independent career, and it is made clear to them—and to their husbands—that a wife with a career is detrimental to her husband's military career. Hence the social advancement of a woman depends on that of the man with whom she is associated. This, in turn, has a negative effect on the sociability of military wives. 'While wives' gatherings have the potential to be havens of support, this potential is often thwarted because the competitive nature of the rank system has turned the occasion into a minefield. Some wives fear, and have reason to fear, that what they say at wives' gatherings will be repeated elsewhere in ways that will harm their husbands' careers.'[114]

The military regards wives as part of a team effort for as long as the marriage lasts, but they are not rewarded as an equal part of the team. They share in some of the benefits of their husbands' promotion (e.g., by moving into better quarters), but in the case of separation and divorce (a not infrequent occurrence given the particular strains to which military marriages are subjected) the wives find themselves thrown back on their own resources, as if their lack of an independent economic base was the result of a personal decision rather than the result of a systematic enforcement of wives' dependence in the military.

How relevant is this atypical example? It demonstrates that the equivalent to 'the corporation man'[115] and the 'two-person career',[116] which we tend to associate with the mid-century, is still around, although no longer the norm. On the other hand, there are a few couples with househusbands supported by their earning wives. But overall, researchers searching for the strictly egalitarian marriage for a long time have been coming up mostly empty-handed.[117]

There is considerable evidence that suggests young couples who start out with a relatively equal set of roles fall into a sex-segregated pattern after the birth of the first child, after which the mother finds herself with the disproportionately larger share of child-care responsibility.[118]

Not only are wives held responsible for the well-being of other family members, they hold themselves responsible as well. A lot has been written about the differences in the socialization of girls and boys.[119] This inevitably carries over into adulthood, unless there has been a powerful countersocialization, such as membership in a social movement that becomes part of a person's identity. The power of various self-help programs, including twelve-step programs, cults, or involvement in social movements such as the feminist movement, all attest to this possibility of adult socialization.

Gilligan's widely cited work has argued that women's moral development differs from men's moral development.[120] While it is problematic to make this a categorical statement, nevertheless it is an empirical observation that is relevant here. Wives take more responsibility than husbands for ensuring a good marriage.[121] This responsibility puts them into the position of pushing for change, so they make demands in marriage, while men respond by withdrawing. There is some evidence that regardless of sex, the partner who is pushing for change tends to demand, and the partner who is asked to change tends to withdraw. Because of the division of labour within families, women are more often in the position of demanders.[122]

Women as a group have more social skills than men as a group, specific examples to the contrary notwithstanding. Women have more friends (both female and male) than men do.[123] However, these skills are not oriented towards having power over other people. It also means that husbands are more likely to receive unconditional support and love from their wives than wives are to receive from their husbands.[124]

Wife Battering[125]

Particular situations may lead to total isolation of women, especially when they are married to or living with highly controlling and possibly abusive men—two character traits that tend to go together. Male aggression against women in intimate relationships is high.[126] A national survey found that at least half of all Canadian women have experienced at least one incident of violence since age sixteen.[127] In Canada, 29 per cent of women who have ever been married or lived common law with a partner have been assaulted by their marital partner and 45 per cent of these cases resulted in physical injury to the woman.[128] A married woman was nine times as likely to be killed by her spouse than by a stranger during the period of 1974–92.[129]

Physical violence and sexual abuse is one area in which we find consistent and important differences between the sexes.[130] Males are much more likely to be abusers and murderers than females, although both male and female children may be victims of abuse. Sexual abuse is very frequent as well: in Canada, 39 per cent of all women have experienced at least one incident of sexual assault since the age of sixteen.[131] The long-term effects of adult survivors of sexual abuse include feelings of low self-esteem or self-hatred, frequent sleep disturbances and nightmares, an inability to trust other people, flashbacks during which the survivor re-experiences sexual abuse as if it was occurring at that moment (which are frightening not just for the survivor but for the people around them), dissociation (which can take the extreme form of multiple personalities), a greater likelihood of drug abuse, alcoholism, eating difficulties, a tendency to hurt themselves, and successful and unsuccessful attempts to commit suicide. In addition, adult survivors of sexual abuse are likely to have difficulties in developing healthy sexual relationships as adults.[132]

Among this list of horrors, one stands out in particular, and it is strongly sex-linked: victims of childhood sexual abuse are at great risk of being revictimized in adult life, especially if they are female.[133] While the majority of victims do not become perpetrators themselves, a minority do if they are male.[134] 'Men with histories of childhood abuse are more likely to take out their aggressions on others, while women are more likely to be victimized by others or to injure themselves.'[135]

Unclear Roles and Muddled Terms

The enormous confusion that has resulted from the dramatic changes in families has affected the terms we use to describe the types of family relationships between various people, such as role descriptions or types of families. If we start with simple role descriptions, what could be simpler than the terms wife or husband? Yet neither of these have clear meanings any longer. In the case of spousal role designation, is a common-law wife a wife or not? The answer to that depends, of course, on how long the couple have been living together, whether they have a child together, and the province in which they live. If they do not have a child and have lived together for two years, they would be considered spouses[136] in British Columbia, but not in Saskatchewan. So is a wife a wife?

What about a husband who is legally married to a woman from whom he never divorced, although he has been living with another woman for many years? Whose husband is he? This is at issue in the case of *McLeod*.[137] She lived with her husband from 1950 to 1979 and bore and raised three sons during that time. In 1979 her husband moved out to live with another woman, although no divorce took place. Legally, *for some purposes*—but not for others!—McLeod was still his wife. When her husband died, she applied for survivor's benefits under the *Canada Pension Act*, but was informed that her late husband's common-law wife was the one who was entitled to the survivor's benefits. However, for the purposes of the Widowed Spouses Allowance, she was considered a surviving 'spouse', so she has been receiving these benefits. In this case, which woman is the wife? To which woman was the man a husband?

As we have seen earlier, the generic term 'spouse' is equally unclear due to lesbians' and gays' challenge to be included under this heading.

CONCLUSION

Spousal roles have been decisively blurred in four ways: high levels of divorce have blurred the boundaries between being married and being not married; the *rapprochement* between common-law and legal marriages has blurred the distinction between these two types of unions; the increasing acceptance of same-sex couples is currently redefining spousal roles as partnerships between two people of the same or opposite sex rather than as husband and wife roles; and the changes within heterosexual legal marriages have led to a blurring—but definitely not to an abolition—of gender-defined roles within such relationships. As a result, there are conflicting definitions—in law, in daily life, in religion, in social policy—as to who is and who is not a spouse, depending on the context. No longer is there any social agreement on the meanings of these terms.

CHAPTER 4

Uncertain Parental Roles

INTRODUCTION

If spousal roles are a lot less clear than they used to be, parental roles are even more confusing. When a couple divorces, the partners cease to be in a spousal relationship with each other. They may be in a postspousal relationship if there is ongoing contact of a financial and/or social and/or emotional kind, but they are no longer married to each other unless they start cohabiting again. Not so with parental roles. If a couple separate or divorce and have children of the union, they continue to be parents to these children, although possibly in a constrained manner.

In this chapter we will examine the extraordinary complexity in parental roles that has developed over the past century in the change from the patriarchal family to the individual responsibility family. All the factors that have affected spousal roles—the increased prominence of common-law unions, the reluctant but emerging recognition of same-sex couples, the frequency of divorce and remarriage, the shift from mostly unpaid to paid work outside the home, plus unpaid work for women—also affect parental roles in an increasingly complex context, but are multiplied by a factor of two or more. The new reproductive and genetic technologies complicate parental roles so significantly that we must regard them as an independent quantum leap in complexity. I shall look at the roles of mother and father in the patriarchal family. I will then examine the changed and increasing complications resulting from the demise of the patriarchal family, and the changes that are currently being wrought through the new reproductive technologies. To facilitate this analysis, I will devise a category system that captures this complexity.

The role designations of mother, father, and child are no longer clear. If a woman has a child outside of marriage, if the child's father is known but has little contact with the child, and if she lives with another man who takes some economic and parental responsibility for this child but does not adopt him or her, which of the two men is the child's father? Are they both fathers? If so, for what purposes? If the couple then separate, which man should be liable for child-support payments? The biological father? The social father? Both? Clearly, the term father is not as clear as one might have supposed.

It gets more complicated when it comes to women and the new reproductive technologies. There have already been several lawsuits in the United States in which women who agreed to carry a child for someone else subsequently sued for custody. Who is the mother of the child in such a case? The woman who gave birth? The woman who was part of a commissioning couple? Does it matter whose egg is involved? Whose daughter or son would a child be in such cases? Our language has not evolved sufficiently to deal with these complicated issues.

After a divorce and remarriage, does a wife whose husband has children (from a previous marriage) who visit regularly have children or not? Is she a partial mother?[1] Statistics Canada uses the term husband-wife family to designate the presence of two (heterosexual) spouses. When dependent children are living with the couple, they are identified as a two-parent family. However, this innocuous term covers diverse possibilities and may, in fact, sometimes be a misnomer. If we are dealing with a blended family, in which a man married a woman with two dependent children, they are then counted as a two-parent family, but the husband and wife clearly stand in a different relationship to the children than if those children were the biological children of both partners. One is a biological parent, the other a step-parent, and the third parent (the biological father) likely has visitation rights that he may or may not exercise.[2] The situation is different yet again if the couple then have another child together. This child is a half sibling to the first two children, and she does *not* visit the two other children's biological father.

If we now assume that the biological father is remarried to a woman who does *not* have custody of her child, is their family a two-parent family or a childless family? (According to Statistics Canada, they would be counted as a childless couple, even though they have three biological children between them.) None of the three combined children (two of his, one of hers) live with them as their primary residence, but they all visit regularly and usually at the same time. During summer holidays, they usually spend four weeks together. How do we characterize the relationship between the three children involved? 'These are my mother's husband's children.' 'This is my father's wife's child.' 'This is my stepsister, but we don't live together.'

Clearly, the current terminology cannot describe these complex situations. This is more than a matter of imprecise wording, it leads to inaccurate research, due to inaccurate categorizations, and hence to inadequate policies.[3]

Finally, parents generate children, but children make people into parents. What this means in practice is 'constantly reinvented or socially constructed as a response to sociohistorical and economic developments'.[4] Looking at this shifting definition in a historical perspective, 'In the past century, under Western masculine hegemony, parenting has been successively encoded in religious strictures, then moralized, medicalized, psychologized, psychiatrized, and more recently legalized …

frequently all of these together in the past decade, in ... the colonization of parents' lifeworld.'[5]

I will look first at the father's role because (complex as this development is) it is vastly simpler than dealing with mothers. First, however, I will present a category system to describe parental roles in general.

A Category System for Describing Parental Roles

Parental roles have always been complex. They start before the birth of a child and may actively continue after the death of a parent. Before the birth of a child, a man is a potential father and a woman is a potential mother, either in the biological sense, by having the capacity to impregnate a woman or to conceive, or as a potential step- or adoptive parent. Legally, a man may be a putative father during this period if there is some uncertainty about paternity. All of this is relevant when we look at how motherhood and fatherhood are socially and ideologically constructed. For instance, women have been refused jobs[6] because of their potential motherhood, while potential fatherhood has rarely been invoked to block men from particular jobs. Since the focus in this chapter is on actual parental roles, I will disregard this aspect here, important though it is.

Furthermore, parental roles can be terminated through a number of legal acts, such as when a child is made a Crown ward or is adopted by another party. This would make a parent a terminated parent. Under various circumstances, such terminations can be cancelled and a parent can become a reinstated parent.[7] Since this section examines the changes in parental roles over the past 100 years, and since this feature has not changed drastically with respect to its existence (although it may have changed in terms of how it is activated), I will disregard this aspect as well.[8] The questions that remain salient for this discussion are the following:

- Is the parent a biological parent? (biological/non-biological)

- Is the parent a social parent? (social/non-social)

- Is the parent the exclusive father or mother or is this role shared with another person? I will call a parent an exclusive father or mother if this person is the only one who stands in that relation to a particular child, and a non-exclusive parent if this role is shared with another person of *the same sex*. The fact that parenting may be shared with a parent of the other sex does not make this a non-exclusive father or mother relationship in this context. (exclusive/non-exclusive)

- Is the parent a full or partial parent? A full parent is one whose rights and responsibilities towards a particular child are not constrained by external factors. He or she has custody of the child, lives in the same household, can interact with the child without supervision, etc. (full/partial)

• Is the parent alive or dead at conception (in the case of the father) and conception and birth (in the case of the mother)? This was not an issue 100 years ago, but is an issue today and hence must be included. (not specified/post-mortem)[9]

• How do these various factors interact? When we apply these questions to fathers, we arrive at a drastically altered picture of fatherhood as it was 100 years ago and as it is today.

THE AMBIGUOUS SITUATION OF FATHERS

Fathers' relationship with their children have always differed from mothers' relationship with their offspring. While it still takes two people to create a child,[10] all mothers used to experience—and most mothers still experience—conception, pregnancy, and birth as a continuous and direct process, while the father, after impregnation, is dependent on the pregnant woman for his experience of incipient fatherhood. The biological aspect of fatherhood has, therefore, always been discontinuous and mediated.

Biological fatherhood is harder to determine (without the help of almost fail-safe paternity tests) than motherhood. This difficulty is recognized in law, which to a large degree has always preferred to identify a father through his legal relationship to a mother. If a man is married to a woman who gives birth to a child, he is regarded as the child's father. If he was not married to the mother, in the past he was not considered a father in the eyes of the law. Indeed, this was one of the bases for legal marriage—to establish the father's right to his wife's children while disentitling his illegitimate children from inheriting. This has changed.

Fatherhood in the Patriarchal Family

There have always been three types of fathers: men who were biological and social fathers, men who were biological fathers only but not involved in raising their children, and social fathers only (e.g., stepfathers).

Around the beginning of the twentieth century, men were fathers to their wives' children. If they produced children outside of marriage, there was no presumed legal or social relationship between the biological father and his illegitimate child (unless the father acknowledged the child as his), and hence no required financial or other responsibility. In this sense they were biological fathers, but non-fathers socially. Illegitimate children were their mothers' children, pure and simple. The mothers might keep them or give them up for adoption, and if they did the latter, the biological fathers would normally be unable to prevent this (had they wanted to do so), as there was no recognized relationship between them and the children.

Marriage dissolution rates through death while there were still dependent children were very high.[11] Therefore, remarriage was quite frequent as well. Upon marrying a widow with dependent children, the husband became the social father of these children, with all the rights and obligations attendant thereof. In this case, he was the *only* father. Divorce, not death, is now the main method of dissolving unions. When divorced fathers or mothers remarry, their former partners may still be alive and interested in the children. A classification of fathers under the patriarchal family[12] looks like this:

Typology of Fathers in the Patriarchal Family:[13]

1. Biological, social, exclusive, full fathers

2. Non-biological, social, exclusive, full fathers

3. Biological, non-social fathers

With time, things changed drastically. As divorce and remarriage became increasingly frequent, and as births to unmarried women have become an important entry point into parenthood, our category system becomes significantly more complicated.

Fatherhood in the Individual Responsibility Family
So far, we have looked at fatherhood as involving one man and a child. However, given the social trends we have observed in Chapter 2, there are many men married to women who have children from previous unions. In such cases, they are in some sort of step relationship to the women's children. The other side of the coin is, of course, that there are also men who are *not* married to or living with the mother of their children. If the mother has custody and forms a union with another man, then those two men share some form of paternity to the children involved. In most cases, men become fathers because they are associated with women who are mothers. Gay cofathers of their partner's biological children are a modern subcategory that affects a small number of people. Whether they are full or partial fathers depends on the circumstances. (I therefore do not specify this variable in the category system.) If we crosstabulate the various types of dimensions that affect the nature of fatherhood, we arrive at the following picture:

Typology of Fathers in the Individual Responsibility Family:

1. Biological, social, exclusive, full fathers

2. Non-biological but social, exclusive, full fathers

3. Biological but not social fathers

4. Biological, social, exclusive, partial fathers

5. Biological, social, non-exclusive, partial fathers

6. Non-biological but social, exclusive, partial fathers

7. Non-biological but social, non-exclusive, partial fathers

8. Gay cofathers, non-biological, social, non-exclusive fathers

The first three types are exactly the same as those in the patriarchal family. Divorce and births to unmarried women have given rise to the four new types. A divorced father who maintains contact with his children and whose ex-wife has not remarried or formed a common-law relationship remains the biological and socially exclusive father, but his fatherhood is partial rather than full (type 4 father). Assuming that the mother has custody, he no longer shares a residence with his children, and his contact will likely be restricted to certain agreed-upon visits. He no longer has the right or opportunity to make the decisions that he was previously able to make, though he may not have exercised that right and opportunity, given the small amount of child care men tend to engage in even when they live in what is called (often misleadingly)[14] an intact family.

If his ex-wife marries, he turns into the type 5 father: everything remains the same as just described for type 4, with the important exception that now there is another male who will acquire some fatherly rights and responsibilities if he demonstrates the settled intention to treat the children as children of the union. This second husband has become, in his turn, a type 7 father (non-biological, social, non-exclusive, and partial) because of father #1, who continues to maintain a relationship with his children.

If the new couple want to have the children adopted by father #2, and father #1 agrees to this, then father #1 becomes a type 3 father (biological but non-social) and father #2 becomes a type 2 father (non-biological but social, exclusive, and full).

A type 6 father (non-biological but social, exclusive, partial) is merely a variation of type 5. This might be a father who adopted a child together with his wife, then divorced his wife, and is now in the equivalent position of a biological father who remains the exclusive but non-custodial and hence partial father of his child.

Fatherhood after the New Reproductive Technologies

The new reproductive technologies have a very minor impact on fatherhood in terms of creating new types: if a wife uses artificial insemination by donor, her husband is simply a type 2 father—there is no significantly new factor added. The only truly new phenomenon is that of a man who becomes a father after his death or, more accurately, whose sperm is used to impregnate a woman after he is already dead. (There have always been instances in which a man became a father after his death if he impregnated a woman, but died before she gave birth.) We thus have to add a ninth type of father: the post-mortem biological father. Our category system now looks like this:

Typology of Fathers after the New Reproductive Technologies:

1. Biological, social, exclusive, full fathers

2. Non-biological but social, exclusive, full fathers

3. Biological but not social fathers

4. Biological, social, exclusive, partial fathers

5. Biological, social, non-exclusive, partial fathers

6. Non-biological but social, exclusive, partial fathers

7. Non-biological but social, non-exclusive, partial fathers

8. Gay cofathers, non-biological, social, non-exclusive fathers

9. Post-mortem biological fathers

What Has Changed?

While there are only three types of fathers in the patriarchal family, we are now dealing with eight types. Because the divorce rate was very low and because illegitimate children (and there were comparatively few of those)[15] belonged only to the mother and not to the father, the norm was that fathers were both exclusive and full. Divorce and remarriage (or common-law union formation), plus unmarried motherhood with subsequent new union formation, have resulted in the emergence of non-exclusive and partial fathers to such a degree that this is now a very prevalent form of fatherhood.

A man may become a partial father through his own actions (by initiating or forcing a divorce),[16] but he becomes a non-exclusive father when the mother acquires a new partner who plays a parental role towards the child. This is important with respect to the locus of action and control. In most instances, men actively participate in their reduction from full to partial father status by participating in the dissolution of the union.[17] Even if there is no other father figure, the non-custodial parent becomes a partial parent.

Once a judge has decided who is entitled to have custody, that person has the right to make decisions concerning the child's lifestyle until the child is old enough to make his or her own choices. The other parent is no longer a 'parent' in any true sense of the word, and effectively becomes an interested visitor in his or her child's life. The access parent has the right to be informed, but not consulted, and must honour the lifestyle established for the child by the custodial parent.[18]

This may or may not signal an actual reduction of the non-custodial father's involvement with his children, since many fathers are not very involved in child care even when they live with their children and the children's mother. The change may be dramatic if they were very involved or it may be minimal if they had little involvement. For some non-custodial fathers, contact with their children actually increases after divorce. Nonetheless, they are still partial fathers.

The appearance of another father figure on the scene for the same children is the truly new aspect. It also sets the scene for considerable potential conflict.

Biological Versus Non-biological Fathers

As noted, biological and non-biological fathers come into contact and possibly conflict with the appearance of stepfathers. When a woman remarries or forms a common-law union with a man other than the father of her children, this man will usually assume the role of stepfather. If he adopts his partner's children, the biological father ceases to function legally as a father, although in some cases the children may continue to regard him as a father.

When no adoption takes place, the situation becomes complicated. The stepfather lives with the children, and hence will inevitably exert an influence on them, for better or worse. In turn, his life will be profoundly shaped by their presence. This may blossom into a rich step-parental relationship, or it may be a barely tolerated coexistence, but in all cases the man and the children share the same residence, as well as a relationship with the same woman (as partner or mother). There is also some economic interdependence/dependence (minimally via the shared residence), and likely some emotional relationship, whether good or bad. In the US, about 35 per cent of the children born in the early 1980s can expect to live with a step-parent before the age of eighteen.[19] The vast majority of stepfamily households are comprised of biological mothers and stepfathers.[20]

The situation with the biological father may be quite different. If he is remarried, he may turn most or even all of his attention to a potential new set of children, whether he is their biological or only their social father. Unless the ex-couple have a cocustody arrangement that involves a 50-50 split of child care, the biological father's contact with his children is likely to be sporadic.

The majority of non-custodial fathers lose any significant contact with their children after divorce. The disengagement process of non-custodial fathers from their biological children is well documented for Great Britain, the United States, and Canada.[21] Recent research on eighty postdivorce fathers in Britain and Canada has shown that, surprisingly, those fathers who were *most* involved (rather than *least* involved) in child care prior to divorce were more likely to lose contact with their children.[22]

> ... rather than there being no correlation between pre- and post-divorce patterns, there appeared to be a strong *inverse* relationship. Fathers who described themselves as having been highly involved with and attached to their children, influential in their development, and sharing 'family work' tasks before the divorce were more likely to have *lost* contact with their children after divorce than fathers who had defined themselves in a more traditional manner, being peripherally involved and reporting lower levels of father-child attachment. The fathers scoring lowest on indices of infant and child care, attachment to their children, influence in various areas of their child's development, and on measures of androgyny before the divorce, were more likely to *remain* in contact with their children after divorce.[23]

The explanation for this counterintuitive finding is in the fathers' adjustment to divorce. Those fathers who were most involved in child care while married experience the greatest role loss, suffer more from their children's absence, and experience the constraints of a visiting relationship more acutely than fathers who were minimally involved in child care while married. For the latter, these experiences are less acute, and for some the change may not have involved a dramatic loss of contact with their children. Indeed, some divorced fathers report an increase in their interactions with their children. Previously very involved fathers may cut off all contact with their children because it is too painful for them to continue in a role they consider to be artificial, insufficient, painful for both sides, and non-spontaneous.[24]

Obviously, there is something wrong with our legal system if it discourages contact between children and those fathers who previously had the most meaningful contact with them. However, in the absence of studies that look at all the participants in this situation that is by definition painful (that is, minimally, the fathers, the mothers, and the children),[25] it is difficult to come up with reasonable policy recommendations for addressing this problem. Further, there is now solid research evidence that children's well-being is *not* related to the amount of continued contact between fathers and children.[26] The issue is one for fathers, therefore, rather than for children.

Joint custody has become a statistically significant type of custody award.[27] However, even when joint custody is awarded, in the majority of cases the actual distribution of caring work is similar to that in sole custody arrangements.[28] What joint custody usually means is joint legal custody, rather than legal and physical custody. In most cases this means that parents have the right to make decisions together about the child's education, health, and religion, while the mother continues to make all day-to-day decisions. The father's 'control is largely passive until the mother makes a decision with which he disagrees. He reserves veto power. He decides whether or not her decision will stand. Her decisionmaking authority is dependent on his concurrence.'[29]

When there are stepfathers involved, depending on the intentions of both fathers, they may be in competition for the same children. Fathers thus become non-exclusive fathers when there is a second father around. While it is possible to be an exclusive partial father (such as a father who shares custody or has liberal access to his child and there is no other father figure around), a non-exclusive father is by definition also a partial father. A man may be an exclusive father to one child and a non-exclusive father to another. Of course, were we to adopt the perspective of children, things would be even more complicated.

Surprisingly, I have found no research that examines the interactions (direct or indirect) between partial fathers who share the same child. While there is information on non-custodial fathers as well as some on custodial fathers, and on the continued interaction (or lack thereof) between the biological father and mother,[30] the interactions between the two men who are partial fathers to the same children seem not to have been examined so far. The whole phenomenon of partial fatherhood (as well as partial motherhood) awaits research.

Cultural Changes in the Father Image

Looking at the types of fathers that have emerged is, of course, only one way of looking at fatherhood. Another way is to look at how we culturally construct fatherhood. A recent analysis examined how fathering has been defined in popular magazines between 1900 to 1989. Fathers are now expected to participate in their children's lives by providing day-to-day physical and emotional care, but, as we have seen in the previous chapter, this shift seems to be almost entirely at the normative level rather than at the behavioural level. There is agreement in the literature that fathers continue to do relatively little child care compared to mothers.[31] As one researcher concluded after a careful analysis of social science research on the issue: 'the new father is a statistical fantasy'.[32] We can note that during the course of this century, parenting has been increasingly conceptualized on an *ideological* level as gender free rather than as equivalent to mothering.[33] Popular mass media in the 1980s have actively contributed to this image,[34] but in terms of actual fathering behaviour, little has changed.

Not only is there no correlation between ideological shifts and actual behaviours, as already noted, but the two may go in opposite directions. This has been argued for the Depression era in the United States. While the culture of fatherhood outside the home suggested increased father involvement during the Depression, the actual conduct of fatherhood inside the home suggests that Depression-era fathers were less willing or able to interact with their children than their counterparts in the 1920s.[35]

Fathers' Rights and Responsibilities[36]

The 1980s saw the evolution of the fathers' rights movement in Canada. This focused on issues of access to children in the case of non-marital and non-custodial fathers.[37] There were several private members' bills that tried to create access enforcement mechanisms. Indeed, in Alberta there were six such bills proposed between 1987 and 1992,[38] all of which eventually died. The bill that got furthest was Bill 124 in Ontario. It was passed by the Liberal legislature in 1988, but the New Democratic government, which succeeded the Liberal government, did not proclaim it as law.

Like the other bills of its kind, Bill 124 would have allowed non-custodial parents (usually fathers) quick entry into court within ten days of a complaint.[39] In Alberta, it was to be within three days. It is ironic that action of such speed was contemplated in view of the decades-long fight to get non-custodial parents (usually fathers) to pay the support they have been court-ordered to pay, and the extraordinary delays or outright lack of success in obtaining such payments.

Support payments are another item on the fathers' rights agenda.[40] A less radical but therefore perhaps more worrying attempt (since it has shown some partial success) is to link child-support payments to access. Since 1987, there have been several cases in which a father was allowed to suspend payments until access time had been provided.[41]

This is ironic, since one of the greatest complaints both women and children make is that most non-custodial fathers do not interact *enough* with the children. If and when fathers decide to fight for custody, their chances of winning are similar to those of mothers.[42] Further, there is a very worrying lack of attention to the issue of violence. Some lawyers and judges will maintain that a man can be a good father even if he is abusive to his wife or ex-wife.[43] This notion must be challenged. Children learn a lot by following examples. If a child observes the father behaving in a physically and/or emotionally violent manner towards the mother, this will damage the child's relationship with the mother and may make the child abusive himself (if male) or become a victim of abuse (if female).[44] Given what we know about the cycle of violence, children must be seen as secondary victims of violence against their mothers. Finally, linking access to support payments is highly problematic in principle.[45] Support is an obligation of being a biological parent, whether or not there is an active social relationship. If we fail to adopt this principle, parents could simply unilaterally decide to stop being parents in terms of financial responsibility, which was typical of the majority of noncustodial fathers until recently and which, unfortunately, is still occasionally the case. Interaction with one's children is part of being a parent, but it is a right that can be lost if one's behaviour is detrimental to the child. The two must be judged independently. Although members of fathers' rights groups present their demands by using a discourse of equality: 'in essence, the demands are to continue the practice of inequality in postdivorce parenting but now with legal sanction.'[46] While fatherhood has undergone some significant changes, these changes do not equal those occurring in motherhood.

FROM CERTAINTY TO UNCERTAINTY: THE REDEFINITION OF MOTHERHOOD

As we have seen, fatherhood has always been mediated through the mother. Contrast this process with the experience of a mother about 100 years ago. A couple have intercourse. About fourteen days later, the woman notices that she has not had her period. She will know fairly soon if she is pregnant. From then on, her pregnancy will progress until birth. The entire process happens within her body. She continually experiences new bodily changes. When she feels the child kicking in the uterus (what used to be called quickening), the presence of a new human being generated within her becomes palpably obvious. Eventually, a second heartbeat can be heard. While she does not control the process, neither does a clinic or anyone else.

Pregnancy and birth today are substantially different from the experience just described, thanks to the use of prenatal diagnostic techniques. If the woman is over thirty-five, she will be urged to have an amniocentesis (which may or may not show some genetic foetal abnormality) and a variety of other tests. Even if she is below the age of thirty-five and in perfect health, and even if neither she nor her partner have any genetic abnormality, she will nevertheless usually have ultrasound tests.

These interventions create a pregnancy experience that is profoundly different from those of women who lived in times during which such tests were not routine. Amniocentesis is usually the prelude to a decision about whether or not to have an abortion. In such cases, an abortion is not sought because a woman is unable physically, emotionally, socially, or economically to carry a pregnancy to term, but because a test administered by medical personnel has revealed that the foetus does not measure up to some externally determined standard. It is therefore not the wish or condition of the mother that results in an abortion but the quality assessment of some third party that suggests this foetus will be substandard. This is a milder form of a mediated pregnancy than that experienced by a woman undergoing *in vitro* fertilization, but it is a mediated process nonetheless.

In a similar way, ultrasound also mediates the pregnancy experience. Before ultrasound, the mother would assess the progress of her baby by being aware of the changes her body undergoes; now it is a machine that provides this assessment. The ultrasound picture can be seen by all who are present, and will be interpreted by the machine operator, i.e., someone other than the pregnant woman. Instead of being the one who interprets the progress of the pregnancy for herself and others, the woman, along with other interested people, becomes a consumer of the various test results.[47] However, before the advent of these new technologies, motherhood underwent changes that parallel those that affected fatherhood, although these changes to motherhood were much less numerically frequent and hence much less typical.

Motherhood in the Patriarchal Family

There have always been three types of mothers:

Typology of Mothers in the Patriarchal Family Model:

1. Biological, social, exclusive, full mothers

2. Non-biological, social, exclusive, full mothers

3. Biological, non-social mothers

Unlike the situation of fathers, mothers became mothers by virtue of giving birth. The mother's relationship was the touchstone against which other relationships could be assessed. While at the beginning of this century an illegitimate child was not even legally considered to be related to his or her father unless the father acknowledged the child as his,[48] there was never any question that the biological mother was the legal mother unless she gave up the child for adoption.

In the case of divorce, of course, the father's right to the children prevailed over the mother's right until the tender years doctrine was generally applied. This was the result of a patriarchal interpretation of the father as the head of the household. Both women and children were seen as his property, and even if one of the dependants left or if the wife was 'put aside', this did not eliminate the father's right over his children.

This changed when judges and others started to rule that children of a 'tender age' belonged with their mother, although the notion of an 'unfit mother' allowed the father to keep the children if he so desired. The conflation of women's sexual behaviour with all other variables meant that an 'unchaste woman'—meaning any woman who had had sexual relations with anyone other than her legal husband—could easily be declared an unfit mother (much in the way in which, until recently, a practising lesbian mother could be deprived of her children just by being a lesbian). She could also be cut off from all economic support.[49]

Motherhood in the Individual Responsibility Family

With the increase in divorce and births to unmarried women, mothers were much more likely than fathers to retain custody of their children. Nevertheless, in Canada (in contrast to other countries) fathers have historically been a significant minority of custodial parents (around 15 per cent).[50] The types of mothers in the individual responsibility model of the family (notwithstanding reproductive technologies) still parallel the types of fathers in this model.

Typology of Mothers in the Individual Responsibility Family:

1. Biological, social, exclusive, full mothers

2. Non-biological but social, exclusive, full mothers

3. Biological but not social mothers

4. Biological, social, exclusive, partial mothers

5. Biological, social, non-exclusive, partial mothers

6. Non-biological but social, exclusive, partial mothers

7. Non-biological but social non-exclusive, partial mothers

8. Lesbian comothers, non-biological, social, non-exclusive mothers

Mothers have been—and continue to be—much more likely than fathers to maintain sole custody in the case of divorce. Although recently there has been a considerable increase in joint custody awards, the woman still has sole custody in the vast majority of cases. In the case of unmarried motherhood, mothers usually have custody of their children, although there are some legal challenges to this from time to time.

Most men remarry after a union has dissolved, and the new wife would be in some ill-defined stepmother role to the child who visits the father. Hence, the biological and social mother is no longer an exclusive mother, as she would be if there is no other mother-substitute, but usually her share in raising the child is larger than that of the non-custodial father. Of course, as noted, there have always been a significant minority of cases in which the father obtained custody and the biological mother was therefore the non-custodial parent. In such cases, some of the comments made about the new types of fathers in the previous section apply to mothers as well. Only when we introduce the new reproductive technologies do matters become very confusing with respect to mothers.

Motherhood with the New Reproductive Technologies

For fathers, the new reproductive technologies added one new category— a post-mortem father. For mothers, we enter a complex labyrinth. Fathers make only one biological contribution to a child: they provide the sperm. Mothers make two biological contributions: they provide the egg and they gestate the foetus. The new technologies have split this unity, and thus have created many types of mothers with which current laws and policies are ill-equipped to cope. In order to list the new types of mothers, we must now distinguish between partial biological mothers— genetic but not gestational, or gestational but not genetic—in addition to the other types already in existence.

Typology of Mothers with the New Reproductive Technologies:

1. Genetic, gestational, social, exclusive, full mothers (what we think of as the norm)

2. Non-genetic, non-gestational but social, exclusive, full mothers (adoptive or stepmothers)

3. Genetic and gestational but not social mothers (birth mothers who have given up their child)

4. Genetic, gestational, social, exclusive, partial mothers (like type 1 mothers but without custody)

5. Genetic, gestational, social, non-exclusive, partial mothers (non-custodial mothers like type 4, but only if the father has formed a new union with a woman who plays a partial mother role)

6. Non-genetic, non-gestational but social, exclusive, partial mothers (e.g., a non-custodial adoptive mother in cases where the father does not have a partner who acts as a substitute mother)

7. Non-genetic, and non-gestational but social, non-exclusive, partial mothers (like type 6, but the father has formed a new union with a woman who plays some parental role)

8. Lesbian comothers, non-genetic and non-gestational, social, non-exclusive mothers

9. Genetic but non-gestational, social, exclusive, full mothers (women who use another woman as a gestator of their own egg in a preconception agreement)

10. Non-genetic but gestational, social, exclusive, full mothers (recipients of a donor egg)

11. Genetic, non-gestational, non-social mothers (provider of a donor egg)

12. Non-genetic but gestational, non-social mothers (gestational carrier for type 8 mother)

13. Genetic but non-gestational, social, exclusive, partial mothers (like type 8, but without sole custody)

14. Non-genetic but gestational, social, exclusive, partial mothers (like type 9, but without sole custody)

15. Genetic but non-gestational, social, non-exclusive, partial mothers (like type 8, but with a second and potentially third partial mother—the gestational mother and/or the father's new partner)

16. Non-genetic but gestational, social, non-exclusive, partial mothers (like type 9 and 13, but with a second and potential third partial mother)

So far, all these types of mothers are alive at the moment of conception and birth. If the genetic and/or gestational mother is dead at these two crucial times, this adds seven more types of mothers. They are, in a categorical sense, only particular subforms of the preceding types, but because of the extraordinary importance of breaking the barrier of death, it is warranted to list them separately here. At this stage, the already complicated format previously adopted no longer suffices. We must now use an identifier to distinguish the various sequences of mothers with respect to the same child in order to keep track. The mother who is mentioned last is the one being categorized.

17. Dead genetic mother #1; gestational mother #2; social, exclusive, full mother #3 (preconception agreement in which the egg of a dead woman is fertilized, implanted in a carrier, and the child is handed over to a third woman)

18. Dead genetic mother #1; gestational but not social mother #2 (the carrier from the previous preconception agreement)

19. Dead genetic mother #1; gestational mother #2; social, exclusive, partial mother #3 (the type 16 mother is now divorced, and her husband has custody of the child, while she has liberal access)

20. Dead genetic mother #1; gestational mother #2; social, non-exclusive, partial mother #3 (same as the type 18 mother, but her former husband has remarried)

21. Dead genetic mother #1 but gestational and social, exclusive, full mother #2 (recipient of donor egg from a dead donor)

22. Dead genetic mother #1; gestational, non-social mother #2 (carrier using dead donor egg in a preconception agreement)

23. Dead genetic mother #1; gestational, social, exclusive, partial mother #2 (type 20 is now divorced and her husband has custody)

24. Dead genetic mother #1 but gestational and social, non-exclusive, partial mother #2 (the former husband of type 22 is now remarried)

25. Dead genetic and gestational mother #1, a woman kept on life support beyond her death so that her foetus will mature and be delivered by Caesarian section

These twenty-five types of mothers (most of which are documented) show the extraordinary complexity that results from the fact that women make two, rather than one, biological contributions to creating a child. This, in addition to the fact that gestational and genetic contributions are now possible beyond death, creates a new template for motherhood.

While unmarried motherhood, divorce, and remarriage have created both non-exclusive and partial fatherhood (with potential conflict between a biological father and a social, non-biological one), the new reproductive technologies have created partial motherhood of quite a different type in addition to the types of non-exclusivity experienced by fathers. Mothers may—and do—face challenges from *the other biological mother*, the one who gestated the child and/or who donated the egg, so partial motherhood may be split in more ways than partial fatherhood.

This makes it obvious that it is not very meaningful to judge motherhood in fatherhood terms—which is precisely what we are doing. A father's biological contribution is simply not comparable to that of a mother either a century ago or now. Egg donation is not comparable to sperm donation, to put it simply. Sperm is externalized—one masturbates and the sperm emerges. Egg retrieval involves invasive medical procedures. Sperm is made up of millions of spermatozoa, while eggs are released one at a time, unless the woman is hyperovulated (which is usually done).[51]

I believe that the type of publicity surrounding the new genetic and reproductive technologies has created a new image of motherhood and fatherhood; what is taken for granted today was still beyond the pale in the early 1980s.[52] These marginal cases thus shape, to some degree, our awareness of parenthood in general.

Comparing Motherhood with Fatherhood

Emphasizing the biological differences between mothers and fathers has been a hallmark of many, if not most, attempts to support sex discrimination. By contrast, proponents of gender equality have often belittled the biological differences between mothers and fathers. Looking at motherhood and fatherhood from a comparative perspective is therefore perhaps even more tricky than comparing wifehood and husbandhood. However, looking at this issue is an essential factor that must be considered.

As we have seen, a father's biological contribution to his child is mediated through the child's mother. In the normal course of events, the woman conceives with the man's sperm, and then generates the foetus inside her body for about nine months. The man can only observe the effects of this process on the mother-to-be rather than experience the generative process himself.

After birth, this difference continues to a lesser degree if the mother breast-feeds the child. While both parents can hold the child, play with her, change her, and interact with her in a variety of ways, the mother continues to have a special biological relationship by virtue of generating breastmilk and experiencing the child feeding at her breast. When she ceases to breast-feed, the interactions of both parents could theoretically be identical, although this is highly unlikely for the vast majority of new parents.

Most people regard children as more the mother's responsibility than the father's. As has been argued, feminist movements 'have been excellent for getting women individual rights and resources (that is, making women more like men) but have been lousy for reassigning obligations (again, that is, making men more like women).'[53] There is decisive evidence that mothers and fathers have a different relationship with their children.[54] Children, both girls and boys, are more likely to feel closer to the mother than to the father.[55]

As far as family law is concerned, theoretically mothers and fathers are equal. Indeed, recent trends in family law express expectations that men and women will take equal responsibility. Counter to what all research shows, 'there has been uncritical acceptance of the empirical proposition that women and men make undifferentiated, exchangeable contributions to parenting.'[56] In practice, the situation is vastly more complicated. In crises, it becomes obvious that a much larger share of the responsibility—indeed, sometimes the entire responsibility—is laid on the mothers' shoulders. One of the worst crises that can happen is when one's child is either sexually abused or is the abuser. Two recent studies have shown that in such cases the state holds the *non-offending mother* responsible for protecting the child who has been abused,[57] as well as restraining the abuser if he[58] is a family member. By contrast, the father is not held equally responsible.

One of the studies[59] that examined non-offending mothers of sexually abused children found that:

Both police and CAS appear to focus their attention on the women. This is due in part to the fact that women do bear the major responsibility for the caring and rearing of children in our society. On the other hand, both agencies are informed by notions that the activities of the caring for and the rearing of children are 'natural' to women. Legitimating ideologies themselves as well as institutions such as the media, police departments, child welfare agencies and families reinforce the notion that women, as mothers, perform such tasks out of some 'maternal instinct' or biological nature.[60]

The consequence of such views is that the non-offending mothers experience a drastic loss of control over their own lives. They may be forced to attend group meetings, are likely to be held responsible for insuring that no contact between offender and victim occurs, and are at risk of losing their children if they fail to be achieve these and other obligations. Most receive little help in coping with an already terrible situation, which is likely to be exacerbated by stresses imposed on the mother—but not on the father—by the various institutions involved.

This process has been defined as making the mother the 'mother protector'. By asking '*how* does the state operate to protect children from sexual abuse?', Krane (1994) found that the child's mother is actually the one designated by the state to protect the child. In the process of shifting this responsibility to the mother, the state reduces a previously multidimensional woman to a largely one-dimensional 'mother protector'. The shift is also one *from* a responsibility at the public level ('protecting' a sexually abused child) *to* the private sphere (the family) via the mother. A mother who has been turned into a mother protector recounts:

I used to have two jobs. I worked at a restaurant on weekends, and I loved that job. Now, I've had to give it up because Joe [her husband] has to go out on weekends, *I* have to watch the kids. *I* can't leave them alone, I didn't need the job for the money but I liked getting out of the house and meeting people and now *I'm forced right back into having to be home on weekends.* If Joe has to go somewhere, heck, he can, *because I'm home!*

I can't work overtime at work either, because *I* have to be home before Charles [the son who abused his stepsisters] gets home from school. My life has changed. *I* have to be there to meet all of them, and *I have to watch out* when they're home. I have no life of my own. I lost one job, well, I had to give it up, because I have to be there watching. I lost my freedom because I have to arrange everything around being at home but I don't find Joe has to. If he says he has a meeting or is going camping with the boy scouts, he doesn't ask 'Are you going to be home?', he just expects me to be there, and that I know better than to plan things for myself.[61]

This outcome was true for all cases (which the caseworkers had selected as typical ones) and corresponded precisely to what Carter (1990) had found. The delegation of responsibility to the non-offending mother is quite explicit. She has to attend meetings, she has to be there, she has to determine who may interact with whom, but the *control* of what will be done is outside her sphere. She merely manages. The conditions are set up by the Children's Aid Society. Most important, even if the husband was the offender, the mother and her failure to protect were the focus of attention rather than the perpetrator and his crime.

In the Man's Image: The Fatherization of Motherhood

Students of the family agree that motherhood has changed, but they use different words to describe the change. Ambert argues that childhood has been 'maternalized'.[62] Fineman suggests that the mother has been 'neutered'.[63] Rothman discusses how the new reproductive technologies allow women to be 'fathers' to their children.[64] Which is it? Maternalization, neutering, or paternalization? Paradoxical as it sounds, I suggest that it is all three. Ambert talks about how more and more fathers are withdrawing socially from their biological children, which has led to the maternalization of childhood.[65] Fineman discusses how the law has substituted an ideology of parenthood for an ideology of motherhood—hence the neutering—but the notion on which this neutered parenthood is based is the male type of parenthood.

The degendering of spousal roles leads to the fatherization of motherhood. This means that a male image of parenting is applied to mothering. As we have seen earlier, motherhood has been culturally (not actually) degendered since the beginning of this century. Motherhood activities were increasingly described as parental activities, thus creating the image (not the reality) of fathers and mothers contributing in similar ways to child care. Meanwhile, the provider role of spousal roles has been degendered as well. If we now conflate spousal with parental roles, as is constantly done, it follows that any man can both earn an income and be an adequate parent—and therefore any woman can as well. The only problem is that there are many more women than men who are responsible for both roles. Combining the provider and parental role is what men have always done—with the proviso that their parental involvement be minimal. Now women are doing both, with little diminution of responsibility in the mother role.

The reshaping of motherhood in the form of fatherhood is most pronounced in the new reproductive and genetic technologies. This takes the form of the mediation[66] of the pregnancy and birth experience as well as how we regard mother and father roles in a technological context. Even those women who do not use high-tech interventions to generate a pregnancy, who therefore have a 'normal' conception and pregnancy, have their experience reshaped by technology and its administration into one that is less direct and more mediated than it was before ultrasounds and other such interventions become routine.

Significantly, we also model motherhood issues on fatherhood issues in the area of reproduction. I will look at only one example from the report of the Royal Commission on New Reproductive Technologies. The commission regards egg and embryo donation as 'offering opportunities to help another woman or couple who is infertile in cases where a donation would be their only chance to become pregnant.'[67] As this has been put forward as the view of 'practitioners and individuals who are infertile',[68] the rest of the discussion is oriented towards how egg and embryo donation should be done rather than *whether* it should be done.

All the relevant recommendations therefore focus on regulating this practice, which is currently carried out in Canada.[69] The commission never considers the importance of the issue in its own right. Considering the changes that the new reproductive technologies have wrought on motherhood but *not* on fatherhood, this is astounding—unless we view it through the lens of fatherhood.

One of the primary functions of families is to provide individuals with a sense of grounding in the social world. Family membership—whether positive, negative, or both—provides a fundamental aspect of our personality formation. By splitting genetic and gestational motherhood, by creating children who are born to women who are not their genetic mothers, we are redefining human life in a most fundamental way, one that cannot be evaluated in terms of some women's desire to give birth to a child. Let us look at some of the commission's considerations of such issues:

> ... there is the issue of multiple parenthood when genetic, gestational, and social roles are separated ... a situation that we know, based on experience with adoption, can have a significant impact on a child's personal and emotional development and sense of identity.[70]

> ... in a caring society, personal autonomy is not a value that trumps all others, and society may see fit to place limits on the exercise of

free choice when the choice concerns an activity that society regards as fundamentally incompatible with values such as respect for human dignity and the inalienability of the person.[71]

These quotes are from the report's chapter on preconception arrangements, not from the chapter on eggs and embryos. However, the comments also apply to egg and embryo donation. Because egg donation is equated with semen donation, a social experiment on a grand scale is endorsed without even an evaluation of the outcomes for those families who have already served as experimental subjects.

The commission simply takes the rules for semen donation and stipulates that they be applicable to egg donation as well. A decisively different female process is therefore regulated according to the standards of an existing male process.

CONCLUSION

Parental roles have undergone tremendous changes, most of which are still not well understood. We have partial and full, exclusive and non-exclusive fatherhood and motherhood, but little research to help us understand how the various types of parents interact. It is clear, however, that there is no longer any congruence between spousal and parental roles in a large number of cases. Recent trends do not lead us to expect that this discrepancy will diminish. The disjunction between spousal and parental roles is a gendered phenomenon. Most mothers retain custody of their children even after union dissolution, while most fathers are non-custodial and non-coresident with their children.[72] Current technological developments have complicated matters by a quantum leap for mothers, but not for fathers.

Legally, the emphasis is on parents rather than on mothers as adequate parents, and therefore less understanding of the needs of a mother who is in the labour force but still responsible for her children's well-being. In crises, the mother may be turned into a 'mother protector', who is held responsible by the state for her children's welfare without being provided with the means of doing so.

When there is a divorce, there is the increasing expectation that both parents will be 'providers', but there is little recognition that women tend to earn less. There also seems to be little awareness of the costs of raising a child, particularly for a lone parent.[73] Courts tend to award low support amounts, if any, most of which are then partially or completely defaulted upon. Overall, it seems clear that parenting—particularly mothering—has become more difficult than it used to be.

CHAPTER 5

Internal Contradictions: Why the Individual Responsibility Model Cannot Work

INTRODUCTION

So far, I have presented two different models of the family and sketched the outlines of a third model, to be considered in detail in Chapter 7. I have summarized some of the social and economic trends characterizing contemporary families, and looked in some detail at the blurring of spousal roles and the complicated process of identifying who is what type of parent to which child. This chapter looks at the suitability of the patriarchal (P) and individual responsibility (IR) models of the family in light of contemporary social and economic trends and the subsequent family structures.

In order to facilitate a systematic assessment of the two models, I will consider each component in sequence. The first question was:

1. WHAT IS THE UNDERLYING IDEOLOGY CONCERNING GENDER EQUALITY?

P: The ideology is one of gender inequality.
IR: The ideology is one of gender equality.

What Is Equality?

"'Equality", like other central political categories, is a contested term.'[1] I will give a brief summary of some conceptions of equality and will (in Chapter 7) present my own preferred approach in dealing with equality issues by striving to reduce *in*equality rather than achieving equality—a subtle but highly consequential shift in perspective.

Equality is mandated in Canada through the *Charter of Rights and Freedoms*. Unfortunately, there has never been a society based on equality, and therefore we are left with developing an approach based on theoretical assumptions rather than on practical experiences of equality.[2]

There have been many formulations of equality over time. These formulations are themselves the outgrowth of specific historical, legal, political, ideological, and disciplinary trends.[3] Among the various formulations there are dichotomies of difference versus sameness, of formal versus substantive equality, and conceptions of equality as equal opportunity, equality as acceptance, equality as same social resources, equality as non-domination, and others.[4]

Difference Versus Sameness

The issue of difference versus sameness is at the heart of many legal dilemmas. It addresses the question 'Do women want "equal" treatment or "different" treatment?'[5] A positive response to *either* alternative leads to problems. In North America, the fundamental antidiscrimination principle is that likes should be treated alike. Legal experts who argue for equal treatment are concerned that legal structures will continue to support or even command an inferior status for women as long as any differentiation on the basis of sex is permitted.

On the other hand, equal treatment falls palpably short if there *are* significant social and biological differences between the sexes, most particularly in family-related issues such as pregnancy and custody. The equal treatment or sameness approach results in conceptualizing pregnancy like 'any other disability',[6] and has resulted in some absurd judgements. One famous example involves the *Bliss* case, in which a pregnant woman sought unemployment insurance payments during a period in which she was considered unemployable because of her pregnancy according to the *Unemployment Insurance Act*. The Supreme Court of Canada rejected her claim that she was being discriminated against on the basis of her sex by stating: 'Any inequality between the sexes in this area is not created by legislation but by nature.'[7] The judgement further cites (with approval) from the reasons for judgement in the Federal Court of Appeal:

Assuming the respondent to have been 'discriminated against', it would not have been by reason of her sex. Section 46 applies to women, it has no application to women who are not pregnant, and it has no application, of course, to men. If s. 46 treats unemployed pregnant women differently from other unemployed persons, be they male or female, it is, it seems to me, because they are pregnant and not because they are women.[8]

With respect to custody, the assumption of equal treatment coupled with the notion that there are no basic or fundamental differences between the sexes means that 'a legal system is established where men and women are constructed as equal rights holders according to their genetic ties to children. The courts are then obliged to admit men as the bearers of rights in the sense of legitimate claims towards children.'[9] This, in turn, has meant that the autonomy of women as child-bearers and mothers has been eroded.[10]

Equality conceptualized as sameness is manifested in law as gender neutrality. Gender neutrality, however, has been recognized elsewhere as one form of sexism rather than as gender equality. How is it possible that the same characteristic is variously identified as either sexist or the solution to sexism?

Gender Neutrality as a Sexist Problem

The answer to this question lies in our understanding of sexism. If sexism is seen as a one-dimensional phenomenon in which various types of manifestations can all be reduced to one base problem—be it called androcentricity, patriarchy, male domination, or whatever—then the solution is to address this one basic problem. *One* problem can be solved by *one* solution. If, therefore, the basic problem is a double standard for women and men, then the solution is to eliminate this double standard and judge everyone according to the same standard. However, this approach will necessarily result in difficulties if there is more than one base problem. In fact, we can distinguish between multiple types of sexist problems that are not reducible to each other. They include:[11]

Androcentricity: Adopting an overall male perspective.

Gender Insensitivity: Ignoring sex as a socially important variable in contexts in which it is important. Given the nature of contemporary society, it seems safe to assume that sex is socially important until it has been shown not to be. This category includes what is usually called 'gender neutrality'.

Sexual Dichotomism: Treating the sexes as two entirely discrete social and biological groups rather than as two groups with overlapping characteristics. It is, in many ways, the mirror image of gender insensitivity. The one ignores the importance of sex, the other exaggerates it, both distort it.

Familism: Treating the family as the smallest unit of analysis in cases where it is, in fact, individuals within families (or households) that engage in certain actions, have certain experiences, suffer or profit from particular costs or benefits, etc.[12]

Double Standards: Evaluating *identical* situations, behaviours, or traits on the basis of sex.[13]

Sexism, then, represents a syndrome of problems that are related but not reducible to each other. Failing to recognize this may inadvertently lead to taking one type of sexist problem and arguing for another problem that appears to be a 'solution'—for instance, a double standard, and arguing for a single standard, even though this may lead to gender insensitivity. In such a case, one type of sexist problem has been substituted for another type of sexist problem. By posing the dichotomous choice of 'same' versus 'different' treatment, this is precisely what has occurred.

Many commentators have, of course, observed problems in the different versus same treatment approach. This has led to at least two responses: withdrawing from the notion of equality altogether and declaring oneself as 'post-egalitarian',[14] or attempting to define equality in substantive rather than formal terms.

Formal Versus Substantive Equality
Here equal treatment is a strictly formal type of equality as contrasted with substantive equality, which is usually defined in one of two ways: equality of opportunity or equality of results. In turn, equality of results is expressed in various subformulations, including equality as acceptance, equality as non-domination, and equality as same social resources.

Equality of Opportunity
This approach serves variously as a political principle, a procedural argument, a cause, and a practice.[15] As a basis for social policy, it will result in the elimination of some discriminatory provisions in which certain groups of people (women in general, married women, people of certain ethnic backgrounds, etc.) are excluded from various jobs, training possibilities, etc. To the degree that it removes legal or administrative barriers, it is mildly useful.[16] However, it is an inherently conservative approach because it accepts whatever hierarchy there is as a given. The promise and intent of the equal opportunity approach is that it will reshuffle who fills *desirable* social positions, but it will not affect the distribution of the positions themselves. Translated into measurement terms, the equal opportunity approach transforms into the equality as equal proportions approach.

Equality as Equal Proportions
This approach is interesting as it underlies a number of useful measures of inequality. Many sociological studies take the proportion of females within a given population as a base from which to compute the over- or underrepresentation in another category. For instance, what is the proportion of female full professors in various disciplines given the prevalence and length of service of female associate professors within a particular area or discipline? Is the rate of promotion the same or different from that of men? If there is a smaller proportion of women who get promoted, and if performance criteria have been ruled out as an explanation, then discrimination becomes a reasonable explanation.

Various statistical methods are based on this logic.[17] The equal proportions model of equality is therefore a useful tool for describing existing inequalities. However, it is not a useful tool for describing gender equality. There are two reasons for this. For one, when this approach is used, it is primarily *desirable* social positions in which the proportions are compared. For example, how many women, Blacks, First Nations people, disabled people, etc., are in various positions of power and influence?

One rarely posits as a desirable outcome that there must be as many homeless women as there are homeless men in order to achieve equality. An exception to this is when negative traits are compared as an indication of inequality. For instance, the incarceration rate for Canadian Aboriginal people is disproportionately high compared to their overall numbers. This is interpreted as an indication of social disadvantage. Theoretically, equality would be improved if we were to either lower the incarceration rate for Natives or raise the incarceration rate for Whites to the same level as that of Natives. Few people, however, would argue that the latter would be socially desirable.

The underlying weakness of the equal proportions approach is that it does not address the overall inequality of a system but simply measures which categories of people are in certain positions. The equal proportions approach, as the measurement version of the equal opportunity approach, is therefore useful for a number of empirical descriptions of inequality. It does not, however, constitute a model of a society that is based on equality.

Equality as Acceptance

This approach has been proposed[18] as a response to three problems within discourses on equality: '(1) it is inapplicable once it encounters "real" difference; (2) it locates difference in women, rather than in relationships; and (3) it fails to question the assumptions that social institutions are gender neutral and that women and men are therefore similarly related to those institutions.'[19] Equality as acceptance means that 'The difference between human beings, whether perceived or real and whether biologically or socially based, should not be permitted to make a difference in the lived-out equality of those persons ... male and female "differences" must be costless relative to each other.'[20]

While attractive (and certainly more preferable than the notion of formal equality), it shares with the equality as equal proportion model the problem that it does not address hierarchy within society. Nevertheless, this approach to equality would result in some very desirable structural adjustments. Littleton uses the example of funding athletic facilities to make this point: 'equality as acceptance would support an argument that equal resources be allocated to male and female sports programs, regardless of whether the sports themselves are "similar".'[21] This approach would therefore go some distance in addressing the problems we encounter with the formal equality approach.

A different version of this type of approach, which is of particular interest because it has actually affected social policy in various countries, is the equality as same social resources approach.

Equality as Same Social Resources

In Scandinavia, in contrast to North America, equality has generally been lodged within the context of social equality.[22] Social equality comes out of a specific social democratic context and cultural heritage. Unlike the liberal tradition, which focuses on the rights of the *individual vis-à-vis* the state, social equality extends citizenship, political, social, and economic rights to those groups that were traditionally excluded. It led to the Scandinavian version of the welfare state, in which 'the state is seen as a tool to be used, not something to be feared, or respected or worshipped.'[23] This contrasts with the Anglo-Saxon idea that the individual and the private sphere, particularly that of the family, must be protected from state involvement.

Many of the commentators on issues of equality between the sexes agree that the family is the forum in which many of the issues discussed here come to the foreground. The equality as same social resources approach argues that the availability of resources is decisive for the equality of women.[24] One commentator formulates this as follows: 'The core is state acceptance of some kind of responsibility for the organization and financing of care for the old, the sick, children and the disabled.'[25] This neatly solves the problem of focusing on difference versus sameness by moving the issue from individual equality to the distribution of social resources.

In spite of the problems that attend debates around equality, clearly one cannot endorse gender inequality as a guiding principle. The issue is to translate the ideology of gender equality in policies in such a manner that it actually reduces or eliminates disadvantages that attach to one's sex. In the following section, we will examine how this has or has not worked within the individual responsibility model of the family.

2. WHAT ARE THE ASSUMPTIONS ABOUT THE LEGAL STATUS OF MARRIAGE?

P: Legal marriage is the basic constituent of a family. Non-legal unions do not generate the same rights and responsibilities as legal marriages do. Children of a non-legal union are considered illegitimate and have no legal claims on their father.

IR: Legal marriages are no longer the sole basic constituent unit of a family. Instead, functioning relationships are recognized as creating this basic unit. Consequently, common-law partners are held responsible for each other's economic support, both during the union and after the union has broken up. There is no legal distinction between legitimate and illegitimate children.

I will break down the discussion of this component into three separate questions.

Should Children of Legal Marriages and Common-law Relationships Have Different Rights and Entitlements?

Today it would be unconstitutional to discriminate against children because they were born outside a legal marriage. Currently more than a quarter of Canadian children are born to unmarried women, so this is a matter of importance to many people. This being so, one of the reasons for legal marriage—which ensured the transmission of a man's property to his legitimate offspring (usually sons)—is no longer relevant. Any proposals that suggest special protections and benefits for families based on legal marriage are at the same time reintroducing discrimination against children born outside of legal marriage. Whether it is intended or not, it is an inevitable consequence.

An increasing proportion of Canadians are living in common-law relationships, some of relatively short duration, some of very long duration. (The same can be said for marriages.) Should the state make a distinction between common-law and legally married couples in terms of any benefits? Should there be differences in terms of property division and support obligations between legally married spouses and spouses in a common-law relationship?[26] A third question of whether the state should single out couples over other groups who live together and/or are economically and financially interdependent (such as siblings, godparents and godchildren, friends who are not sexually involved with each other, etc.) will be addressed in Chapter 7. This question is not in the purview of either the patriarchal or individual responsibility model.

Should the State Make Distinctions between Legally Married and Common-law Couples?

For centuries, common-law unions used to be the norm for the majority of people. In Europe and America the Christian Church insisted that marriage was a holy sacrament. Over several centuries, marriage thus came to be regarded as something that needed the blessing of institutions other than that of the participating families. This eventually resulted in state regulation as to who could marry whom under what circumstances, and how they could divorce or separate. Depending on how far back we go in history, we can point to periods when common-law unions were either the norm or the exception.

The answer to the question of whether the state should distinguish between the two types of unions depends partly on what one sees as the family's function for the state. 'The family' is usually credited with being the building-block of society. Families socialize the children and prepare them to become the next generation of citizens who will earn money and pay taxes, thus enabling the state to continue to function. Families also take care of their own members—looking after them when they are sick, providing emotional and instrumental support for each other, consuming some things together (and others individually). In so far as this is beneficial for the state, the state has an interest in encouraging these types of groupings.

The question then is whether legal marriages perform these types of functions better than common-law unions. There is no empirical evidence that this is the case.[27] In general, some families (of whatever type) function better than others. Some legal marriages involve emotional, physical, and sexual abuse, as do some common-law unions and some same-sex unions.[28] Other families of either type of union function superbly, and many function sufficiently well to generate members who are able to pull their own weight in society. There is no compelling reason for the state to make a distinction between the two types of families, but many compelling reasons *not* to make distinctions. If the conservative thinkers are correct and unattached men pose a threat to society,[29] then men are being attached to women and possibly children through either type of union. In so far as stability is desirable, this would argue for giving every shred of support to common-law unions, since there is some evidence that social support increases the stability and happiness of a union.[30]

Should There Be Differences in Property Division and Support Obligations between Legally Married and Common-law Spouses?

Matters are more complicated with respect to cohabitants' obligations towards each other. As we have seen in Chapter 3, cohabitation has become more like marriage in terms of frequency, social acceptance, support obligations, and the status of children of the union, while legal marriages have become more similar to common-law unions with respect to last names. In some provinces, there are still distinct differences between legal marriages and common-law relationships with respect to property division upon union dissolution by death or separation. There is some evidence that people in common-law unions wish to avoid the legal commitments of marriage.[31] It is problematic to remove this space of freedom, given the great diversity of unions that exist. There is a distinct difference between a young couple living together, having a child together, and then splitting up, and an older couple living together after they have raised children generated with another partner. If a middle-aged couple decide to move in together at the age of fifty-five and to split at age sixty, and if both of them have children in their thirties, the partners may wish to protect their assets for themselves and for their children—with whom they have had a close relationship for over thirty years—rather than with a partner with whom they were associated for five years. If a partner entered into such a relationship with a low capacity for self-support and leaves the relationship in the same way (that is, he or she was not economically harmed by being in the relationship), and if there was no shared child rearing, what is the justification for support?[32]

Treating all common-law relationships like legal marriages in terms of support obligations and property division ignores the very different circumstances under which people may enter a common-law union. If they choose to marry, they make a positive choice to live under one type of regime. If they have chosen not to marry, is it the state's task to impose a marriagelike regime on them retroactively?

The state has a direct interest in property division and support payments only if it can reduce the number of people dependent on the state for support; otherwise it is demonstrably not concerned with the fact that some of its citizens are poor and others are rich. Here we are dealing with notions of economic dependence/independence and interdependence. I will come back to this question under point 7.

3. What Are the Assumptions About Household/Family Memberships' Incongruence/Congruence?

P: Household and family memberships are treated as congruous at the nuclear level. Hence, a spouse is equated with a parent.

IR: Household and family memberships are mostly treated as congruous at the nuclear level. This being so, a spouse is equated with a parent. Conversely, an external parent is *largely* treated as a non-parent.

We are dealing with two issues here that need to be examined separately: the incongruence/congruence between household and family memberships and the conflation of spousal and parental roles.

Incongruence/Congruence of Household and Family Memberships

As we have seen in chapters 2 and 3, there is a high degree of incongruence between household and family memberships due to high rates of divorce, births to unmarried women, and remarriage or union formation. As we have seen in Chapter 4, this has resulted in a multitude of types of fathers and mothers. One household may encompass people who belong to two (or maybe more) family units that are not shared by other household members. The assumption of congruence between household and family memberships is therefore misplaced, since it does not reflect reality. This is the primary problem shared by both the patriarchal and the individual responsibility models. It is precisely because we make this assumption that spousal and parental roles are conflated.

The Conflation of Spousal and Parental Roles

Under the patriarchal model, spousal and parental roles were mostly congruous. Because people remarried mostly after widowhood, the widowed person's children automatically became the stepchildren of the new marriage partner. This part of the historical backdrop may partially explain why we still treat spouses as parents.

Today, however, the situation is vastly more complicated. In the majority of cases, the other parents are still alive but do not live with their children. This has led to the generation of partial non-exclusive fathers (and some mothers). It raises the issue of the rights and responsibilities of both fathers (assuming there are only two) in the case of non-exclusive fatherhood (or two mothers in the case of motherhood).

Biology Versus Intentionality

When it comes to support, many divorced or unmarried fathers default partially or completely on support payments,[33] and mothers carry the sole or major burden of economic responsibility for the children. Hence, if a lone mother finds a new partner, and the biological father has defaulted on paying support, there may be an attempt to get the second man to assume some financial responsibility for the children if that second union dissolves as well. This then pits two men (sometimes more) against each other, with the custodial mother and children caught in the middle. Often at stake is the question of the importance of a man's *intent* to treat the woman's children as the children of the marriage versus the biological fact of fatherhood on the part of the natural father. If a man can show that he did *not* intend to treat the children as the children of the marriage, he is more likely not to have to pay support if and when the relationship dissolves. This seems an unsatisfactory arrangement all around. The biological father is often relieved of his responsibilities, while a man who is not the biological father may be given a financial responsibility past the duration of the relationship just because he was decent in his behaviour towards the children during the relationship.[34]

While there is no clear-cut reason why the second man should *not* ever assume any responsibilities, there certainly seems to be no reason at all to allow the biological father to escape his. The biological father's responsibilities should cease only with the adoption of a child by another person, regardless of whether or not the new partner takes over responsibility for new biological or social children with the mother: 'it should not be possible to remarry or procreate one's way out of existing child support obligations, which should be treated on the same footing as an outstanding loan or any other financial commitment.'[35]

The Necessary Disjunction between Rights and Responsibilities of Parents

Support is, of course, only one of the relevant issues. Continued contact with the child in the form of access, visitation, and general input into the child's socialization process (assuming that physical custody is not shared) is another. There are at least two different views on whether this issue should be treated as integrally related to support payments or not.

People who argue that the two are related make at least two different points. First, fathers are less likely to default on paying support if they have close and intimate relationships with their children. Second, obligations should be balanced by rights. In other words, fathers should not be obliged to pay support for their children if they do not get the benefit of their children's company. However, research does not support the notion that close contact between non-custodial fathers and their children encourages regular and sufficient support payments.[36]

Let us turn to the second point: support payments should be balanced by rights to a child. First, it is important to note that problems with access are relatively infrequent. A follow-up study on the effects of the divorce legislation found that 'Most men and women in sole custody arrangements ... indicated that they were satisfied with the present arrangement.'[37] In most instances when there are problems, it is that mothers and their children would like more frequent contact, not less, between the children and their father.[38] In some instances, of course, a non-custodial father wants access while the custodial mother does not. In such cases we need to ask why. Is it because contact with the father is not deemed to be beneficial to the children and/or detrimental to the mother, or is it because the mother is vindictive and wants to impede contact between the father and his children?

Contact with the father may not be desirable because he is violent to the children and/or to the ex-wife. In such circumstances it seems appropriate that his access be severely circumscribed. If we link support obligations to rights, this would suggest that abusive men either have no financial obligations towards their children (if we wish to minimize contact between them and their children) or that children must associate with such fathers, even if this is not to their benefit. Either outcome seems morally wrong as well as bad policy, since it would financially reward bad fathers or force children and their mothers into contact with violent men.

If the mother is trying to prevent access for reasons of her own, then this problem needs to be rectified. However, this must be achieved by legal means other than stopping support.[39] Children are dependent upon the care of others. Their needs are not reduced regardless of whether or not they visit their father. Their needs are absolute and immediate. Therefore, it is necessary to recognize the fundamentally asymmetrical relationship between parental rights and obligations: obligations are absolute, while rights can be lost. Losing the rights should not imply that a parent is also freed of his or her obligations. Income tax regulations are another aspect of this asymmetrical relationship. At present, non-custodial parents can deduct their child-support payments, and recipient custodial parents must declare it as income.[40] This makes sense if we equate household membership with family membership. It does *not* make sense if we assume that the two are incongruent. The father would not be able to deduct his child-related expenses if he were living with the child and the mother. What has changed is the household composition, not the family constellation.

Treating household and family memberships as congruent is highly problematic given the high degree of incongruity (which shows no signs of abating!). In the case of second or subsequent unions, it leads to the ambivalent treatment of the biological father as largely a non-father in terms of his responsibilities, and treats the non-biological social father (if there is one) as a substitute. This tactic is a concrete example of the lack of recognition of partial, non-exclusive fatherhood. Justice Fleury in *Primeau* v. *Primeau*[41] states that 'A parent-child relationship is not one that can be terminated unilaterally by the parent or the child. The same result should follow in either the case of the natural parent or the "deemed" parent.' He equates social with biological fatherhood, ignores the partial nature of biological fatherhood, and decides that a social, non-exclusive, partial father has all the obligation for support while the biological, non-exclusive, partial father has none. Clearly something is out of kilter here.

Enforced Quasi-spousehood of the Ex-wife

Failing to separate the effects of rulings on people as parents versus people as spouses occurs when custodial mothers (there seem to be no cases of custodial fathers in the same situation) are prevented from moving to another place of residence, even if they have a better job offer and/or wish to move together with a new partner or for any other reason, because they cannot move the children without the consent of the access parent, who denies this consent. This is truly perverse. Under the patriarchal family, the man's domicile was, by definition, also the woman's domicile, no matter where she wanted to live. With the reform of all provincial family laws, this stipulation was eliminated. A husband can no longer force his wife to live in his home or in his city of residence. A husband also no longer has the right to prevent his wife from taking any job she wishes to accept. However, *after* the couple has split up, an ex-husband can suddenly constrain an ex-wife's activities as if they were married in a patriarchal manner.

A landmark decision[42] by Justice Abella recently broke this regressive interpretation of the *Divorce Act*. This case involved Mary Richards, who had custody of her child, and her ex-husband, Lee MacGyver, an ex-alcoholic and abusive man, who had liberal access. Some time after the divorce, Richards became involved with Ron White. They planned to marry. The ex-husband's petition for shared custody was denied. White was transferred to the United States, and MacGyver obtained a court order that the child should continue to reside in North Bay. On appeal, the mother's custody was confirmed and the move was approved. The father appealed to the Court of Appeal. In denying this appeal, Justice Abella argued that:

... the court should be overwhelmingly respectful of the decision-making capacity of the person in whom the court or the other parent has entrusted primary responsibility for the child. We cannot design a system which shields the non-custodial parent from any change in the custodial parent's life which may affect the exercise of access. The emphasis should be, rather, on deferring to the decision-making responsibilities of the custodial parent, unless there is substantial evidence that those decisions impair *the child's not the access parent's* long-term well-being.

We must also forcefully acknowledge that the custodial parent's best interests are inextricably tied to those of the child. The young child is almost totally dependent on that parent, not on the parent seen during visits ...

... one reaches the admittedly difficult conclusion that a parent with custody, acting responsibly, should not be prevented from leaving a jurisdiction because the move would interfere with access by the other parent with the child, even if the relationship between the child and the access parent is a good one.

To conclude otherwise may render custody a unilaterally punitive order. No court could—or would—prevent a parent with access from moving anywhere or at any time he or she chose. Lee MacGyver could, for example, anytime he chose, and for whatever reason he chose, decide to leave North Bay for anywhere he chose, whether or not a court deemed the move 'necessary' ...

I have difficulty understanding why, then, the courts should not feel equally constrained in interfering with the right of the custodial parent to decide where to live.[43]

In a more recent judgement, the Supreme Court ruled on a similar issue. While using quite different language and reasoning, they were nevertheless prepared to let a custodial mother move with her child to Australia to pursue her studies, even though the non-custodial father had an excellent relationship with the child.[44]

4. WHAT IS THE APPROPRIATE UNIT OF ADMINISTRATION?

P: The family household is treated as the normal unit of administration.

IR: The family household is treated as the unit of administration (with a few exceptions).

Both the patriarchal and individual responsibility models treat the family household as the unit of administration. If we accept that household and family memberships are in many cases *not* congruous, then it becomes highly problematic to treat the household as the administrative unit for many purposes.[45]

The Familism-Individualism Flip-flop

Taking the household or the family rather than the individual as the smallest administrative unit may lead to what has been described as the familism-individualism flip-flop.[46] The familism-individualism flip-flop occurs when policies that are meant to benefit families end up hurting certain families because entitlement is based on family or household status. It is a counterintuitive outcome.

The reasons behind this phenomenon may be diverse. One is the notion that public support must not usurp the functions that are properly carried out by family members for each other. Therefore, support that is available for people who are not family members if they render certain services is not available for family members who provide the same services. For example, if a family takes in foster children, they are paid a certain amount of money per child. If they raise their own children, they will not get the equivalent amount, or if the mother or family is on welfare, they will be regarded by some as 'welfare bums' rather than as citizens performing a vital service for the community.

The familism-individualism flip-flop is particularly obvious and tragic in cases of disability, where family members (often wives/mothers) get caught in a vicious trap. What is supposed to be encouraged—that family members render support to each other—is in fact made impossible. The following is a fictional but realistic example:[47]

> Emily Apple and her paraplegic husband, Louis, have been married since March 1990. She wants to provide the extensive daily care he needs in their apartment and work three days per week at nursing. But if she earned $770 per month at part-time nursing, her husband's $655 a month disabled allowance would be cut to $189 monthly. If she worked full-time, it would be cut off completely. She is afraid she may have to separate and let the province take care of her husband in a $250 per day chronic care hospital.

The familism-individualism flip-flop here works as follows: its underlying ideology is that family members should take care of each other financially as well as by providing care. Hence, a disabled person's allowance is reduced if another household/family member has income above a certain level. The couple are treated as an administrative unit, rather than Louis as an individual who is entitled to his disability allowance *because of his disability*, which requires care on an ongoing basis, regardless of other factors. The effect is that in the name of maintaining the family, it has become impossible for the wife in this case to render the care she is willing and able to render, which is exactly the opposite effect of what the policy proposes to achieve.

Another example can be found in the income tax provisions. The 1987 (and later) provisions concerning child care stipulate that child-care expenses are payments made to any resident of Canada, except those paid to:

- the mother or father of the child

- a supporting person of the child

- a person for whom either you, or a supporting person of the child, claimed a personal exemption

- a person under twenty-one who is related to you or your spouse; for this purpose, a 'related person' could be a child (including an adopted child), brother, or sister of you or your spouse, but does not include a niece or nephew

Example: Lynn and Paul married and have an eight-year-old daughter. They paid Lynn's nineteen-year-old sister to care for their daughter while they were at work. Neither Lynn nor Paul may claim these payments as child-care expenses because the money was paid to a related person who is under twenty-one.

While this is not as extreme a position as used to be the case with child-care expenses, it is a good example of the familism-individualism flip-flop. Let us assume that Lynn's sister, Deborah, is preparing to go to university in the fall and needs a summer job to earn money for her tuition. She is perfectly willing and eager to babysit for her sister and brother-in-law, and is a good and dearly loved friend to her niece. Lynn and Paul are pleased to have such a good arrangement for the summer because their daughter has just recovered from an illness and needs some special care, which they know Deborah is able to provide. However, they are not so well off that they could forego claiming their child-care expenses. Regretfully, they decide that they cannot afford the best arrangement for their child, which is to have Deborah take care of her. Deborah decides to search for another job.

Deborah discusses her situation with her friend, Marjorie, and finds with astonishment that she is in a similar situation. Deborah and Marjorie decided to trade jobs: Marjorie babysits for Lynn and Paul, Deborah for Marjorie's sister and her husband. Both sets of parents are able to deduct the child-care expenses paid to Deborah and Marjorie, yet Marjorie is not as good a babysitter for Lynn's daughter as Deborah would have been because she is less familiar with the special needs of the child.

Deborah and Marjorie thus do the same work for someone who is unrelated as they were planning to do for their respective nieces. In one instance the expense can be claimed, while in the other it cannot.[48]

Taking the household (which is equated with family membership, given assumption #3) as the administrative unit therefore creates difficulties, and excluding people from benefits on the basis of their family status may prevent family members from helping each other.

Further, the administrative focus on the household instead of on the individual has meant that women have qualified for benefits in their role as wives rather than as individuals or as mothers. Those countries who have developed liberal welfare regimes (the United States, Canada, Australia, and Great Britain) end up with a dual insurance/assistance model: 'first-class (insurance) benefits tend to go to men and second-class (welfare) benefits to women'.[49]

The next two points will be dealt with together since they are intimately related.

5. What Are the Assumptions Concerning Economic Responsibility/Dependency?

P: The husband is responsible for the economic well-being of the family household. The wife and children are treated as the husband's economic dependants whether or not they actually contribute to the household through paid or unpaid labour.

IR: Husband and wife are equally responsible for the economic well-being of themselves, each other, and any dependent children. Children are considered dependants of both their parents, and spouses are considered interdependent rather than one as the dependant and the other as the head of the household.

6. What Are the Assumptions About Care and Service Provision for Family Members in Need of Care?

P: The wife/mother is seen as responsible for providing care and services to family members in need of care.

IR:Fathers and mothers are equally responsible for providing care and services to family members in need of care.

The assumption of economic dependency on which the patriarchal model is based is inappropriate for at least three reasons. First, most of the wives and mothers are in the paid labour force today, thus contributing financially to the economic well-being of the family.[50] Second, this assumption is premised on a notion of work and its value, which ignores the contributions made through unpaid family work (see below). Lastly, it conflicts with the assumption of gender equality. Therefore, an assumption of automatic female dependence (rather than interdependence) is inappropriate even when the wife is a housewife without an independent income.

The assumption concerning care provision in the patriarchal model likewise conflicts with the assumption of gender equality. Assumptions #5 and #6 of the individual responsibility model seem appropriate if taken on their own, but become very problematic when taken together and particularly in conjunction with assumption #7.

With the introduction of gender equality, discriminatory laws have been repealed or reformed. This, however, is only one aspect of the changes that have taken place. Under the patriarchal model, the conceptualization of wives and children as the economic dependants of their husbands/fathers was premised on the understanding that economic contributions necessarily involve money transactions.[51] With the switch to equality, a reconsideration of this premise became necessary. It was replaced with a new premise consisting of two logical components: (a) unpaid housework, including child care, is economically valuable, even though no money changes hands; and (b) husbands and wives contribute to the economic well-being of the family *by virtue of being married to each other.*

While the first premise constitutes a long overdue correction in the way work (both paid and unpaid) is valued, the second premise is problematic, given the pervasive inequality in who is actually doing the housework and caring work in families.[52] It is, however, an explicit component of family law today. For instance, the *Ontario Family Law Reform Act* states:

> The purpose of this section is to recognize that child care, household management and financial provision are the joint responsibilities of the spouses and that *inherent in the marital relationship there is equal contribution*, whether financial or otherwise, by the spouses to the assumption of these responsibilities, entitling each spouse to the equalization of the net family properties ...[53]

This is a very clear statement, but not one that reflects reality. In fact, in many marriages there is an unequal contribution in financial as well as 'child care' and 'household management' terms. Women's financial contributions to families range from 0 per cent to 100 per cent, with the average hovering around one-third, since on average women's earnings are lower than men's earnings. Presumably, men's contributions to child care and household management also range from 0 per cent to 100 per cent, with the average also hovering around one-third, since that is about the average contribution men make to family affairs in terms of unpaid work.

These two differential sets of contributions, however, do *not* even out for two reasons: women and men do not assort themselves in marriages so that they reflect the averages, and the variations among women (and possibly men) are so strong that they form very distinct subgroups. While the majority of wives are in the labour force, about one-third are not. The women in the labour force tend to do as large a share of household management and child care as the women *not* in the labour force.[54] The contribution of these women to the family welfare therefore has increased both in absolute and in relative terms, while the contribution of the husbands has remained stable. Beyond that, although the average incomes for the sexes are as cited, this does not mean that it is true in all marriages. In about one-fifth to one-quarter of all marriages, the wife earns as much or more than the husband, but in all likelihood, she continues to do the larger share of housework.

The notion that the contribution to the family is inherent in the marital relationship therefore covers a multitude of situations in which this is patently not the case. Ironically, the assumption that wives are economically vulnerable because of their marriage was one of the driving forces behind the various attempts at family law reform in the 1970s and 1980s. 'The fact that a woman earns a lower wage creates an economic incentive for the couple to further the male spouse's career.'[55] The majority of wives have taken on the role of financial coprovider, which was largely reserved for the husband in the patriarchal model, while the majority of husbands do not take on the role of care coprovider and cohousewife, which used to be reserved for wives and is still mainly carried out by women. In other words, women have added the primary male role to their responsibilities, but men have not added the primary female role to theirs.

All of this becomes legally relevant only after a union dissolution when family property must be split. If the emphasis could be shifted towards more equal contributions *while a union is ongoing*, it would be a much more socially meaningful matter. Even with the assumption of equal contribution, after a divorce a woman and her children are likely to be much poorer than the man. This is a well-documented fact, and the reasons for it have been discussed in Chapter 3.

The degendering of contributions as a matter of *fact* rather than as a social goal has not contributed to a substantive improvement in the situation of women and children, but instead is one of the factors that worsen the situation. Because women and men are declared to be able to support themselves, the *Divorce Act* stipulates that after union dissolution, each spouse must be self-supporting as soon as possible. The effects of this stipulation range from the reasonable to the absurd. The ability to support oneself depends on one's previous employment history, the overall job situation, one's training and educational background, one's responsibility for small children (or other people in need of care), and the support one receives for executing such caring tasks. Just as the man is *assumed* to contribute equally to child care and household management by virtue of being married, so the woman is *assumed* to be able to become equally self-sufficient because women in general are likely to be or to have been in the labour force. However, many women have interrupted involvement in the labour force, so they are greatly disadvantaged by this assumption of degendering.[56]

7. WHAT IS SEEN AS THE APPROPRIATE PRIVATE-PUBLIC DIVISION OF RESPONSIBILITIES?

P: The public has no responsibility for the economic well-being of a family if there is a husband/father present, and no responsibility for care provision if there is a wife/mother present. However, if one of the spouses is missing or incapacitated, and if there are children, public assistance is seen as legitimate (although not always rendered).

IR: The public has no responsibility for the economic well-being of a family or for providing care if there is either a husband/father or wife/mother. It will provide temporary help if one of them is absent or incapacitated, but the basic assumption is that a parent is responsible both for the economic well-being and care of dependent children.

Here is the crucial point where assumptions #5, #6, and #7 unite. In the patriarchal model, assumption #7 follows logically from assumptions #5 and #6. If the person who is responsible for either sex-specific function is absent or unable to fulfil his or her function, it is logical to replace the functions of this person.

The problems arise with the individual responsibility model. In the patriarchal model, the husband and wife were considered able to fulfil two functions (economic provision and care). They were each assigned one function on the basis of their sex. In the individual responsibility model, the husband and wife are each assigned both functions (economic provision and care). So far, so good. However, the next step in the individual responsibility model's logic is that since *either* person can fulfil either function, one person can do both. This is by no means a logical step to take. If we apply this logic to any other set of tasks—for instance, digging a hole in the sidewalk, with one person operating the crane and the other doing the ground work—either person can do either job, but both are needed in order to complete it. If there is only one person, it will take him or her at least twice as long.

When caring for an inevitably dependent person—to use Fineman's phrase[57]—and earning money, the option of doubling the time does not exist, since the need for care is absolute and always present. The failure to recognize that one person cannot possibly care for dependent people on a full-time basis while earning money at the same time is the major problem with the individual responsibility model.

This is evident in discussions about welfare mothers,[58] who are seen as a drain on the public purse, as dependent on the state, and as unwilling to work—even though they are working (albeit in an unpaid capacity) and rendering an extremely important service for the state: raising their children. If both parents failed to raise the children, the state would have to pick up the cost of doing so, at much greater expense than what a welfare mother currently receives.

Broadening the basis of discussion somewhat and combining assumption #1 (gender equality) with assumption #7 (the public/private division), it is apparent that gender equality can be achieved only if women and men both have the opportunity to earn an equal and independent income. Enough has been written on this topic to make it unnecessary to belabour the point. The issue that is less recognized (though the point has often been made) is that gender equality is unthinkable as long as caring for dependent family members remains strictly a private matter. The failure to act on this issue is one of the reasons why we continue to have economic inequality between women and men,[59] which in turn makes it seem reasonable that men will give priority to employment requirements over family work requirements, while women do the reverse, so one set of inequalities reinforces the other. The vicious circle can only be broken if we finally recognize that care for children and other inevitable dependants is a socially useful service that requires public support.[60]

And here we come back to the issue of spousal support[61] after dissolution of a legal marriage or common-law union. If an economic disadvantage has occurred *because* of membership within a union, there seems to be a good reason to ask the economically stronger partner to make up (at least partially) for this disadvantage. However, it is important to realize that this will *not* create economic equality between ex-wives and ex-husbands, nor will it even raise a substantial proportion of women and children above the poverty line. One estimate was that if we had support awarded in 100 per cent of the cases and 100 per cent enforcement of such payments, this would raise approximately 1.8 per cent of all women above the poverty threshold. Even allowing for a generous margin of error, obviously the overall proportion of women who would be helped through better awards and enforcement of support payments is minuscule.[62] Alternative policies therefore need to be instituted. This point will be discussed in Chapter 7.

8. What Are the Assumptions with Respect to Heterosexuality/Homosexuality?

P: Homosexuality is seen as an illness or a crime and partners within same-sex couples are not publicly recognized as having any social, economic, or legal obligations towards each other. It is seen as irrelevant for family policy, since same-sex couples are regarded as antithetical to the nuclear family.

IR: Same-sex couples are starting to be recognized as a valid family form.

The assumption of the patriarchal model is out of sync with current reality. The assumption of the individual responsibility model is more in sync, but could be strengthened to make the sex of partners irrelevant for most purposes.

Conclusion

The individual responsibility model of the family thus has distinct advantages over the patriarchal model of the family, yet it has several inherent flaws nevertheless. It is premised on the notion of gender equality rather than inequality, but this equality tends to be conceptualized in formal terms, thus failing to address substantive aspects of gender inequality, particularly the need for public support for care of inevitable dependants.

The individual responsibility model has started to recognize common-law couples as functioning families, and has abolished the legal distinction between legitimate and illegitimate children, while at the same time (and more problematically) extending support obligations to common-law spouses.

Household and family memberships are treated as congruous in both the patriarchal and the individual responsibility models. This is highly problematic because as we have seen, household and family memberships are incongruent for many people, households, and families. Furthermore, the resultant conflation of spousal and parental roles results in serious problems and lies at the root of some recent Supreme Court decisions, which seriously impede the achievement of fuller gender equality. Likewise, the family household is treated as the normal unit of administration, resulting in a familism-individualism flip-flop, which may actually penalize people for living in a family situation, producing results that are the opposite of the professed intent of policies.

Assigning each adult the responsibility for economic well-being and care for inevitable dependants without giving any concomitant systematic public support for this central function mocks the notion of gender equality. It is neither theoretically possible nor practical in current reality to postulate gender equality without providing sufficient social resources for the care of dependants.

Finally, the incipient recognition of same-sex couples as a viable form of the family is a distinct advance over the patriarchal model of the family.

CHAPTER 6

From Refurbishing the Past to Abolishing the Family: Three Proposed Solutions

INTRODUCTION

All critics agree that the current approach to families—that is, the individual responsibility model of the family and policies built on this model—do not work. This is behind the current notion that 'the family' is in crisis. There seem to be three predominant directions for change: a return to the patriarchal model of the family (without naming it as such), pushing gender equality between spouses to its logical end, and abolishing legal marriage and the nuclear family as a norm. I will look at one proponent of each of these positions, and then discuss the social responsibility model of the family in the next chapter.

A RETURN TO THE TRADITIONAL NUCLEAR FAMILY

David Popenoe has been an outspoken critic of current families and family policies. He sees the American family (and families in all highly industrialized countries) in decline. The family has been robbed of its functions, and its decline lies at the root of the gradual dissolution of Western societies (and, incidentally, of the US's feared loss of its position as world leader).[1]

Popenoe does not simplemindedly blame only families or women in particular but recognizes (and discusses in some detail) the importance of other global, regional, and local trends. He discusses how to link the father firmly to the family. He identifies unattached men as the source of many societal ills: 'every society must be wary of the unattached male, for he is universally the cause of numerous social ills'[2] and hence sees as a major issue how 'to get men to marry the mothers of their children'.[3] His argument that families, and children in particular, are in crisis is persuasive (and shared by others who do not share his view of the appropriate solutions).[4] His solution is to bolster and buttress the nuclear family.[5] 'I do not necessarily mean the traditional nuclear family, characterized by male dominance and a stay-at-home wife', he writes. 'I refer instead to the nuclear family in more general terms—consisting of a male and female living together, apart from other relatives, who share responsibility for their children and for each other.'[6]

In order to 'rebuild the nest', the US (and, by implication any other society) would be 'well advised to establish as a paramount national goal the promotion of intact, nuclear families that can successfully raise children.'[7] In order to achieve this goal, two broad efforts must be made: 'the promotion of long-term, monogamous marriages, especially when children are involved; and the provision of additional resources to the parents of young children so that parents will be able to do a better job of childrearing.'[8]

To achieve the first, Popenoe proposes a two-tier system of divorce law: 'marriages between adults without minor children would be relatively easy to dissolve, but marriages between adults with children would not. Properly conceived family life and sex education in the schools might help. Rigorously enforcing economic support from divorced fathers and stigmatizing "deadbeat dads" would probably yield more male responsibility, as well as marginally more money for children.'[9]

'How to get men to marry the mothers of their children ... rests on a combination of fewer unplanned births through widespread birth control, and finding ways to lock the father into the union (at least when the child is young).'[10] In addition, families (that is, presumably, nuclear families with a locked-in male only, since all others are part of the problem we have to overcome) need more money as well as time. 'For children in America today there is a national time-famine, brought about mainly by father absence and by both husband and wife being in the labour force.' Therefore, 'We should enact policies that make work more family-friendly, including parental leave, flexible hours, compressed work weeks, more part-time work (with benefits), job sharing, and home-based employment opportunities. Another possibility is more "career sequencing", in which parents deliberately postpone careers to provide more time for young children.'[11]

Is Popenoe advocating a return to the patriarchal family? At first blush, it seems not. He consistently endorses the progress made by women in the past 150 years and explicitly advises liberals, and especially feminists, that they need not fear 'that society will shift back to the traditional nuclear family, with all of its rejected moral baggage'.[12] Before addressing this question systematically, it is helpful to look at his image of the past.

First of all, it is important to note that recent historical research has shattered the view that almost all families in the past who did a fine job in raising their children were nuclear families. It is part of a monolithic approach to families to underestimate diversity by looking for uniformity, and to assume that just because people are married, they also love each other and actively participate in the socialization of children, etc. The *structure* of a family is equated with *a capacity to adequately carry out certain functions*. For instance, the assumption is that a married couple will do well in raising a child, while a lone parent (usually a mother) will do less well or even badly.

This is putting the cart before the horse. Instead, we should ask under what circumstances specified functions (such as adequate socialization of the children) are carried out and then support the structures within which this takes place. Popenoe, of course, believes that he has addressed this question. In his view, the nuclear family is 'the family structure that unquestionably works the best'.[13] However, the past is by no means an indication that the nuclear family structure works best. Recently we have become aware of the extent of child abandonment in Europe. Both illegitimate and legitimate children were abandoned. 'At their height levels of abandonment ranged from 20% to over 35% of all births in such cities as Paris, Vienna, Milan, and Florence.'[14] In nineteenth-century Russia, as many as one-third to one-half of the abandoning mothers were married, and in Spain, until the 1870s about half the abandoning mothers were married.[15] A sign that nuclear families unquestioningly work best? Further, the degree of violence of all types—physical, emotional, sexual, up to and including uxoricide and famicide[16]—that has been (and continues to be) common in nuclear (as in other) families should make it impossible to argue that this one family form 'unquestionably' works the best.

If men are locked into a marriage, women and children will also be locked in,[17] regardless of the quality of the marriage. There is considerable evidence that people locked into an unhappy marriage may do as much or more damage to their children than if they divorce,[18] quite apart from the unhappiness that results for the adults. Popenoe does not discuss the issues of violence and abuse at all—prime reasons why a divorce may be preferable to maintaining a marriage. He does suggest increasing benefits to nuclear families, but forcing a male to stay in a marriage is not, *per se*, necessarily a means of raising a family out of poverty.[19]

In order to assess whether Popenoe's vision is a repackaging of the patriarchal family, I will briefly consider the eight components of the patriarchal family and examine to what degree they describe his vision of the new familism. I will leave the question concerning gender equality for the last. On the surface, Popenoe endorses gender equality. However, when looking at the assumptions behind the other aspects of his vision, things become starkly patriarchal.

Marriage would confer a much more important legal status than it does today. He worries about how to make men marry the mothers of their children. Once married with children, divorce would be made more difficult. I worry instead about a unit in which people will stay only through coercion. As Stacey has argued, the fact that divorce is as high as it is today is:

> ... a sad, revealing commentary on the benefits to women of the traditional nuclear family ... even in a period when women retain pri-

mary responsibility for maintaining children and other kin, when most women continue to earn substantially less than men with equivalent cultural capital, and when women and their children suffer substantial economic decline after divorce, so many regard divorce as the lesser of evils.[20]

... Without coercion, divorce and single motherhood rates will remain high.[21]

It is interesting that Popenoe talks about the problem of coercing men into marriage without mentioning that this also locks in women and their children just as securely—or rather, as used to be the case, much more securely—since they will have fewer economic options. The underlying assumption is clearly that women will *want* the men to be present, which the divorce literature tells us might be true in some cases, but untrue in most of them.[22]

However, perhaps the most worrying aspect of this notion is that it would result in a further deterioration of the already very tenuous situation of lone parents and their children. This is inevitable, given Popenoe's premise. He worries that women have been able to survive outside of marriage with their children, and sees it as a central factor in the escalating rates of divorce and lone motherhood.[23] In order to *decrease* the attractiveness of lone parenthood, then, Popenoe cannot afford to support lone mothers since this might make them unwilling to keep the men around. Note that I have shifted the actor here. As far as Popenoe is concerned, the male is the one who acts and who needs to be coerced into marriage. The picture changes when we conceptualize the woman as an independent actor as well.

Household and family memberships are conceptualized as congruent, and any discrepancy is clearly identified as the major problem that we have to overcome. Hence, the unit of administration is the household/family. New benefits will be made available to the congruent unit and, by implication, only to this unit since this is the type of family we wish to strengthen and foster, while trying to minimize the number of families in which there is a discrepancy between the family and household memberships. On the other hand, Popenoe holds fathers responsible for child support, even after divorce. In the absence of social support for the resulting lone-parent family, however, the majority of these families will be below the poverty level (as is the case today) and, as we have seen earlier, he cannot afford to provide public support for these families because this would damage the push for nuclear families. This is a vicious circle that has often trapped policy makers.

In spite of several bows to women working in the labour force, 'It is highly relevant that the traditional family role of men in almost all societies has been that of a protector and provider, precisely so that mother and infant could be closely attached. In the absence of a husband or other helping relative, mother-infant attachment obviously becomes problematic.'[24] This makes all families without a male deviant, and it makes it clear that a gendered division of labour, with all its implications, is an integral (if mostly undiscussed) part of Popenoe's vision.

Both father and mother are identified as potential caregivers, and the language is often carefully gender neutral. Two 'parents can devote more attention to a child than a single parent',[25] but since there is no notion of publicly subsidized day care, since parents' input in child rearing is irreplaceable, and since men's provider role is crucial, it seems that the 'career sequencing' would have to be a primarily female phenomenon (as it is now). Nonetheless, some of the policy measures Popenoe mentions in this context in order to make work more family-friendly would be very welcome and helpful for whichever parent avails herself or himself of them. In any case, as far as Popenoe is concerned, it is clear that it is the family who must care for the child. External care provision (unless it is given by some other relative) is again seen as part of the problem rather than as part of the solution.

Indeed, providing care for children is clearly and repeatedly identified as the single most important task of the nuclear family. According to Popenoe, while society should subsidize the provision of care in the nuclear family, presumably by allocating money through variously undefined policy instruments (the tax system, direct transfers, etc., come to mind), it is the family, with the father locked into a marriage, who bears sole responsibility for child care. Care for other dependants (the elderly, chronically ill, disabled, etc.) is not the focus of attention and therefore not included here.

Popenoe gives little explicit attention to same-sex couples, but since he does not include them in his definition of the nuclear family, which consists of 'a male and a female living together', they are clearly undesirable forms of families. They are considered of no real importance as family forms since most gay and lesbian couples do not form 'family units', in Popenoe's view, so they are not worthy of any public support, but are part of the problem we need to solve.

Now let us return to the first point: the ideology concerning gender equality. As stated earlier, Popenoe endorses the notion of gender equality and assures us that his approach will not result in a return to the traditional family, characterized by male dominance and a stay-at-home wife. However, by forcing the man to stay with the family, Popenoe forces the woman to stay with the man, and by decreeing that nuclear families are better than all other alternatives and making it harder to leave a marriage when there are children, he clearly makes a female-headed, lone-parent household a deviant family form. Male violence, particularly against women and children, is prevalent. How will this be dealt with?

Popenoe argues that there is a biological need for the family because unattached men need to be civilized by attaching them to women and children. This will be fostered by 'appropriate' family life and sex education. What about 'appropriate' socialization of males through 'appropriate' sex education, anger management training, peace education, and family life education to teach an abhorrence for the use of violence in all its forms? In addition, all students could be taught negotiation and conflict resolution skills, thus enabling them to deal constructively with inevitable interpersonal conflict. Further, since dual-earner families suffer from a time deficit (true!), and given that there is pervasive gender inequality in society, it will be the obvious choice that women will have to be the ones who sequence their careers, especially since (as Popenoe informs us) in all societies men have traditionally been the providers and protectors (from the aggression of other males!).

Since the only family worthy of support would be the nuclear family, this would leave all other families in the lurch: lone-parent families, same-sex families, the first families of men who themselves are in new nuclear families, extended families, and other family constellations. In most of these families, women struggle to raise children on their own. Women who are not attached to men therefore would not be eligible for social support for raising their children since they are the problem that must be overcome. It seems safe to conclude that Popenoe's 'new familism' is, in fact, the old patriarchal familism, dressed up with a few rhetorical statements concerning gender equality and a few useful specific policy proposals. Okin, however, has a very different vision than Popenoe.

GENDER EQUALITY IN FAMILIES IN THE GENDERLESS SOCIETY

Okin (1989) has examined theories of justice and their applicability to women, in light of the currently existing social structure of families in the US. She concludes that all theories reviewed have serious flaws (some more so than others). At one extreme, some theorists have argued that justice as an ideal does not apply to families, which are 'governed by virtues nobler than justice and therefore not needing to be subjected to the tests of justice to which other fundamental social institutions' must be subjected.[26] Okin, on the other hand, argues that 'justice is a virtue of fundamental importance for families, as for other basic social institutions.'[27] She demonstrates that at present families are not based on justice because marriage, as it is currently constituted, makes women and children vulnerable.

What is of particular relevance here is Okin's model of a 'humanist justice' in which families are based on social justice. To achieve this she advocates a genderless society, and proposes some social policies that facilitate a move towards the just family. First, she proposes that 'public policies and laws should generally assume no social differentiation of the sexes. Shared parental responsibility for child care would be both assumed and facilitated.[28] Second, she argues that 'the demands of work life throughout the period in which a worker of either sex is a parent of a small child'[29] must be rethought. To this end she proposes eliminating all sex discrimination, including sexual harassment, and establishing provisions for employees, in large-scale workplaces, parental leave, flexible working hours, on-site day care in large-scale workplaces, and government subsidies to give all children access to high-quality day care. Third, Okin suggests that children's education must make them fully aware of the politics of gender, that boys and girls should take home economics, and that schools be required to provide high-quality after-school programs.

Fourth, she turns her attention to unattached parents and their children. She argues that pregnancies among single teenagers would be reduced in a genderless society, and that men would remain financially responsible for their children, with governmental back-up if a man is unable to pay child support. In the case of single parenthood after separation and divorce, 'it seems inconceivable that separated and divorced fathers who had shared equally in the nurturing of their children from the outset would be as likely to neglect them, by not seeing them or not contributing to their support, as many do today.'[30] Fifth, Okin makes another very important assumption:

> Because these parents had shared equally the paid work and the family work, their incomes would be much more equal than those of most divorcing parents today. Even if they were quite equal, however, the parent without physical custody should be required to contribute to the child's support, *to the point where the standards of living of the two households were the same.*[31]

Sixth, Okin considers the need to protect the vulnerable, who she defines, in this context, as traditional housewives, noting that there is only a minute percentage of househusbands. In order to avoid economic dependence of wives in 'gender-structured' marriages, she advocates that 'both partners have *equal legal entitlement* to all earnings coming into the household'.[32] This would be achieved by having employers make out wage checks divided equally between the earner and the partner, and would constitute a public recognition of the value of labour in families that is currently unpaid.

Lastly, the same fundamental principle would apply to separation and divorce: '*Both postdivorce households should enjoy the same standard of living.*'[33] Alimony and child support would continue until the youngest child enters first grade, but child support should entitle the children to a standard of living equal to that of the non-custodial parent.

While many of these suggestions are admirable (and have, of course, been made before), we need to ask if they would actually lead to gender equality or a genderless society, and what would happen in the process. Lastly, I will look at how this approach relates to the individual responsibility model of the family.

There are a number of problems with what Okin proposes. One is singling out gender inequality without putting it into the broader context of general social inequality and the paradoxical interaction between change within the family and society at large. Okin asks: 'Without just families, how can we expect to have a just society?'[34] In turn, we can ask: Without a just society, how can we expect to have just families? In the interaction between the two, change will occur unevenly as it always does. How far can we push family policies that *assume* gender equality in the absence of such equality in the rest of society, and vice versa? We again face here the problem of formal versus substantive equality.[35] This is intimately connected to another problem, which is shared by many authors and legal thinkers in particular: treating a statistical fact (women's incomes tend to be lower than those of men) as if it were descriptive of individual cases (wives have lower incomes than their husbands). As we have seen in Chapter 2, this is not always true and may lead to considerable problems when policies are devised on this basis without adequate flexibility to reflect the realities of all situations.

Yet another problem is an insufficient consideration of the life cycle of a family. Although Okin does consider families that are formed outside of marriage or that emerge through the break-up of a marriage, she does not consider what happens if one of the former spouses remarries and has another biological child and possibly stepchildren with the new partner. How does this affect the first family's entitlement to a standard of living equal to that of the higher-earning ex-partner?[36]

Looking at her policy suggestions, the first point is to both assume and facilitate gender equality in task allocation. While there is no argument about facilitating equal participation of women and men in the caring functions of society, at present our family laws *assume* that this is so when it is blatantly *not* so. As we have seen in chapters 3 and 4 (and as Okin documents) at present men in general do *not* contribute equally to this work by any stretch of the imagination. Assuming that women and men make equal contributions may lead to undervaluing the actual contributions of women (and some men) who do most of this work.

Okin's second and third proposals—reshaping paid work to accommodate parental (rather than just maternal) caring responsibilities, and reshaping the education system around the same issues—would help alleviate the problem to some degree, but they would do so slowly. People of various ages, classes, ethnic backgrounds, etc., would be affected differently. This is not an argument against these proposals. In fact, I find them very attractive. I am simply pointing out that we are talking about a process that would take an entire generation, assuming that we have the social consensus and the political will to implement the suggested changes immediately.

With respect to family formation outside of marriage, better access to birth control and an infrastructure that supports family planning would almost certainly reduce teenage pregnancies.[37] However, it is not clear if fathers who are more involved in child rearing would continue to be so after separation and divorce. Indeed, Kruk found the opposite (see Chapter 4).

When it comes to maintaining the same standard of living between the ex-spouses, we run into the problem of an incomplete life cycle approach to families. What happens when the higher-earning man remarries and has another child and his new wife brings yet another child into the marriage for whom he accepts financial responsibility? Does this mean that his first family's living standard must be lowered because he now has more children to look after? Assuming that these families are not rich, this might push either family or both families below the poverty line. Should they both drop below the poverty line? Alternatively, if the man marries a wife who has a very high-paying job and they have no children, is the first wife entitled to a portion of the second wife's earnings (when the second wife has no obligation to the first wife) just because there should be equality in incomes? If the custodial first wife marries a rich man and their newly formed unit has an income equal to that of the ex-husband's household, should the ex-husband no longer be obligated to continue contributing to his children's financial welfare? If the ex-wife has been the higher earner all along, plus the primary caretaker, does she have to pay her ex-husband to equalize their incomes?

Similar questions need to be raised regarding the notion that employers should divide pay cheques between the employee and the spouse, in case one is a housewife or a househusband. What happens if the wife works part-time and intermittently, as is often the case today? Will the employer have to adjust the pay cheques frequently in such cases? What if the non-earning partner is a man who does *not* contribute to the family care and who would *not* spend his money on family needs?[38] Will the pay cheque still be split and the family reduced to a level below which they can survive? There is considerable evidence that women tend to spend their money on family needs, while men tend to keep a portion for their own private use, regardless of the amount of money available and the needs of other family members.[39]

On the other hand, if one makes the division of pay cheques voluntary, those earners who are already sharing incomes would be the ones most likely to choose this option. Would splitting pay cheques be contingent on whether or not there are dependent children? What if the partner is an invalid and *receives* more care than he or she gives to the spouse? Is this person still entitled to half the pay cheque?

Most important, however, some of the family issues cannot be solved only within the family; they need a societal contribution that is better justified in terms of a societal obligation towards children and dependent adults than by reference to equality between spouses. While the latter addresses *intra*familial justice—which is certainly important—it brackets the issue of *inter*familial justice.

Comparing Okin's approach to the individual responsibility model of the family certainly endorses gender equality. She does not address the issue of the status of legal marriage, but her proposals could probably accommodate common-law as well as same-sex relationships. She treats household and family memberships as largely congruent, but she recognizes that there is some incongruence to the degree that she addresses the role of the absent parent. The unit of administration is not explicitly addressed, but in so far as she advocates splitting income between ex-spouses, she regards first families as the unit of administration. Okin attempts to find ways to reduce incongruity. At best this could be accomplished within one generation (about twenty-five years) if all the educational reforms (which sound very good) were instituted immediately. In the meantime, we would be left with what we have at present: an assumption of equal contribution and congruity as the norm in the face of widespread unequal contribution and incongruity.

Okin regards husbands and wives as equally responsible for the economic well-being of themselves, each other, and any dependent children, and both parents are equally responsible for the care of children—if they live together. She does not deal adequately with parents who do not live with their children and who may have formed new families.

When it comes to the appropriate private-public division of responsibilities, Okin's emphasis on universally accessible day care does shift some of the responsibility for child care to the public. However, it is also clear that the marital couple still have the primary responsibility. Given that Okin's model does not deal adequately with first and second families and the conflicting demands they make on both households, it does not allow for a transition to the genderless society, nor would it deal adequately—even if we *did* achieve a genderless society—with the necessary transfers of money from families without children to families with children. All in all, Okin's vision of a genderless society has many appealing aspects, but it has the same major weaknesses as the individual responsibility model.

REPLACING MARRIAGE AS A LEGAL CATEGORY WITH THE MOTHER-CHILD DYAD

Fineman has argued that 'The institution of "Mother" has been transformed in law, collapsed and merged with "Father" in the generic concept of "Parent".[40] In this way, the mother has been neutered. The couple, consisting of a sexualized tie between a man and woman, is, unlike earlier times, privileged as foundational and fundamental in family law. This sexual family is socially and culturally considered the 'natural' form to experience intimacy. This unit is responsible for 'inevitable dependency'. Dependency is inevitable 'in that it flows from the status and situation of being a child and often accompanies aging, illness or disability'. Caretakers become dependent as well, but their dependence is a *derivative dependency* that flows 'from their roles and the need for resources their caretaking generates'.[41]

> Women, wives, mothers, daughters-in-law, sisters are typically the socially and culturally assigned caretakers. As caretakers they are tied into intimate relationships with their dependants. The very process of assuming caretaking responsibilities creates dependency in the caretaker—she needs some social structure to provide the means to care for others ...
> ... the notion of the natural family ... masks inevitable but unacknowledged dependency and perpetuates our official and public rhetoric ...[42]

Dependency is shifted from the state to the private grouping, which 'is premised on having a specific structure—the continuation of the historic, essential division of labor within the family ...'[43]

Fineman argues that the 'egalitarian family as an articulated ideal is premised on the couple-based family unit. As such, it generates tension in so far as one of the goals to be attained by the partners is equal career or market proficiency.'[44] We 'must abandon the pretence that we can achieve gender equality through family-law reform. The egalitarian family myth remains largely unassisted by other ideological and structural changes in the larger society and is belied by the statistics reflecting the ways women and men live.'[45] She proposes to end marriage as a *legal* (but not social, emotional, religious, etc.) status, and instead to place inevitable dependants and their caregivers in a group within which family privacy is maintained.

> The caregiving family would be a protected space, entitled to special, preferred treatment by the state.
> The new family line, drawn around dependency, would mark the boundaries of the concept of family privacy. Specifically, I envision a redistribution or reallocation of social and economic subsidies now given to the natural family that allow it to function 'independently' within society. Family and welfare law would be reconceived so as to support caretaking as the family intimacy norm.[46]

To describe this family, she uses the metaphor of the Mother-Child, in order to draw on the powerful resonances and positive images of Mother. 'Mother is a metaphor with power to make the private visible.'[47] She does *not* assume that all women either wish to mother or are capable of doing so, and she states explicitly that men can and should be mothers. The concept also stands metaphorically for all types of caring relationships in instances of inevitable dependency. 'This unit, graced as the new family norm, would provide the structural and ideological base for societal subsidies and policy. Our special family-law rules, no longer oriented to protecting sexual families, would bolster nurturing units.'[48]

Fineman's approach has the singular advantage of dealing directly with the issue of dependency rather than indirectly through the couple. This takes her approach out of the framework of either the patriarchal or the individual responsibility model. On the other hand, she does not address all of the issues that are currently dealt with by family policies. Her important concept of 'inevitable dependency' is coupled with 'derivative dependency', which develops as a result of caregiving. There are other types of dependencies (such as emotional or financial dependencies between adults) that are neither inevitable nor derivative. She does not explicitly deal with these, but obviously regards them as private issues that are not regulated by law (or at least not by family law). The same applies to *inter*dependencies between adults, since her intent is to remove the couple relationship from the centrestage it has held. Hence she has no comments on such issues as support payments or the sharing of responsibilities for one (or more) inevitably dependent people. Her modal unit is between one adult and one inevitably dependent person— the Mother-Child metaphor she employs.

Fineman has little to say on gender equality, except that the way it has been interpreted in law does not lead to its realization. She clearly states that she would abolish marriage and all couple relationships as a legal concept, thus eliminating the need for legal recognition of common-law relationships at the same time. The question of household and family memberships thus becomes irrelevant, and the administrative unit is the caregiver-dependant relationship. The only dependency that Fineman deals with is the one between an inevitable dependant and his or her caregiver. The *implicit* assumption about care provision seems to be that it is delivered by only one person, with the substantive help of the public, which protects and supports this special relationship. Caregiving is redefined as socially useful and necessary, and rewarded accordingly. Homosexual unions are as irrelevant as heterosexual ones, but it would be equally irrelevant whether a caregiver is lesbian or gay.

Fineman's vision, then, is one that transcends both the patriarchal and the individual responsibility models. It presents an alternative view, but does not address all the issues currently affected by family laws and policies. In the next chapter I will pick up some of the points she makes.

CONCLUSION

We have considered three starkly different visions of where family policy should be directed. All three share the premise that our current approach is inadequate and leads to serious problems, although what is considered problematic varies considerably. This is particularly true of Popenoe and Fineman. While Popenoe sees all family forms other than the nuclear family (defined as a female-male couple with their dependent children) as problematic, Fineman sees the emphasis on this type of couple and its designation as the social norm as a major problem. Okin implicitly accepts the primacy of the couple, but problematizes the current absence of gender equality, defined in both formal and substantive terms.

Both Okin and Fineman thus criticize major premises on which Popenoe bases his approach. Fineman also criticizes the central notion of Okin's approach—that gender equality can be achieved through family law reform. She focuses instead on a redefinition and reallocation of societal resources, but does not examine all the functions families today perform. In the next chapter I will examine some of these other functions.

CHAPTER 7

The Social Responsibility Model of the Family

THE IDEOLOGY CONCERNING GENDER EQUALITY

In this chapter I will ask how each of the eight questions *should* be answered, given the current social and political realities. In order to do so, I will have to go back to some basic issues. As we have seen in the preceding chapter, an ideology of gender equality is not a straightforward matter. Both Popenoe and Okin confess adherence to such an ideology, with vastly different ways of trying to implement it, while Fineman professes disillusionment with the ideology as it is currently operationalized in law. However, it is impossible to argue for gender *in*equality because equality is constitutionally mandated, and because gender inequality is the ideological basis of the patriarchal model of the family, with all its horrific effects on women and children. The task is to devise a way of dealing with gender equality in a manner that avoids the problems inherent in the individual responsibility model of the family, but it must not translate into a gender-neutral approach. Instead, any legal or policy approach premised on gender equality needs to be non-sexist (that is, avoid all the problems of sexism as described in Chapter 5).[1] This, however, does not yet provide us with a vision of an equal society *in principle*.

The existing models, while partially helpful for various purposes, do not in and of themselves provide a vision of what a society based on gender equality would look like. Do we need such a vision when all we are interested in is family policy? I believe we do. The failure of gender-neutral legislation—which would be an obvious solution in many instances if we were living in a society in which gender equality was already the norm—alerts us to the need that we cannot expect full gender equality at the lowest level of societal organization (the family) when it is absent at the highest level (the nation and the world).

Families are not isolated microcosms. They are organizational structures in which most of us live for much of our lives, hence their importance for our personal welfare. These structures interact with society at large. For instance, if we do not value dependant care at the societal level, we will not give it credit when determining pension entitlements,[2] nor will we see it as real work and deal with it appropriately, etc. This will have inevitable effects on the care provider, which will, in turn, affect familial relations and shape life outcomes.

Replacing the Ideal of Gender Equality with the Ideal of Minimal Stratification

Given that we live in a complex society, the imagination fails when we try to invent a society based on equality for all its members (sex being only one of the criteria around which societies are stratified, although the most universal one).[3] The simplest formulation is still the one in the Communist Manifesto: 'From each according to his [or her] ability, to each according to his [or her] needs.'[4] But even with this formula, who determines what a 'need' is? Is access to artistic materials or privacy as great a need as access to food, clothing, and shelter? Is there a hierarchy of needs? Who determines what the hierarchy is? Who assesses ability? If an individual is gifted but lazy, what are her or his abilities? Should laziness be regarded as a natural trait, or should people be required to contribute on the basis of their potential? Who determines what their potential is? One can imagine the many law cases centred on these issues.

Even under the most simplifying conditions, then, it is hard to imagine what an equal society might be like. We live in a highly complex society that is based on a complex division of labour, which requires people to develop specialized skills. For example, a farmer cannot do the job of an airplane pilot without specialized training. Differentiation is a necessary aspect of any complex society. Differentiation, however, inevitably leads to stratification (Holter 1970). Hence for a complex society, some measure of inequality is inevitable. Our goal therefore shifts from moving towards a society based on equality to one in which inequality is minimized. The task, then, has turned from envisioning a society based on equality to envisioning a society that is minimally stratified.

Conceptualizing a Minimally Stratified Society

The first step is to realize that inequality/equality is a multidimensional phenomenon in all circumstances. If we can define salient dimensions of inequality, we have taken a step towards defining a minimally stratified society. The following twelve dimensions are not exhaustive, but they are indisputably important:[5]

1. The lifespan

2. One's body

3. Human worth

4. Reproductive processes

5. Work

6. Property

7. Services

8. Knowledge and information

9. Political power

10. Lifestyles

11. Symbolic representations

12. Affective relationships

These dimensions can be used to ask empirical questions. Are there any differences in the likelihood of survival on the basis of race, sex, sexual orientation, religion, ethnic background, etc? Are there differences in access to various types of work, and what are the working conditions within these occupations? What is the likelihood for a member of a particular group to wield political power? If the characteristic under investigation is not predictive of a person's placement within any particular dimension, then the society is minimally stratified *along this particular characteristic.*

We can think of these dimensions as a system of communicating pipes. If one of the pipes (a dimension) is long and thin, there is a lot of inequality in this dimension. For instance, when the highest income earner within a society receives $20 million yearly and the lowest $4,000 yearly, the property dimension is very long and thin. If the tax system were to levy a 100 per cent tax on all income above the limit of $100,000, and raise the lowest income to $10,000, this would bring the two end-points much closer together. The property dimension would then be condensed and look like a fat roll rather than like a thin hose. Therefore, one way of reducing inequality is minimizing the differences *within* any or all of the dimensions.

The other aspect concerns the degree to which the various pipes communicate. If they communicate very well, a person or group will be at about the same level in each of the dimensions, either at the bottom, the middle, or the top. This means that one's status in one dimension carries over into one's status in another dimension—and thus contributes to a high degree of stratification. By contrast, when one's status in one dimension is irrelevant to one's status in another dimension, this suggests that there is less stratification.

Our formal definition of minimal stratification is as follows: *a society or institution is minimally stratified if (1) within each dimension of stratification inequality has been reduced to its possible minimum, and (2) if placement within one dimension has no effect on one's placement within another dimension.*

The first component of this formulation posits minimal stratification as a moving target. For instance, many disabilities are a natural source of inequality. However, as technological means become available to reduce stratification—for example, wheelchairs—we may need special provisions to accommodate wheelchairs (by legislating ramps or other means of access for people in wheelchairs) in order to minimize unequal access to services.

The second component of our definition of minimal stratification addresses the fact that inequality is inevitably a multidimensional phenomenon. If people are clustered together in high (élite) or low positions *across* various dimensions, there is a high degree of stratification. If the people who have no jobs or have access only to low-paying jobs with little autonomy are also poor, have a lower life expectancy, are generally treated as if they were of lower human worth, have their reproduction controlled by others (e.g., via involuntary sterilization), have little or no property, have less access to services than people in positions of higher placement, have less access to knowledge, etc., there is a high degree of stratification. By contrast, free access to health services for all on an equal basis, free education (from kindergarten through graduate school), easy access to various sources of knowledge through public libraries, and important institutions within a society such as the law, government, etc., that respectfully treat all as of equal worth, indicate less stratification.

A society would be minimally stratified on the basis of sex if:

- women and men lived to their fullest possible biological lifespans

- had equal control over their own bodies

- were considered and treated as of equal human worth

- had equal control over their own reproductive processes

- had equal control over property

- had equal access to all types of work and equal degrees of control over working conditions

- had equal access to all paid and unpaid services, and received as many services as they rendered

- had equal access to the means of knowledge creation and its transmission, including all forms of education and information (including the capacity to determine what counts as news or as information of general importance)

- had an equal chance to wield political power

- had the same degree of control over their daily lifestyles

- had equal control over symbolic representations in religious images, church rites, secular rites (e.g., the conferring of medals, honours, orders, etc.), in visual depictions (e.g., pornography, erotica, films, videos, pictures, billboards, advertisements, public statues, stamps, etc.), in verbal depictions (poetry, fiction, essays, biographies, etc.)

• and with respect to symmetry or asymmetry in affective relationships

Affective relationships can be very important from the familial level up to the national level. However, the issue is whether or not affections are symmetrical or asymmetrical. In general, the party who cares less has more power within a relationship than the party who cares more. Canada, for instance, cares a lot more about what the United States thinks about it than vice versa. For our purposes, this dimension is not relevant in a policy context.

We have not achieved the degree of gender equality as described, but nevertheless there is significantly greater gender equality today than there was 100 years ago. This approach also allows us to describe different types and degrees of gender inequality between various countries, e.g., Saudi Arabia and Canada. If we were to answer the questions for women in Saudi Arabia and Canada, we would find that in most dimensions (and maybe in all), gender inequality is greater in Saudi Arabia than in Canada.

FAMILIES UNDER MINIMAL STRATIFICATION

Minimal Stratification at the Societal and Familial Level
In order to say that families are premised on equality, we need to demonstrate that in society there is minimal stratification on the basis of sex and marital status.[6] As we have seen, this is far from the truth. However, we still need to consider the respective position of spouses as spouses.

Inequality/Equality between Spouses
The question, then, is whether people are equal with respect to the various dimensions listed previously *in their capacity as spouses*. This analysis can be performed for specific couples or for couples in general. I will analyse inequality/equality of couples in general, and restrict the discussion to heterosexual couples for the time being.

Regarding lifespan, is there something about marriage that increases or decreases the lifespan of husbands and wives? As Jessie Bernard[7] has argued a quarter century ago, being married is good for men. Married men tend to live longer than single men. The same is not true for women. Recent data suggest that there may be a slight levelling of this effect, but that overall this relationship still holds.[8]

Of course, factors other than being married also influence life expectancy. For instance, poorer people have lower life expectancies than richer people. In Russia between 1990 and 1993, there was a horrifying drop of five years in life expectancy, which can only be explained by the rapid social transition Russia has experienced since 1990.[9] By contrast, control over one's body is intimately linked to marriage. Until 1983,[10] a man had the legal right in Canada to have access to his wife's body for sexual purposes whether she was willing or not—in other words, he could legally rape her.[11] This changed when marital rape became a crime.[12] Rape is only one form of using another person's body for one's own purposes. Physical violence is another. As we have seen, women are more likely to be assaulted by their dates, boyfriends, and common-law or legal husbands, and often by their ex-boyfriends or ex-husbands.

Operationalizing (i.e., transforming) human worth into measurable variables is difficult. At the societal level, we can look at the existence, extent, and degree of active and effective protection of human rights laws. At the familial level, the law assumes by now that husbands and wives are of equal worth in so far as it assumes equal responsibility and ability. The law no longer assumes that the male is the 'master' of the wife or the 'head' of the household, as was the case under the patriarchal model. Whether or not spouses attribute equal worth to each other is a strictly empirical question that varies from couple to couple.

As far as reproductive processes are concerned, equality takes two forms: being able to reproduce if one wants to and is capable of doing so, or not to reproduce if one does not want to. Either partner can prevent reproduction if both sexes have equal and *independent* access to birth control, or where both are in an equal position to refuse to engage in sexual relations. For women, access to abortion is crucial.[13] To generate a child, it takes either the active cooperation of a couple or the power of one person (presumably the male) to force himself on the other. Since reproduction necessarily involves at least[14] two people, there can be no such thing as a 'right to reproduce' for an *individual*.[15]

Work includes access to all types of jobs, control over working conditions, as well as the performance of unpaid work. Since women continue to be disadvantaged in the labour market, there is no equal access to all types of jobs for women and men. Control over working conditions tends to be associated with greater autonomy in higher-level jobs. Women have less access to higher-level jobs and therefore less control over working conditions than men. If wives modify their career aspirations because they have to tailor their own jobs around those of their husbands or because of family demands, both the family and the labour market reduce women's access to higher-paying, prestigious jobs. However, the number of such jobs is limited for both women and men. Realistically, most people are looking for a job with decent pay and decent working conditions. The fact that part-time workers are not protected in the same way as full-time workers works to the disadvantage of more women than men.

When it comes to unpaid work, we noted earlier that women are more likely than men to perform unpaid family work. This tends to go along with marriage, and is therefore a continuing and important aspect of inequality between spouses.

Property includes all types of assets—money, bonds, stocks, and other property. Realistically, most people have only two major types of property: their earning capacity (which is a direct function of the type of job they have) and their house. With respect to jobs, we have already noted that women tend to be clustered in the lower-paid, less prestigious jobs. However, family law in Canada decrees that all business assets acquired during a marriage be split equally upon separation. In spite of such equal sharing, the woman, on average, ends up with less property than the man. There are four factors for this inequality.

First, if the major form of property consists of job-related benefits (primarily lifelong earning capacity), then the fact that the wife obtains half the assets of what the husband has accumulated during the marriage reimburses her partially for the past, but continues to leave her disadvantaged for the future from the day of separation onwards. Unless she receives personal support, she will have to support herself on her own salary. If the marriage has impeded or interrupted her career, this will affect her for the rest of her work life and indeed even her retirement years.

Second, the wife usually has custody of the children, and since the assets are split between the adults rather than between all family members, two or more people (the wife and the children) receive as much as one person (the husband). Third, support payments for children are usually inadequate, are not usually readjusted for inflation, and are, on top of that, more often than not defaulted upon. Fourth, although the value of the matrimonial home is split upon divorce, given the wife's lesser average earning prospects, she will be less likely to be able to purchase a new home or buy her husband's share of the existing home. If the wife had a better job than the husband, only one of the aforementioned factors apply, namely, that she is likely to have custody of the children and therefore an equal split of assets will economically disadvantage the parent who has child custody. However, the other factors should work in her favour.

Services are either paid or unpaid. As noted earlier regarding unpaid services, husbands tend to receive more of these services from their wives than vice versa. As for paid services, what services are available at what price? Is an equal amount of tax money spent on services for women and services for men in their roles as wives and husbands or as mothers and fathers? What is the proportion of tax money spent on child care, homemaking services, and support for families in general versus services that benefit primarily men? For example, women depend more on public transportation than men do, yet public subsidies for private cars cost more than subsidies for public transportation.[16] Why is it that in times of fiscal crises, public transportation is usually reduced, rather than shifting some of the public costs of private cars to car owners?[17]

Daily lifestyles will vary greatly from couple to couple. The primary issue is not who manages a chosen lifestyle, but who chooses it. Is it a joint decision or a decision imposed by one of the partners? Does one spouse control the other's lifestyle by regulating the other's activities, determining who the other may associate with, planning daily routines, or identifying and regulating appropriate types of behaviour, etc.?

In this culture, women are disadvantaged when it comes to symbolic representations. Most public statues are those of males. The God figure in the major monotheistic religions is invariably male. Advertising and the media relentlessly objectify the female body. Within a marriage, one's name is perhaps the most powerful symbol. Wives retaining their surname indicates gender equality; taking their husband's surname indicates inequality.

Finally, affective relationships within marriage are very important. In general, the person who cares most about a relationship is in a weaker position than the one who cares less. Women are taught and socially expected to carry out most of the emotion work needed to maintain and sustain a marriage. Men are encouraged to think of themselves as independent, and this may carry over into their emotional relationships.[18] This is an important aspect of understanding inequalities, but out of the purview of public policies, since obviously the degree of caring about a relationship neither should nor could be regulated by the state.

It is meaningful to regard inequality as a multidimensional phenomenon. Policies that either reduce inequality within any given dimension and/or that place the spouse who is generally in a lower position in various dimensions into a higher position in other dimensions serve to reduce inequality. If we focus on minimizing inequalities that are the result of being married or being a parent instead of on equality (particularly that form which results in equal treatment), we have a strong tool at hand that allows us to assess whether particular policies create, maintain, leave unaffected, or reduce inequality in a given situation. Our first component of the social responsibility model of the family, then, is this: *(1) There is an ideological commitment to minimizing stratification on the basis of sex.*

MARRIAGE AS A LEGALLY PRIVILEGED RELATIONSHIP

The Supreme Court of Canada has gone on record repeatedly to defend heterosexual marriage (whether legal or common law) as an institution that deserves to be privileged in terms of access to certain benefits. In *Egan* v. *Canada*, a gay man asked to receive the spousal allowance to which he would have been entitled had the person he lived with been of the opposite rather than the same sex. In rejecting his claim, the judges argued:

> ... [the] ultimate raison d'etre [of marriage] ... is firmly anchored in the biological and social realities that heterosexual couples have the unique ability to procreate, that most children are the product of these relationships, and that they are generally cared for and nurtured by those who live in that relationship. In this sense, marriage is by nature heterosexual. It would be possible to legally define marriage to include homosexual couples, but this would not change the biological and social realities that underlie the traditional marriage.[19]

The question is whether children are generally cared for and nurtured by those in a heterosexual relationship. That depends. If we interpret this to mean that children are nurtured by the same heterosexual couple who provided the genetic input, then this is increasingly not the case, as we have seen in chapters 2 and 4, due to the number and proportion of children born to unmarried women[20] or whose parents divorce or separate. These children are subsequently nurtured mostly by their mother with help from the mother's spouse (if there is one), whether this person is the biological father or not. In the latter case, the parallel to the situation of lesbian mothers is striking: in a lesbian relationship, the children are nurtured and cared for by their mother and her partner (in this instance, another woman). The judges conflate parental and spousal roles, which is common enough but leads to a number of difficulties.

The spousal allowance is available to any heterosexual couple, either married or common law, after they have lived together for at least one year. As the dissenting judges in *Egan* v. *Canada* note, capacity to procreate is irrelevant in this context. An elderly heterosexual couple who had lived together for only one year, and who had never raised children together, could receive this allowance if they met the other eligibility criteria. Given the context, then, the conflation of spousal and marital roles is particularly drastic. Justice LaForest addresses this conflation as follows:

> I am not troubled by the fact that not all these heterosexual couples in fact have children. It is the social unit that uniquely has the *capacity* to procreate children and generally cares for their upbringing, and as such warrants support by Parliament to meet its needs. This is the only unit in society that expends resources to care for children on a routine and sustained basis ... whether the mother or the father leaves the paid workforce or whether both parents are paying

after-tax dollars for daycare, this is the unit in society that fundamentally anchors other social relationships and other aspects of society.[21]

However, as we have seen, it is *not* the only unit that has the capacity to procreate, nor is it the only unit that generally cares for the children. Indeed, we find an increasing discrepancy between biological and social fatherhood. If there is any unit that is unique, it is the mother-child unit.[22] We cannot privilege legally married couples or heterosexual couples in general to promote good child care or greater social benefits for society.

We can no longer justify benefits to couples, whether married or common law, just because they raise children for the state because heterosexual relationships (legal or otherwise) are no longer an acceptably accurate proxy variable for raising children. Are there other reasons to privilege the couple relationship? Justice LaForest cites a second function of this relationship: it 'is the unit in society that fundamentally anchors other social relationships and other aspects of society.'

There is considerable evidence that one's intimate relationships do serve as anchors for other relationships and influence how one experiences other aspects of society. When dealing with adults who are neither inevitably dependent nor in a status of derived dependency (from providing care on a full-time basis), there are at least two separate issues. Is it in the state's interest to encourage adults to live together? Therefore, should benefits be available to those in such arrangements? Does living together create an obligation to support each other beyond the duration of the union? This point will be addressed later. Here I will restrict myself to the first question.

Having disposed of the argument that the child-caring function takes place only within heterosexual nuclear families, the question is whether the function of 'anchoring' is sufficient to warrant special status for heterosexual relationships. If the answer is no, it would involve a shift in policy that would improve the situation of some couples and prove detrimental for others; those who have their benefits decreased because of family income would gain, while those who receive benefits simply on the basis of couplehood (e.g., the spousal exemption) would lose.

If, on the other hand, one wants to argue (and there is justification for this argument as well) that it is beneficial to society if individuals live together in supportive groupings, this would suggest that all such groupings, regardless of the adults' sex, should be privileged. In addition, a further argument could be mounted that groupings of more than two who decide to live interdependently should likewise be eligible for the same (prorated) benefits as couples, whether heterosexual or homosexual, legally married or not. In either case, there is no reason to privilege heterosexual unions over other unions. Our second component of the social responsibility model of the family is this: *(2) Functioning relationships constitute a family unit. Legal marriage is present but not privileged over other relationships.*

Assumptions about Congruence/Incongruence in Household/Family Memberships and Marital and Spousal Roles

As we have seen in previous chapters, incongruence between household and family memberships is widespread and shows no signs of abating. Basing policies on an inaccurate *assumption* of reality invites problems. The reasonable approach to take, therefore, is to make no such assumption. However, this is not a simple matter. We need to look at familial relationships across households as well as within households.

Given that parents have responsibilities for their children, there is no reason for such responsibilities to cease if a parent no longer lives with his or her children.[23] We must recognize that parents who do not share a household with their children still have financial responsibilities for them.

It gets more complicated with respect to coresident spouses of custodial parents (stepfathers and sometimes stepmothers). Step-parents acquire partial parental rights through their actual caring behaviour. With respect to support obligations for children after union dissolution, it seems sensible to allocate some responsibility to step-parents *depending on the length of the union and the age of the children*. A potential rule of thumb might be that support obligations for non-biological children should not exceed the length of the union.[24] Since the biological father's obligations would continue no matter what, some support would be available. How this would translate into practical policies if, for instance, the biological father was poor or absent and the social father was rich will be discussed in the next chapter. The third component of the social responsibility model of the family is this: *(3) At the nuclear level, household and family memberships may be, but are not assumed to be, congruous. Therefore, spousehood is not automatically identified with parenthood, and parenthood is not automatically identified with spousehood.*

THE UNIT OF ADMINISTRATION

Given that there is no longer an assumption of congruity between household and family memberships, it does not make sense to take the household as the unit of administration for most purposes. (There are a few exceptions, such as billing for items consumed on a household basis: the family residence, utilities, etc.) Instead, we should take the individual as the unit of administration. This is neither far-fetched nor different from what Canada does at present or did in the past *in some instances*. The current Canadian health insurance system works on an individual basis: that is, every citizen and permanent resident is entitled to access to basic health services *as an individual.* Children are listed as their parents' children, but are entitled to the services *in their own right.* If they were to move and live with an aunt, a godparent, or a foster parent for a year, they would still be entitled to health care.

Similarly, the family allowance used to be paid to the primary caregiver (the mother), *unless the primary caregiver was someone else*, in which case it was paid to that person. In other words, the family allowance was attached to a child and went with it if care providers changed.[25] At present 'the Canadian income taxation system [is] moving amendment by amendment into a system based upon marital status.'[26] Individual taxation, as opposed to couple taxation, 'ensures self-determination and helps achieve more equality for women by alleviating the tax opportunity costs of marriage.'[27]

A similar system could be adopted for adults in need of care: the care allowance is attached to them as individuals. If they are able to make such decisions, they decide to whom it is paid, whether to a family member or to someone else. If they are unable to make such a decision, the care allowance goes to the actual care provider. This would eliminate the familism-individualism flip-flop and allow family members to provide care for inevitable dependants without being financially penalized for it. The fourth component of the social responsibility model of the family, therefore, is this: *(4) The individual is the unit of administration (with a few exceptions).*

Assumptions Concerning Economic Dependency/Interdependency and Care Provision

First, we need to distinguish between different types of dependency. There is inevitable dependency with its correlate of derived dependency. There is interdependency created through living together and mingling one's affairs. There is also temporary dependency, such as when an adult goes to school and becomes economically dependent on another adult. Such dependency is neither inevitable nor derived, nor does it necessarily take place within a context of interdependency (which implies mutual contributions), but it is nevertheless real and important.

Inevitable dependants include children or adults in need of care because of chronic or temporary illness, disability, senility, etc. Under the individual responsibility model of society, caring for these people is the family's responsibility. It usually becomes the responsibility of women within the family (in practice, although not in law). It is thus conceptualized as a private task, a part of 'housework' or 'family work'. The concept of housework refers to unpaid work performed by a household or family member for another household or family member or for oneself, and includes maintenance and personal service functions.[28] There are many other definitions that have been proposed, but usually housework or family work is defined by the nature of the task: instrumental tasks such as shopping or cleaning; emotion work such as kin-keeping and counselling; outside work (e.g., yard work), inside work (e.g., vacuuming); daily and repetitive tasks such as meal preparation; and infrequent and non-repetitive tasks such as doing minor repairs, etc.

If we look at the picture through a different set of lenses and ask who benefits from the unpaid work performed at home, quite a different picture emerges—some of the work is socially useful, and some is privately useful. A simple test suffices to identify which is which: would the public pick up the cost of care if it was not provided by a family member? If the answer is yes, we are dealing with a *socially useful* type of care rendered by private individuals often in their homes, such as care for inevitable dependants. If the answer is no (such as when a wife renders services to a physically and mentally fit husband, adult child, for herself, or for some other adult), then it is a *privately useful* service.

The state profits directly from care for inevitable dependants in two ways: private care is often (not always!) of a better quality than institutionalized care, and it is definitely cheaper. The state thus saves large amounts of money. It is therefore in the state's interest to support caregiving for inevitable dependants by any means available.

However, is this care useful to the state only when it is rendered by a family member? And just who is a family member? This is obviously a question with a fluid answer. At some point, common-law spouses were considered non-family; now they are, for all intents and purposes, defined as family. Same-sex couples are edging their way up there. With partial fatherhood, non-biological fathers (and mothers) have been awarded family status even though the biological parent may still be around and even though the couple may not be married but living in a common-law relationship.

Before looking at an example of non-familial caring, we need to note that dependency has at least two components relevant in this context: (1) dependency on the actual rendering of the care (diapering, feeding, playing with, constantly watching an infant; providing food, possibly dressing and providing other practical help for a dependent adult); (2) economic dependency of both the inevitable dependant and his or her caregiver, who is a derived dependant because providing care on a full-time[29] basis makes it impossible to earn a living on a full-time basis.[30]

I will now look at one empirical example of caring behaviour between non-relatives in order to provide some substance for a discussion of dependent relationships between non-kin.

Helping Relationships among Non-kin

Kinship can be defined as relationships between people connected by blood, marriage, or adoption. We ascribe special qualities to these relationships, yet there are kinship relations that are largely (sometimes entirely) inactive, and there are relationships with people with whom we are not connected by either blood, marriage, or adoption, which can be as multifaceted, important, and as abiding as kin relationships.

Sometimes, such relationships are constituted as fictive kinships: they are given a fictive kin relationship, reflected in such as comments as 'She is like a sister to me', 'I consider him my son', 'This is your aunt Fatima', etc. Some cultures, especially in Latin America, have a formalized system of godparenting, which assigns culturally understood rights and obligations to the participants in a godparent relationship.

In North America, this is less often the case. In a comprehensive study of friendship,[31] Rubin has explored the many ways in which kinship and friendship are similar and dissimilar, and how they are experienced differently by women and by men. One of the most important differences between the two kinds of relationships is that kinship is socially—and often legally and economically—supported. Relatives will inherit from a person who dies intestate and has no close immediate family. On special occasions that mark life events, such as weddings, the birth of a child, a bar or bat mitzvah, important anniversaries, or a funeral, family are expected to participate, and this expectation is conveyed to us in a multitude of ways. For example, when such an event involves a partner in a heterosexual couple, friends, colleagues, and neighbours will assume that this affects the other partner and make comments to that effect. They may not make such an effort if dealing with a same-sex couple. There are many printed cards that celebrate heterosexual couples' relationships. How many cards that celebrate anniversaries of same-sex couples can be found in department stores? Relatives may fail to include the same-sex partner as a daughter- or son-in-law, etc.[32]

Such is not the case for friends: 'friendship, in our society, is secured by an emotional bond alone. With no social compact, no ritual moment, no pledge of loyalty and constancy to hold a friendship in place, it becomes not only the most neglected social relationship of our time but, all too often, our most fragile one as well.'[33]

While friendship is largely experienced as a conditional relationship, kinship is an unconditional one. One does not choose most of one's relatives (one *does* choose some, such as a spouse in our society, although not his or her relatives, who become in-laws through marriage), but one always chooses and is chosen by one's friends.

Some friends take over economic and social obligations for each other. One example of this is the following case-study of John. Other forms of taking on responsibilities include becoming a godparent to a child, letting friends in need stay with one, or providing services in emergencies. Friends also tend to share entertainment and fun occasions, take vacations together, etc.

Most people do have some friends, but there are marked differences in the way women and men practise friendships. Rubin found that women are much more likely than men to have close friends. She found that married men in particular do not usually have friends other than their wife, whom they tend to refer to as their 'best friend', if they name anyone as a friend at all.[34] Most of the women she interviewed, by contrast, whether married or not, had no difficulty in naming friends, including a 'best friend', who was generally not their husband.

Most men have 'friends of the road' (people with whom they *do* things) rather than 'friends of the heart' (friends with whom one is connected through *being* rather than *doing*). Women tend to have both kinds of friends.[35] The differences in numbers is overwhelming: of the group of men *most likely* to have friends (those under forty and living in urban centres where they were more apt to have been influenced by the feminist movement), less than one-fifth had a friend who held an important place in their emotional lives.[36] In other words, more than 80 per cent of the men had no close friendship outside of their marriage. For women, however, friends are very important, even when they are married. Friends may be a lifeline in times of stress, and a source of joy at other times.

However, legally enforcing friendships would probably destroy them, since by their very nature they are voluntary relations. This is, of course, what makes them fragile, but also so particularly gratifying. Since a friend cannot be forced to participate in one's life, friendship is a gift always newly given. Marriage, by contrast, is a gift that, once presented, can only be withdrawn under excruciatingly difficult circumstances.

Today, the line between family and friends is perhaps more blurred that it was in the past. Middle-aged people date again after a union dissolution, and present their 'friend' to their friends and family. Friendships may or may not involve sexual relations, which may or may not lead to an intended permanent relationship. Such friendships, if they involve a heterosexual couple living together, may turn into a common-law relationship. Of course, if the couple is of the same sex, we currently recognize such a relationship as something more than a friendship—e.g., by allowing an employee to declare her or his same-sex partner as a beneficiary in a company benefit plan—but we still do not put them in the same category as a common-law relationship in all respects.

Helping relationships among non-kin are as old as helping relationships among kin. It is, however, difficult to discern the extent of such relationships, either then or now, so I cannot present statistics on the issue. Instead, I will present the following case-study of one man and his helping relationships over roughly a twenty-year period.

Case History: The Story of John[37]
by Meg Luxton

John was born in 1946 and raised in a working class community in Canada. At 16 he started paid employment as a production worker for a large industrial manufacturer where he worked until 1994 when he was laid off as part of a major restructuring at the plant. At the time of his lay off, 6 people were directly dependent on him for financial support and three were indirectly benefiting from the subsidized rent they received from him. Of the nine, only two, his elderly parents, would be officially recognized as 'family'.

Snapshots of each of the census years of his adult life suggest that the actual relations he was involved in (co-residence, economic pooling and sharing both within his household and with others, and caregiving and committed long term emotional relations with friends and children) would be largely undetected by the current assumptions of census collecting.

More importantly, his life long commitment to his community was never recognized formally. He could not claim dependents on his income tax, he could not get benefits for them from his workplace, and as he noted, if any of them were ill he would not be included in medical consultations nor could he get funeral leave if any of them died.

In 1976 John was living alone in a small house he had bought outright from his savings. A close friend of his, Jane, who had two young children—Patricia aged 5 and Michael aged 3—had to move out of her apartment; so John invited them to move in with him. For five years the four of them lived together. The two adults never had what either of them considered a 'spousal relationship'; they were not lovers and they maintained separate personal finances. However, they contributed equally to all household and child care expenses by pooling money in a joint household account and they shared practical and emotional care giving of the children.

In 1981 Jane and the children moved into a different house with her new lover. After a few months John invited two men, Peter and Stephen, who were friends from work to move in with him. Peter had a 5 year old boy David who moved in too. The three adults never had what any of them would consider a 'spousal relationship' but they pooled all their money into one account, and shared all the household tasks including the practical and emotional care of David. John continued to do child care for Patricia and Michael who came to the house frequently; he also gave Jane a monthly allowance to help support the children.

In 1986 both Peter and Stephen had been laid off and had moved to other cities to take jobs. While David moved with Peter, he came to visit John every summer for a month and they remained in close contact by phone and letter writing.

Soon after, an old high school friend of John's moved in. Tony had shared custody of his 7 year old daughter, Kathy, who lived for six months in a different city with her mother and six months with Tony. John and Tony kept separate accounts but shared household and child care expenses equally. They shared household work and when Kathy was living with them, John shared child care. John continued to be actively involved and responsible for Patricia and Michael. He continued to give them a monthly allowance of several hundred dollars per child. He also continued to have David come for summer visits.

By 1991 John had moved into a new house. He still owned the first house, which he rented for cost to Jane who lived there with her new lover and their new baby. John had moved into the new house because it was next door to his elderly parents and by living so close he was able to provide regular care to them. He saw them on a daily basis, often eating with them and providing financial support. He continued to provide substantial financial support to the children. He paid Michael a monthly allowance to cover room and board while Michael studied at a community college, he paid the full costs of rent and day care for Patricia and her baby Sarah (born in 1991) and when David was accepted into university, John agreed to pay his tuition and residence costs for fours years of study.

Year	Co-residents	Economic sharing	Caregiving
1976	Jane (28) Patricia (5) Michael (3)	household	child care
1981	Stephen Peter David (5)	total income	child care
1986	Tony (40) Kathy (7) [6 mo/yr]	household allowances	child care
1991	none	subsidized rent and allowances to several people	child care

This particular case is one of an extraordinary degree of sharing on the part of one individual. Even if the degree of sharing is generally less, we can nevertheless assume that the extent to which friends and other significant others help each other is considerable. What does this mean for policy purposes? Should such relationships be recognized as familial?

The answer to this question is not simple. It is not always in everyone's interest to be recognized as someone else's family member. When the effect of such recognition is a court order to pay support, the payer may very well prefer not to be regarded as a family member. On the other hand, when the recognition implies access to certain benefits, entitlements, services, or information about or access to one's significant other (for instance, when she is in the hospital), the same person who might prefer not to be regarded as a family member in terms of economic responsibilities might very well prefer to be considered a family member in this context.

There is nothing illogical in such a variable stance. People may be willing to volunteer for responsibilities that they would refuse if the same responsibilities were forced upon them. In the case of John, should he be forced to continue to pay support to the various parties he supported while employed, even if it meant selling his house? On the other hand, while he voluntarily accepts the responsibility, should he be entitled to write it off his income tax or be able to claim the children on his medical and dental plans?

Potential Regimes for Dependency Relations among Non-kin

There are three questions that need to be addressed in this context. First, should responsibilities for dependants, once undertaken, become permanent? If no, it is a one-time voluntary regime; if yes, it is an ongoing involuntary regime. Second, should responsibilities be mutual? If yes, it is a symmetrical regime; if no, it is an asymmetrical regime. Third, should responsibilities that are voluntarily undertaken (at least in the first instance) be socially recognized or not?

Applying the first two questions to John's case, we arrive at four types of regimes: (1) the ongoing, involuntary asymmetrical obligations regime; (2) the voluntary asymmetrical regime; (3) the ongoing, involuntary symmetrical regime; and (4) the voluntary symmetrical regime.

Drawing on the *ongoing, involuntary asymmetrical regime*, one can argue that John assumed a parental relationship through his previous behaviour, which generated certain expectations among his dependants, which in turn entitle them to continue to be supported by him. This would be similar to the construction of support obligations to make a claim for ongoing support from stepfathers who behaved in a parental manner towards their wives' children, and who are ordered to pay support after the union dissolves. The judge therefore orders John to sell his house so that David can complete his last year of studies.

Alternatively, *the voluntary asymmetrical regime* leads one to argue that John provided for these people out of the goodness of his heart, and that it would be perverse to penalize him for his previous generosity at a time when he is no longer able to continue his support. Such perverse logic would, one might argue, actively discourage generous behaviour on the part of people who might otherwise be so inclined. Under this regime, none of the former dependants would be able to sue John for continuing support.

Third, *the ongoing, involuntary symmetrical regime* takes this thought one step further. It suggests that the people John supported for so long now have an obligation to support him. The group of people he supported each have a moral and *legal* obligation to support him as much as they can. For instance, rather than having John sell his house so that David can continue his studies, David would have to drop out of college to support John so that he does not have to sell his house. One might argue that this obligation would only extend to the adults because they had an option to accept or reject his support when he first offered it, while their minor children were in no position to reject the offer. On the other hand, one might also argue that these children were the direct beneficiaries of his generosity, and hence share the obligation, much as adult children are required (in law, although usually not in practice)[38] to support their parents if the latter are in need. Under this regime, John may therefore sue any of his non-kin former dependants to help him maintain his house.

Finally, under the *voluntary symmetrical regime*, John's former dependants band together voluntarily, pool their resources, and find a way to help him maintain his house. They do this out of a feeling of moral obligation, and John would not be able to sue any of them.

Of the four regimes, the voluntary asymmetrical regime seems the most compelling. Little would be gained (and potentially much lost) in trying to force people to support non-kin whom they supported for some time out of benevolence. Nor would it be appropriate to enforce a hypothetical reciprocal responsibility when no such contract for interdependency was made initially. However, John is still not happy. This regime does not address the issue raised by John: that he had no right to attend important social functions, that his dependants were not recognized as dependants in terms of social policy, and that he did not receive any tax benefits, etc.

This is where the *socially recognized, asymmetrical voluntary regime* comes in. This regime would recognize that outside of marriage and parental relationships, all other relationships are voluntary and partial. In terms of support, this would mean that John no longer has such a support obligation if he is no longer willing or able to provide for the others. Nor would they be obliged to provide for him, unless they voluntarily chose to and were able to do so. However, during the time that John was providing for them, he would have been able to deduct his support payments as if these people had been related by blood, marriage, or adoption. To the degree that he participated in child care, he would have acquired the right to participate in social functions associated with the children. For instance, he would have been eligible for bereavement leave had one of them died, or sick leave in case one of them was ill (provided his company had such a benefit). The socially recognized, asymmetrical voluntary regime, then, would recognize the actual contributions people make, avoid penalizing those who are most decent and generous while rewarding those who behave selfishly, and not impose support obligations between unrelated adults.

In terms of social policy, the socially recognized, asymmetrical voluntary regime makes sense. The state benefits to the degree that one contributes *in a tangible manner* to the care of an inevitable dependant, or enables someone else to do so through economic support. Further, if anyone supports an adult who is a temporary dependant and who would otherwise claim support from the state, the state also benefits. It would therefore make sense that such people receive whatever benefits are available on a prorated basis, so that for each dependant there is a maximum amount that can be claimed (this is to avoid fraudulent schemes). That is, John would have been able to claim the support he was paying to the various people as long as they were partially financially dependent on his contribution.

With respect to support obligations, it seems sensible to make a distinction between legal marriage, which is a quasi-contractual situation that is deliberately entered into, and all other situations in which such contracts were not undertaken. This provides an answer to the previously raised question of support obligations between common-law couples and common-law spouses' obligations towards their stepchildren in the case of union dissolution. In both instances we are dealing with dependency relations among non-kin. Applying the socially recognized, asymmetrical voluntary regime would suggest that *legal* (not necessarily *moral*) support obligations cease with union dissolution. Of course, in the case of adults who live together, division of assets would still have to be achieved, and if one partner to a union was disadvantaged *because of the union*, she (or he) should have the right to compensatory payments, e.g., for taking advanced training to better one's job prospects, etc. We are now ready to formulate the fifth component of the social responsibility model: *(5) All dependency relations are socially recognized, regardless of whether they are between kin or non-kin. Adult members of an interdependent unit are responsible for their own and each other's economic well-being. Fathers and mothers are both responsible for their children's economic well-being, whether or not they live with them.*[39]

CARE PROVISION FOR A FAMILY'S CHILDREN

Given the first component, both mothers and fathers are responsible for caring for their dependent children by providing the care themselves, or by paying partially or totally for their share of the care provision. This fundamental responsibility does not change even if one parent does not live with the children.

As discussed in Chapter 4, it is important to make a distinction between parental rights and obligations. Failing to do so would allow abusive or otherwise irresponsible men (and some women) to divest themselves of their financial obligations by misbehaving. The sixth component of the social responsibility model is this: *(6) Mothers and fathers are both responsible for providing care for their children. Parents retain parental responsibilities—which are not tied to parental rights—even if they do not live with their children.*

THE APPROPRIATE PRIVATE-PUBLIC DIVISION OF RESPONSIBILITIES

As we have seen earlier, providing care for inevitable dependants has a high *social* value, not just a private value. Social policy should recognize this as an important family function that deserves public support in a tangible form. However, there are two categories of inevitable dependants: children and adults. It makes sense to distinguish between the two because children are acquired through the (hopefully) voluntary cooperation of two adults, who therefore share the responsibility, with society, for these children's welfare, while adults do not voluntarily become inevitable dependants.

If no family care is available, the state will carry the cost of care for inevitable dependants. Family members may often prefer to care for adult inevitable dependants without being able to absorb the costs for this. Under the individual responsibility model, the familism-individualism flip-flop would make caregiving by family members difficult and sometimes impossible. However, if we regard the cost of care for inevitably dependent adults as a social responsibility, it would enable family members to afford to actually provide the care if this is possible and mutually desired.

Regarding children as inevitable dependants, society already takes a relatively large responsibility for them. Public education for children as of the age of six is a form of caregiving that allows parents to work in order to earn money (and schools cost taxpayers a considerable amount of money). Therefore it is the first six years that are particularly crucial. It would make sense to look at child care as a threefold responsibility, shared equally between father, mother, and society. If every child had access to free day care, this would provide care for the time equivalent of one full-time job, leaving sixteen hours for each of five days and twenty-four hours for Saturday and Sunday during which the parents would have to look after the children. Of course, there are a number of other ways in which parents and society share the responsibility for children, such as financial compensation, day care on a sliding scale, summer camps, etc. There is considerable social support for public support of care for inevitable dependants. Fully 85 per cent of a national sample of Canadian respondents agreed that there should be support payments for families who care for an elderly family member, and of those, 70 per cent would be willing to pay additional taxes to fund such an initiative. The support for a national subsidized child-care service is not quite as high, but still very considerable: 77 per cent would support such an initiative, and 73 per cent of these would pay additional taxes for such a goal.[40]

What is often not considered, however, is that if there is really only one parent, this parent—under our current individual responsibility model of the family—is supposed to carry the load of two. This makes little sense. Therefore, when there is only one parent, the state needs to replace the contribution that would otherwise be made by the second parent. As stated previously, this does *not* include lone-parent families in which the second parent is alive but not coresident, since his or her responsibilities remain unchanged. Only if this parent is dead or unable to contribute his or her share would society take over that share of the responsibility. The seventh component of the social responsibility model of the family is this: *(7) The public shares the responsibility, with both parents, for the care of dependent children. If one parent is really absent or unable to contribute his or her share, society will pay the cost of his or her contribution. The cost of care for inevitably dependent adults is a public responsibility, while the delivery of the care may be rendered by a family member.*

ASSUMPTION CONCERNING HETEROSEXUALITY/HOMOSEXUALITY

This issue has, in effect, already been addressed previously. It makes no difference whether members are of the same or opposite sex in terms of benefit for the state or for the members of an interdependent unit. Same-sex couples should be able to marry legally or have an alternative but equivalent domestic partnership arrangement. Once this is possible, if they fail to marry legally, they would be treated like a heterosexual common-law couple. The eighth and final component of the social responsibility model is this: *(8) There is no distinction between same-sex or opposite-sex couples in terms of their treatment by the state.*

COMPONENTS OF THE SOCIAL RESPONSIBILITY MODEL OF THE FAMILY

1. There is an ideological commitment to minimizing stratification on the basis of sex.

2. Functioning relationships constitute a family unit. Legal marriage is present but not privileged over other relationships.

3. At the nuclear level, household and family memberships may be, but are not assumed to be, congruous. Therefore, spousehood is not automatically identified with parenthood, and parenthood is not automatically identified with spousehood.

4. The individual is the unit of administration (with a few exceptions).

5. All dependency relations are socially recognized, regardless of whether they are between kin or non-kin. Adult members of an interdependent unit are responsible for their own and each other's economic well-being. Fathers and mothers are both responsible for their children's economic well-being, whether or not they live with them.

6. Mothers and fathers are both responsible for providing care for their children. Parents retain parental responsibilities—which are not tied to parental rights—even if they do not live with their children.

7. The public shares the responsibility, with both parents, for the care of dependent children. If one parent is really absent or unable to contribute his or her share, society will pay the cost of his or her contribution. The cost of care for inevitably dependent adults is a public responsibility, while the delivery of the care may be rendered by a family member.

8. There is no distinction between same-sex or opposite-sex couples in terms of their treatment by the state.

CONCLUSION: CAUTION IS THE MOTHER OF WISDOM

While I personally find the resulting social responsibility model of the family rational, just, practical, and hence attractive, some cautionary remarks are nevertheless appropriate. It is easier to derive principles in theory than to apply them in real-life situations, especially if the proposal is one that would involve a radical shift. Not only does it require enormous political will, but also no complex social system ever changes in all of its aspects simultaneously and in the same direction. Therefore, applying principles that could (if initiated all at once and at the same time) provide a more just and efficient basis for all relevant policies may (if initiated in a piecemeal fashion) in effect increase inequalities if the principles are not applied very cautiously. One needs to be constantly on the lookout for unplanned, undesirable effects.

Further, even if the principles were all adopted at once as the basis for all current and future policies, there would still be considerable leeway in how they would be translated into concrete reality. And of course, other issues—such as whether the state has the money for a particular desirable policy—cannot simply be ignored.

To address some of the problems, in the next chapter I will discuss how the social responsibility model of the family could be applied to some important issues.

Practical Applications of the Social Responsibility Model

INTRODUCTION

If we had a social responsibility model of the family, first and foremost, we would not have children living below the poverty line. Unfortunately, this is not the case today. Recent provincial welfare reforms and the federal devolution of control over provincial spending[1] have resulted in a substantial deterioration of the situation of welfare recipients, 38 per cent of whom are children![2] In a social responsibility model we would support care providers for inevitable dependants. There would be a host of other initiatives: we would socially recognize all those who support others, we would not discriminate against people on the basis of their family status, we would (with a few exceptions) treat people administratively as individuals, etc. In short, we would encourage caring relationships and the voluntary assumption of responsibility for others.

A coalition of national organizations and community partners has made a number of proposals for a set of national social security policies for families with children. These recommendations fit within a social responsibility model of the family. They include:

• A progressive children's benefit system to protect and enhance the living standards of families with modest incomes, to reduce child poverty, and to recognize the additional costs all families incur by raising children

• A federally organized child support assurance system to protect children from the loss of basic income support resulting from separation or divorce

• Federal financing of a comprehensive child care system, complemented by parental leave policies …

• A national education endowment program to ensure that youth from families with low and modest incomes can afford postsecondary education

• A comprehensive employment insurance system to protect income support to workers during periods of transition[3]

Unfortunately, the tide seems to be running against such changes. This is deplorable. The importance of a good and internally coherent safety net for everyone has been demonstrated time and again.[4] Given a large deficit and public debt, social programs are being slashed rather than expanded.[5] In 1994–5, total federal program spending was 16 per cent of the GDP, and it will fall to just 13 per cent of the GDP by 1996–7.[6] The United Nations has ranked Canada as one of—sometimes *the*—most livable countries in the world because of its social infrastructure, which was built in the past. As we reduce our investment in the social capital of the country, we will develop a social deficit that will result in a reduced quality of life for all of us.[7]

There is, of course, a large debt and deficit.[8] Are there alternatives to slashing social programs?[9] Indeed, there are. The yearly amount of $90 billion worth of tax expenditures exceeds the yearly $40 billion spent on social programs by more than half.[10] It amounts to three-quarters of the $120 billion spent yearly on all direct federal programs. If we focus our attention on reducing these expenditures, it would allow us to leave our social spending intact or to enhance it.[11] The National Council of Welfare has suggested that an additional $10 billion of tax revenue could be raised annually by eliminating selected tax deductions.[12] They propose that half of this be used to reduce government deficits, and half to enhance social security programs.[13] Other very concrete and practical proposals for generating revenue have been made as well.[14]

Regardless of overall spending patterns, small changes occur constantly because the political push is strong enough to demand them, because Supreme Court decisions require new policy or legislative responses, or because of other reasons. The sum of small changes may add up to large changes, so it is important to look at all the small changes. If they go in the right direction, they will form the basis for a more rational scheme of family support than the one we have inherited from the patriarchal and individual responsibility models.

There is one particular danger, however. Any changes in public policies will shift benefits and burdens somewhat. If one aspect gets shifted *while others are not*, the net effect may be negative, although the change might have been desirable in principle had other things changed as well. In such instances, compensatory measures are essential or else the change should be delayed. It is therefore helpful to define a set of policy goals and to require that any policy initiative further at least one of these goals without moving us further away from any of the other goals.

The characteristics of the social responsibility model can be reformulated as policy goals:

- minimizing sex stratification

- providing collective support for inevitable dependants

- providing collective support for care providers of inevitable dependants

- giving social recognition to all those who partially or completely support temporary dependants, whether they are related or not

- facilitating self-support and autonomy for every individual

- giving social and legal recognition to lesbian and gay families[15]

A recent inventory of federal programs that support families in Canada lists forty-seven programs, ranging from very specific ones such as the National Adoption Desk, the Family Violence Prevention Program for Native Peoples, or the Foster Care Payments and Income Tax over the Federal Social Housing Program to the broadest programs such as the Child Tax Benefit.[16] In addition, each province and territory has a host of programs. I will examine only selected issues. I am partially guided in my selection by recent court cases that have highlighted some aspects of various policies. I will move from specific issues to more general ones.

TAXATION OF ALIMONY OR MAINTENANCE INCOME

Taxation of child-support payments has been much in the public eye due to the publicity surrounding the case of Suzanne Thibaudeau,[17] a divorced mother of two who receives child-support payments of $1,150 per month from her ex-husband, and who has to declare this as income, while the ex-husband may deduct his payments from his income for tax purposes. At issue was whether the custodial mother and recipient of the child-support payments should pay taxes on this money, or whether the non-custodial father and payer needs to declare this as part of his income. The Supreme Court decided ultimately that the deduction/inclusion scheme as it has been since 1942—namely, that the payer may deduct his expenses, and that the recipient must pay tax on the child support received—was appropriate.

The case was followed in the press and generated a number of letters to the editor. It seems that most people who supported Thibaudeau were women, while most who supported the status quo were men.[18] This was certainly the case in the Supreme Court. The two women judges—L'Heureux-Dubé and McLachlin—supported Thibaudeau's request, while the men supported the status quo.

It is interesting to reflect on the history of the deduction/inclusion scheme. It was first introduced in 1942 when the patriarchal model of the family ruled undisputedly, and was explicitly justified in order to help the non-custodial ex-husband. Excerpts from the House of Commons debates prove this point:

Mr Hanson (York-Sudbury): ... Has the minister met the alimony case, the man who is divorced, who has an income of, say, $10,000?

Mr Isley: I certainly have.

Mr Hanson (York-Sudbury): Such a man who has married again is in a very tight spot. I think he ought to have a little consideration; that should be allowed as a deduction.

Mr Bence: I was going to say a word on that point. It seems to me most unfair when a man is divorced and is supporting his ex-wife by order of court, he should not be allowed to deduct, for income tax purposes, the amount paid in alimony. If that were done, the ex-wife could be required to file an income tax return as a single woman, as she should, and she would have to acknowledge receipt of that income in making up that return. In many cases the man has married again, but still he must pay a very high tax on the $60, $70 or $80 a month he must pay his former wife. I am not thinking of it so much from the point of view of the husband, though I believe he is in a very bad spot. In the cases with which I have become acquainted, the husband has defaulted in his payments because he has not been able to make them, and in those cases it is the former wife who suffers, and accordingly I believe she should be given as much consideration as the husband.

Mr Ilsley: I agree that there is a great deal of injustice to the husband, and perhaps indirectly to the wife, under the law as it stands now, and much consideration has been given some method by which the law might be changed ...

Mr Green: I really think it is an impossible situation, with the tax so greatly increased as it has been this year. After all, our law recognizes divorce, and once the parties are divorced they are entitled to marry again. In some cases that have been brought to my attention the husband has remarried and had children by the second wife, but is forced to pay income tax on the alimony that he pays the first wife, and I suggest that the position is absolutely unfair.

Mr Ilsley: I agree that it is, in a great many cases.[19]

This debate reflects an exclusively male point of view. There is no discussion of child support at all. 'Alimony' may include spousal as well as child support, and there is no discussion of the potential effects of this policy on women and their children (except a pious but empty sentiment that it may be in the interests of women, since men will be defaulting less often).[20] The second wife and her children are mentioned. The man's family is therefore defined by his household members, not by his parental ties, which is characteristic of both the patriarchal and the individual responsibility models. In the conflation of spousal and parental roles, he is seen as the father of a potential second wife's children, but is not regarded in that role when it comes to his first wife's children, just because he is no longer married to her.

Beyond equating household membership with family membership and conflating spousal and parental roles, there seems to be no recognition of parental responsibility. Justices Cory and Iacobucci maintain that:

> … the legislation in question confers a benefit on the post-divorce 'family unit'. It is clear that the divorced parents still function as a unit when it comes to providing financial and emotional support to their children and that both parents remain under a legal obligation to provide this support. The fact that one member of the unit might derive a greater benefit from the legislation than the other does not, in and of itself, trigger a s. 15 violation, nor does it lead to a finding that the distinction in any way amounts to a denial of equal benefit or protection of the law.[21]

This statement demonstrates one of the biases common in the family literature: the sexist bias.[22] By looking at a benefit in terms of its effect on the 'family unit', without regard to its disparate effect on the individuals making up this unit—which is, of course, precisely what is at issue here—the problem has been defined away. This is the case also with Justice Gonthier's opinion who concurs with Justice Garon that the court establishing the amount of alimony must take the tax consequences for both payer and recipient into account without worrying about *how* it must be taken into account. The absurd logic of the stance has been conclusively demonstrated by L'Heureux-Dubé, with the help of a hypothetical example:

> Let us suppose that, in a new initiative designed to respond to the high costs of maintaining separate households, the government decided to provide a net subsidy of $1,000 to all separated couples with children in order to help them meet their children's financial needs. Let us further suppose that this $1,000 subsidy was accomplished by giving $2,000 to the *non-custodial spouse* and by clawing back $1,000 in income tax from the *custodial spouse*. Finally, let us assume that although the new program provides that the custodial spouse may attempt to claim his or her rightful share of the net subsidy via existing procedures within the family law system, no formal mechanism is implemented to insure the equal division of these additional benefits and liabilities. Does such a program confer an advantage upon *non-custodial spouses* and a disadvantage upon *custodial spouses*? Does it create an unequal burden or benefit?[23]

The notion of divorced or separated couples as a 'family unit' is entirely inappropriate. It conflates spousal and parental familial relationships. The non-resident father is a family member of the children, *not* of his ex-wife. She is most definitely not a member of his family, although they share financial responsibility for the two children.

The majority opinion thus conflates spousal and parental roles and treats the parents as a family unit when they are not. Justices Cory and Iacobucci treat Thibaudeau and Chaine (Thibaudeau's ex-husband) as a *couple* when the issue is parental status, not ex-spousal status. If Thibaudeau and Chaine had never been married, and he was paying the same amount of child support for his children, the tax situation would be identical. Their marital status is therefore entirely irrelevant. By failing to distinguish between spousal and parental roles, Cory and Iacobucci conform to the individual responsibility model of the family.

By contrast, L'Heureux-Dubé argues that she 'must respectfully disagree with my colleagues who conclude that the appropriate unit of analysis is ... the couple.'[24] By looking at the issue at hand as a parental rather than a spousal matter, she concludes: 'With all due respect, I cannot see the logic in designing a system, whose central purpose is to benefit children, in such a way that it begets as its primary beneficiary that half of the separated or divorced 'couple' that does not have custody of, and therefore primary responsibility for, those same children.'[25] This is in line with the social responsibility model of the family, which separates spousal and parental roles, thus recognizing non-custodial parents' ongoing responsibility towards their children without postulating a fictional couplehood for the divorced ex-spouses.

McLachlin adds another important consideration to the matter. She points out that the current deduction/inclusion scheme is based on a double standard that operates against custodial parents. First, the non-custodial parent may deduct child support from his taxable income, while the custodial parent 'cannot deduct amounts she spends on maintaining the children'.[26] Second, the custodial parent 'must also pay the tax that the non-custodial parent would ordinarily have had to pay on the income devoted to child support.'[27] Third, the non-custodial parent need not include in his or her 'taxable income the amounts which the custodial parent spends on maintaining the children.'[28]

Looking at the issue from the perspective of minimizing stratification between the sexes, we find that custodial parents are mostly mothers who, as a group, are much poorer than non-custodial fathers. In so far as tax consequences are *not* always taken adequately into account in setting support payments, having the recipient pay tax on monies received from the other parent increases rather than decreases inequality. Of course, the current practice is based on the outmoded assumption that women are their husbands' economic dependants.[29] On this ground, too, the current tax provision is contrary to the social responsibility model of the family. Without using these terms, this is part of the logic underlying the reasons for judgement by both L'Heureux-Dubé and McLachlin.

Under a social responsibility model, then, child support would not be deductible for the non-custodial parent and would not be taxed as income for the custodial parent. Changing the current provision so that the non-custodial parent may not deduct his payments and the custodial parent need not pay income tax on the monies received would save the federal government a substantial amount of money each year.[30] This money could be used to fund some other program, such as dealing with the pervasive poverty of lone-parent families.[31]

Happily, the public fall-out from the *Thibaudeau* case was such that the federal government decided to change the tax rules, even though the Supreme Court had decided to uphold them. In March 1996, the federal government announced that as of 1 May 1997, the recipients of child-support payments will no longer have to pay tax on these payments, and the payer will not able to deduct the payments from his (occasionally her) income.[32] The money thus saved will be used to improve the Working Income Supplement, which goes to low-income families.

CHILD-SUPPORT PAYMENTS

So far we have only looked at the taxation of support payments. However, in order to have something to tax, there first needs to be a support payment that is provided regularly and is of an adequate amount. Even with the switch to a no-deduction, no-inclusion system, this is a much greater stumbling block that the taxation questions. There is general agreement that so far, the awards made and the collection of payment mechanisms have been faulty.[33] Divorce or separation and flawed economic support results in the poverty of the majority of women and children as a consequence of union dissolution. In 1993, only 16 per cent of all single-parent, mother-led families received child or spousal support of an average amount of $3,604.[34] However, 71 per cent of them received welfare.[35] If there are cuts in welfare, these are the people who will suffer the most. Thibaudeau—important though her case is—therefore represents an atypical minority of lone-parent mothers.

There are various models to address the problem of child-support awards, all of which are based on some type of formula. These include the *income shares model*, which is based on the concept that the child should receive the same proportion of parental income that he or she would have received if the parents had continued to live together;[36] the *equal living standards model*, which is based on the notion that the two postdivorce households should have similar living standards after divorce;[37] the *cost-sharing model*, which identifies an actual dollar amount that is deemed necessary for the child's needs, and then apportions the cost between the two parents according to their ability to pay;[38] and the *fixed percentage of income model*, which assigns a fixed percentage of the non-custodial parent's income to child support.[39]

Besides the level of payments, the degree of compliance is equally important. If a non-custodial parent is supposed to pay a high amount of child support but fails to do so, the custodial parent is no better off than if no amount had been awarded. Australia has taken some significant steps, more far-reaching than other countries, to collect child-support payments. It introduced its reform in two phases. In phase 1, starting in 1988, a Child Support Agency within the Australian Taxation Office was established. Payers deposit their support payments directly to the agency or have it automatically deducted from wages or other sources of income. The agency then sends the cheques to the payee. In phase 2, levels of payments were set.[40]

The problem with all of these schemes is, of course, that they will be effective only if non-custodial parents (mostly men) have enough money to pay a decent amount of child support. Where this is missing, the best formula plus enforcement mechanism will not generate enough income for the children and their custodial parent.[41]

Looking at the new support guidelines that will come into force as of May 1997, we find that they will improve the situation somewhat for two reasons. The payments are marginally higher than current payments if the tax consequences are factored in,[42] and the level of support will be compulsory by law unless there are exceptional circumstances. With the exception of those non-custodial parents who fall below the specified threshold and who therefore contribute no child support, almost all other non-custodial parents would have to make some payment to the custodial parents. The amounts, however, do not even begin to cover day care, let alone other expenses.[43] For low-income families, at least, there must be some social support for the child. Poverty will not be eradicated only by improving the child-support systems, but the system must be improved nevertheless. Child-support payments, for the majority of lone-parent families, can only be *one* factor in a set of policies designed to eliminate poverty among children. This is a goal to which Canada has committed itself.[44]

In addition, we need to consider how child-support payments would affect welfare entitlements. Seventy-one per cent of lone-parent mothers receive welfare. If welfare is reduced dollar by dollar for any child support received, the mother and her children would not be better off. Non-custodial fathers would have to pay their fair share, which is desirable, of course, but it would not solve the problem of poverty among children and their mothers.

FINANCIAL SUPPORT FOR ALL LONE-PARENT FAMILIES

The child-support assurance system is a modified version of the income shares model, with a collective component added:

> All nonresident parents would be required to share their income with their children. The sharing rate is a proportion of the nonresident parent's gross income and is determined by legislation. The resulting child support obligation is withheld routinely from income just as income and payroll taxes are withheld. The child receives either the full amount owed or a minimum benefit set by legislation and provided by the government, whichever is higher.[45]

Only this last approach addresses one of the major issues regarding poverty among lone-parent families.[46] Important as the support payments are, they alone will not solve the problem of poverty among these families, even if we had the best possible system in place in terms of setting levels and 100 per cent success in enforcing them. Overall, the level of poverty among women and children would be marginally improved, and there would be somewhat greater fairness in the mothers' and fathers' shared financial responsibility for children. Both are important goals, but neither would solve poverty.

A child-support assurance system would have some very significant advantages. Custodial parents and their children would be assured of a certain minimum income, and the money would be certain to arrive on time and without default or delay. It would raise the children above the poverty level. Much of this money would come back to the agency that distributes the cheques via wage garnishing and other mechanisms. Other amounts would come from welfare. The rest would have to be generated through other means, as mentioned earlier in this chapter. The state is much better than most people at collecting money from its citizens. It has the mechanisms in place. Mothers would still receive higher amounts than the minimum if their children's father had the means to pay, but, whatever the circumstances, they would at least have the minimum. It would be more dignified than welfare. There would be no need to check for a 'man in the house',[47] since the mother would be entitled to the child-support payments whether or not she had a lover.

A child-support assurance system would be in accord with the social responsibility model of the family, in so far as it did *not* conflate spousal with parental roles, would enforce the non-custodial parent's ongoing economic responsibility towards his children, and treat the custodial parent as the administrative unit. However, in isolation, this approach would create other problems.

FINANCIAL SUPPORT FOR ALL LOW-INCOME FAMILIES

Let us construct a hypothetical example. Abby and Abdul are married and have two kids. She earns $16,000, he earns $40,000. Abdul loses his job, and three months later they split up. They have used up their savings. Abdul is unable to pay child support. Abby applies for Child Assurance Support and receives $500 per child per month. Within half a year, she meets Ben. They fall in love, and shortly thereafter he moves in with her. Ben has a steady job that pays $22,000 per year. Abby continues to receive her Child Assurance Support.

Their neighbours, Carol and Claudio, who also have two children, each earn $19,000. The total earned income of Abby and Ben is therefore identical to the total earned income of Carol and Claudio, but the former receive a very substantial government subsidy while the latter do not. Carol and Claudio are upset. Their taxes go to support a benefit for Abby and Ben, for which they themselves are ineligible. Abby and Ben would like to marry, but decide not to so as not to lose their Child Assurance Support payments.

If we use parents' marital status to determine eligibility for public child support, this would help those parents who suffer a particular disadvantage, but in the process the system would create a new inequity. On the other hand, there does need to be some substantial recognition of the special needs of lone parents.[48] The assured child support would therefore need to be complemented by a child benefit that is available to *all* parents, regardless of marital status. This type of thinking is consistent with the current Child Tax Benefit. This is an important support for parents. Over 2.2 million Canadian families with about 4.6 million children[49] were receiving monthly payments in 1993. The amounts paid are calculated using information from the income tax returns filed by both parents, but they were much less than the amounts discussed above.[50]

However, comparing the Child Tax Benefit to the children's benefits paid by other comparable countries, we find that Canada's contribution is the lowest of eleven OECD countries.[51] This benefit needs to be increased substantially to make a significant dent in poverty.

CHILD-CARE EXPENSES

At present, a parent may deduct child-care expenses up to a certain level in order to earn money or prepare for doing so by participating in an approved training program, for instance. There is no longer a double standard with respect to mothers and fathers, so the condition of gender equality is satisfied.

Gender equality was at the centre of a highly publicized law case recently in *Symes* v. *Canada*.[52] Elizabeth Symes, a lawyer, argued that she should be able to deduct, as a business expense, the salary for the nanny who was looking after her two children. The case was eventually lost at the Supreme Court of Canada. As in *Thibaudeau* v. *Canada*, the Supreme Court of Canada was split along gender lines: all the male judges held that the appeal should be dismissed, while the two female judges held that it should be allowed. Section 63 of the *Income Tax Act* stipulates that a taxpayer may deduct $2,000 per child annually (up to a maximum of $8,000) for child-care expenses if the child care is needed to enable the taxpayer to earn income. In the case of a couple, the lower-income earner must declare the child-care expenses. Symes paid between $10,075 and $13,359 per year for the nanny. Deducting the entire expense would therefore have made a tangible difference.

Justice Iacobucci, writing for the majority, concluded that the cap on child-care deductions 'has not been proved to violate the appellant's right to equality'.[53] This is premised on the foregoing conclusion that s. 63 does not discriminate on the basis of sex. After considering whether child-care expenses are appropriately characterized as personal expenses (not necessarily), he asked whether they were business expenses. The answer to this was no, because 'Traditionally, expenses that simply make the taxpayer available to the business are not considered business expenses since the taxpayer is expected to be available to the business as a *quid pro quo* for business income received.'[54] He did deal briefly with the question of the meaning of having children: '… I am uncomfortable with the suggestion that the appellant's decision to have children should be viewed solely as a consumption choice. I frankly admit that there is an element of public policy which feeds my discomfort … I suggest it is more appropriate to disregard any element of personal consumption which might be associated with it.'[55] The question before the court was the propriety of the result of s. 63 of the *Income Tax Act*, rather than an evaluation of how the act operates as a child-care system. However, when dealing with s. 1 of the *Charter* in his deliberations, Iacobucci states:

> With respect to the *Act* itself, it is certainly relevant to consider how income tax deductions affect the class of taxpayers who need help with child care. In particular, I advert to the well known fact that tax deductions operate as upside-down subsidies … In my opinion, it would be strange indeed for this Court to consider uncapping a child care expense deduction, without even considering the very real drawbacks of tax deductions in equality terms.[56]

By contrast, Justice L'Heureux-Dubé (writing for herself and McLachlin) argued that it is clear that the interpretation of a business expense 'is premised on the traditional view of business as a male enterprise [that] has itself been constructed on the basis of the needs of business*men* … As a consequence, the male standard now frames the backdrop of assumptions against which expenses are determined to be, or not to be, legitimate business expenses.'[57] She then compares the position of female lawyers with that of male lawyers, finds that female lawyers need paid child care significantly more than male lawyers, and concludes that child-care expenses are indeed business expenses and that: 'The definition of a business expense under the *Act* has evolved in a manner that has failed to recognize the reality of businesswomen. It is thus imperative to recognize that any interpretation of s. 63 which prevents the deduction of child care as a business expense may, in fact, be informed by this partisan perspective.'[58]

L'Heureux-Dubé then addresses the question of the appropriateness of using an income tax deduction to alleviate the high cost of child care and suggests that 'Perhaps child care should not even be subsidized through the tax system but, rather, provided for in another manner.'[59] However, she argues, this was not the question at issue. The question was simply hinging on an examination of the advantaged position that some business*men* hold in relation to business*women*—and there is evidence that child care affects women differently than it does men.

What is the result of looking at the issue of deducting child-care expenses from the perspective of the social responsibility model? Looking first at minimizing gender stratification, the stance depends on one's perspective: if comparing businesswomen with businessmen, then allowing the deduction would increase gender equality. On the other hand, if looking at it from the more general perspective of gender equality, as well as equality in general, then anything that will increase the use of a regressive policy instrument (as any deduction is) would be counter to this goal. There are several reasons why this is so. First, poorer women will have to partially finance richer women—the nanny's taxes will go to partially finance her employer's costs. In times of budget deficits and debts, and in line with the arguments presented at the beginning of this chapter, it would not make sense to increase deductions further.[60] Second, any measure that is disadvantageous to poor people is particularly disadvantageous to women because there are more poor women than there are poor men. Conversely, any measure that improves the situation of poor people will also disproportionately improve the situation of women. With respect to minimizing gender stratification, then, the best approach would be to abolish the child-care deduction in its entirety and to replace it with a credit, unless a child already attends a day-care centre that is paid for with public monies.

Marriage and family and household memberships are not at issue in this matter, but the unit of administration may be. The judgement takes the parent as the appropriate unit of administration and determines the status of the tax deduction on the basis of the parent's status as a business person. Alternatively, we could consider the child as the appropriate unit and devise a benefit that would be linked to the child (as the old family allowance used to be). This would, again, argue for a universal taxable transfer of a set amount rather than a tax benefit that is tied to the income of one parent.

Regarding economic dependency, responsibility for care provision, and the division of public and social responsibilities, it would not be possible under a social responsibility model of the family to allow only *one* parent to be eligible for a benefit when in fact there are two. If the benefit was converted into a universal transfer that would, however, be taxable (so as to ensure progressivity of the tax system), it should be attributable 50 per cent to each parent. This would mean lone parents would be entitled to 100 per cent of the transfer, but pay only 50 per cent of the tax liability (and this would, of course, apply equally to any other parental-status benefit). The other parent (whether living in the household or elsewhere) would be taxed for the other half. If there was no second parent, one half of the tax liability would be forgiven. With respect to same-sex couples, lesbian or gay couples who adopted a partner's child or who both adopted a child would be treated in exactly the same manner.[61]

We have now arrived at a substantially different benefit than the one that currently exists in the *Income Tax Act*: a refundable child-care credit that is paid to every parent who is not already receiving an equivalent or higher benefit through subsidized child care and which is taxable 50 per cent to each parent, whether or not the parents live with the children.

CHILD CARE

Would this type of provision satisfy the public responsibility for child care? Not really. If we assume that a small child needs care twenty-four hours a day, seven days a week, and that adults need to be economically responsible for themselves, it follows that the public's share of responsibility for child care should equal a full-time job, which I will equate with forty hours a week (eight hours per day for five days per week).[62] That still means that the parents must provide child care for sixteen hours per day and night for five days a week, and for twenty-four hours per day for the weekend.

There is a substantial literature that suggests child-care monies are better expended by establishing and supporting public day-care centres than by transferring the monies directly to the parents.[63] It would also make good economic sense to provide child care for all children who need it. This would generate jobs for the child-care workers[64] and enable mothers to work for pay, while allowing children to profit both from the social setting of day care and the home setting of individualized attention. Financing does not have to come from the federal government alone. Part of it can come from municipalities,[65] from employers,[66] and from parents according to their ability to pay.

Assistance to parents is available in other forms, of course. Free public education is a major one, as is medical insurance for all individuals, assistance to homemakers, relevant and useful school curricula, and many other services and institutions. We will briefly consider certain kinds of assistance relating to couples.

Spousal Amount

Legal or common-law spouses who are supporting a spouse who has little or no independent income may claim this exemption. Same-sex spouses, however, may not claim this exemption. Privileging a heterosexual couple is in accord with the individual responsibility model of the family and conflicts with the social responsibility model. There are problems with the current provisions. First, people who are in substantially the same situation as a heterosexual couple (namely, same-sex couples and non-sexualized groupings such as siblings or friends living together) are excluded. Second, its format is regressive, since it is a deduction. All deductions, by definition, provide a greater benefit to higher-income earners than lower-income earners, and are of no benefit to the people with the lowest incomes who do not pay taxes. Third, we may question why a couple who both work or an unattached tax-paying individual should subsidize, via their taxes, a husband who receives services from his wife in the form of unpaid housework.

If we want to bring this benefit into accord with the social responsibility model, we have three possibilities: first, extend the benefit to other groupings; second, transform the benefit but pay the monies to the dependants; and third, abolish it and use the monies thus saved for other purposes.

Transforming the Spousal Benefit into a Benefit for Wholly Dependent Adults

There is no good theoretical justification for limiting the spousal benefit to legal and common-law spouses. A lesbian and gay couple would fulfil the same functions for the state as would a heterosexual couple, and so could a pair of sisters or brothers, or any other group of adults who live together and are economically and emotionally supportive of each other. In so far as this enhances people's mental health, makes them more resilient in times of crises, allows them to pool their resources, and thus makes them more productive, it can be regarded as desirable for the state to support such groupings. Such adults would not be on welfare, and would possibly use the support to upgrade their qualifications, thus increasing the human capital. In such a case, it would make sense to transform the benefit into a benefit for wholly dependent adults. If a person wholly supports more than one other adult, he or she would be able to claim all of these dependants. If a person partially supports one or more other people, he or she could make partial claim(s). The benefit would constitute a modest reward for engaging in pro-social behaviour for the person who supports the others. It would recognize that the supporting individual is paying for something that would otherwise be the state's responsibility for funding.

However, problems remain. As long as the benefit is a deduction, it remains regressive. This could be remedied by converting it into a refundable credit. The other problem is how we see the role of the wholly dependent adult. Is this a person who renders services to the provider? If so, why should this be subsidized or supported by the state? Or is this a strictly benevolent action on the part of the provider and therefore deserves some assistance? These two problems could be partially addressed by changing the spousal benefit into a refundable tax credit paid to the *dependants* themselves.

Transforming the Spousal Benefit into a Refundable Dependants' Tax Credit

I have so far painted a rather idyllic picture of the groupings, whether it be a heterosexual or same-sex couple, or some other grouping. As we have seen in the preceding chapters, familial groupings include the most loving, caring, and supportive relationships as well as the most brutal, abusive, dangerous, and exploitative ones. Rather than pay the benefit to the taxpayer, then, the amount could be paid to the dependant. This would constitute a modest step towards a guaranteed annual income for individuals.[67] The amount of money within the household would remain roughly the same,[68] only the benefit would now go to the dependant rather than to the provider. The dependant would therefore be able to contribute modestly to her or his own support, and if the provider was abusive, the dependant would at least have a small amount of money as a personal resource. Research has demonstrated conclusively that even small amounts of money paid directly to dependants (in this case, family allowances paid to housewives) are disproportionately important for the recipients, since in some cases it is the only money under their control.[69]

Transforming the spousal amount into a refundable dependants' tax credit would seem like the better policy instrument. However, the question still remains as to why the public should support a couple, one of whom receives services from the other, since not all taxpayers will themselves receive an equivalent full-time service (because they are unattached individuals, or women who do the housework in addition to their paid jobs, or husbands who have wives with full-time jobs that do not allow them to devote as much time to housework as full-time housewives).

The problem with both the current spousal amount, the proposed wholly dependent adults' benefit, and the dependants' tax credit is that they do not differentiate between those adults who have no income because they render private services to another physically and mentally fit adult (such as a healthy husband) and those who do socially useful work by caring for inevitable dependants (children or adults in need of care).

Transforming the Spousal Amount into a Care Provider's Refundable Tax Credit

If a housewife looks after a physically and mentally healthy husband, she contributes unpaid work to the relationship and he contributes the money. She renders services that are privately useful to the man, but these services do not have a *direct* social value. If this same housewife looks after one or more dependent children, or her disabled husband, or another adult who is unable to care for herself or himself, she is rendering a *directly* socially useful service. If she failed to render this care, the state would have to pick up the cost, which would be higher.

It would therefore seem desirable to recognize that this particular housewife[70] does work that is useful for society by providing her with a modest care allowance. Even though it is mostly symbolic in monetary value, it might be a very potent symbol of recognition. It would reallocate money from childless households to households with children,[71] which is what should happen if we want to reduce and eventually eliminate poverty among children. By itself it would not achieve this, but it would move us in the right direction without requiring new funds.

FAMILY STATUS FOR THE PURPOSE OF EMPLOYMENT BENEFITS

Another category of benefits are those related to employment.[72] Under the social responsibility model of the family, familial relationships are recognized on the basis of the existence of actual relations, rather than on the basis of pre-given designations. John, who supported six people, only two of whom were recognized as family (his parents), was concerned about the lack of social recognition for his ongoing relationships with his other dependants.

One benefit is bereavement leave in the case of the death of a family member. This issue came to prominence in the case of *Mossop* v. *DSS*, in which a member of a gay couple was denied bereavement leave when the father of his long-term lover died. If the father of a heterosexual employee's spouse had died, he or she would have received bereavement leave. The case was eventually lost on the ground that Parliament had not intended 'family status' to include gay and lesbian partners. One commentator on the case, who was involved in writing an intervenor's factum, raises some trenchant questions around this issue:

> Why, many of us wondered during the construction of the factum, use the category of 'family' at all? Should I not receive paid leave to attend, say, Elvis Presley's funeral, I asked at one point, if his death means more to me than the death of someone whom others would regard as a member of my 'family'? Would my unrequited regard for Elvis make him a member of my family? It may be true that people take leave more often to mourn the death of those others regard as closest to them, but was the determination of who 'counted most,' in this way, not very subjective? The example was not meant to be funny; it raised a serious issue …
>
> The factum's response to the 'Elvis Presley problem' as the concern about limits came to be known, is that the definition of family need not be meaningless or arbitrary, but should be linked to the purpose of the legislation, or the benefit at issue. For example, the purpose of bereavement leave is to acknowledge that individuals need to mourn the loss of those close to them, or support others who must mourn … The crux of the argument is that a definition of family in the context of employment benefits ought not to be limited to those whom the state, or an employer recognizes as a family member but expanded to include people the employee cares about, respects, depends upon, or with whom he or she shares a special relationship … Two remedies could solve this problem: the employer could limit the number of days of bereavement leave for all employees, to be used at their discretion, avoiding entirely the need to define family. Or, if the employer were wed to the idea of bereavement leave only for a category of people known as 'family members,' the employer could permit employees to supply a list of those they regarded as family, honouring the subjectivity of the definition.[73]

This seems like a very sensible proposal that could be implemented immediately. It does not cost the government any money, and the cost to employers would be minimal or non-existent; if people are distressed, their work performance is likely to suffer, so allowing bereavement leave makes sense for both the employee and the employer. The employee can deal with his or her distress or that of a close family member, and return to work with the issue more resolved than it would have been had there been no time off at all.

PARENTAL LEAVE

Canada lags far behind the Scandinavian countries with respect to providing parental leave. Sweden has had a parental leave scheme since 1974 that has been upgraded periodically. By 1989, parents were jointly entitled to twelve months' leave under an insurance system that provided 90 per cent replacement of earnings, plus an additional three months at a relatively low flat-rate level, plus ninety days' child sick leave. This leave is available to both mothers and fathers, and may be divided according to their preferences.[74] In the beginning, Swedish fathers were slow to take the leave (in 1974, only 3 per cent of eligible fathers took the leave). However, in 1989, 44 per cent did so.[75] Fathers who have taken such a leave are more likely to share equally in the responsibility for child care, as compared to fathers who have not taken such a leave.[76] While such a policy is admirable, it is important to note that it is only one factor in reconciling unpaid family work and paid work,[77] and that many women (and more men) do not benefit from them.[78] What is also needed is to 'move negotiations around parental leave from the realm of individual decision-making, based on what is best at the time for the family or for individual family members, to a more broadly based consideration of organizational structures, labour justice, community action, and the interconnection between employment and family spheres.'[79]

CONCLUSION

The intent of this chapter was not to provide a brand-new and comprehensive set of policies for families but to examine whether the social responsibility model leads to policies that differ from those derived from the individual responsibility model, and to see whether such policies can be implemented on a piecemeal basis, since it would be politically and administratively impossible to reform everything at once. The answer to both questions is yes. However, *should* we move towards such a model? I would argue that it is essential that we do so.

Old family structures have fractured, and no amount of nostalgic wishing is going to change this fact. Therefore, we need to devise policies that will recognize facts as they are and not increase problems for families that are already under great stress. Beyond this, we desperately need policies that recognize the socially important work performed within families and that support those who do most of this work: women (and of course all men who do the same). The transformation of formerly rigid structures need not be a bad thing, but if nothing replaces them, we will be in trouble—and so far, we have only seen the beginning of it. At present, governments everywhere are backing away from supporting individuals within families. The opposite is needed. We need to recognize the vital importance—in every sense of the word!—of the work carried out within families and, to the degree that it is socially useful, give it social support.

APPENDIX 1

Excerpts Concerning Family Relationships from the Canadian Federal Tax Guides, 1970-1994

The purpose of these excerpts is to demonstrate the shifting definitions of dependency/interdependency between spouses, children, and other dependants over time. Changes are therefore only defined as such in terms of eligibility criteria, not changes in terms of amounts of money and time periods (both tend to shift each year). Further, slight changes that do not substantially affect eligibility criteria have been ignored.

All citations refer to the federal tax guides for the years quoted. The tax guides were from different provinces, however, as found in the National Archives. All emphases are in the originals.

1970

12. Other Deductions: '... claiming a deduction for Canada Pension Plan contributions you made in respect of a personal employee such as a housekeeper or a gardener, or for alimony or separation allowance you paid' (p. 6).

18. Married or Equivalent Deduction:

A person who is married for any part of the year may claim married exemption for the full year, subject to the provisions regarding income received by his spouse. Thus, a man who married in December or a man whose wife died in January may be able to claim married exemption as though he were married for the full year.

... there are certain circumstances in which an unmarried person may claim the equivalent to married exemption (p. 9).

19. Other Exemptions: Wholly Dependent Children:

... a child includes a son, daughter, or grandchild, and certain nieces and nephews. In the case of a niece or nephew, a claim is allowable only if in 1970 either (a) you had complete custody and control of the child, or (b) the child was resident in Canada and also the mother was a widow or was separated or divorced and not receiving alimony or a similar allowance for the child's maintenance, or the father was mentally or physically infirm (p. 10).

1971

12. Other Deductions Include: Substantially unchanged.

18. Married or Equivalent Deduction: Substantially unchanged.

19. Other Exemptions: Wholly Dependent Children: Substantially unchanged.

Other Dependants: 'A claim may be made ... for the support of a person on whom you were wholly dependent when you were a child' (p. 10).

1972

23. Other Income: Includes 'alimony or separation allowance' (p. 12).

31. Child-Care Expenses:

> The child care expenses ... can only be those incurred to permit the mother, or in some cases the father, to work. Babysitting expenses for other purposes are not eligible. A father who was separated must have a written agreement of separation. He becomes eligible to claim child care expenses the date the agreement is signed (p. 16).

32D. Alimony or Separation Allowance Paid: Show the name and address of the person to whom it was paid' (unchanged) (p. 17).

36. Married Exemption: In essence unchanged, but it continues: 'The spouse for whom an exemption is being claimed, however, must report all income received throughout the year on his or her own tax return' (p. 17).

37. Equivalent-to-Married Exemption: May be claimed 'for a dependant living with you and may be affected by the dependant's "net income"'. (p. 17)

38. Children and Other Dependants: Essentially unchanged for nieces and nephews. Also unchanged for *Other Dependants* (p. 18).

1973

30. Child-Care Expenses: Unchanged (p. 17).

31E. Alimony or Separation Allowance Paid: Substantially unchanged (p. 18).

34. Married Exemption: Unchanged (p. 18).

35. Equivalent-to-Married Exemption: Substantially unchanged (p. 18).

36. Children and Other Dependants: Eligibility for nieces, nephews, and other dependants is substantially unchanged (p. 19).

1974

7. Taxable Family Allowance Payments:

Family Allowance payments must be included in the income of the person who claims a personal exemption for the child in respect of whom the allowance was paid. If neither parent claims a child, the person to whom the cheque is made out must report the payments as income.

In the event both parents must report a portion of the total benefits, a letter reconciling the total benefits must be attached (p. 7).

18. Other Income: Includes 'alimony or separation allowance' (p. 10).

33. Child-Care Expenses: Substantially unchanged, but with the following addition: 'Payments made to your estranged spouse should not be claimed ...' (p. 15).

34E. Alimony and Separation Allowance Paid: Unchanged from 1973 (p. 16).

43. Married Exemption: 'A person who is not legally married is not entitled to a deduction for married exemption or the equivalent to married exemption for a person to whom he is not related.' The rest is substantially unchanged (p. 17).

44. Equivalent-to-Married Exemption: Unchanged. '... there are some circumstances under which a single, divorced, separated or widowed person may claim this exemption' (p. 17).

45. Children and Other Dependants: Nieces and nephews unchanged (p. 17). Other dependants substantially unchanged (p. 18).

1975:

7. Taxable Family Allowance Payments: Substantially unchanged (p. 8).

18. Other Income: Unchanged.

33. Child-Care Expenses: Substantially unchanged, except for addition: 'Alimony or separation payments paid to your estranged spouse should not be claimed [for this purpose]' (p. 17).

34E. Alimony or Separation Allowance Paid: The beginning is unchanged, but there is the following addition: 'Alimony or separation payments to a third party on behalf of or for the benefit of your estranged spouse or children of the marriage in the custody of your estranged spouse also qualify as a deduction ...

For example, if you made rental payments on behalf of your estranged spouse pursuant to your written separation agreement ...' (p. 18).

38. Married Exemption: Substantially unchanged (p. 19).

39. Equivalent-to-Married Exemption: Substantially unchanged (p. 19).

40. Children and Other Dependants: Exemption for wholly dependent children is essentially unchanged. Nieces and nephews substantially unchanged.

1976

7. Taxable Family Allowance Payments: Substantially unchanged (p. 7–8).

32. Child-Care Expenses: 'The child care expenses claimed ... can only be those incurred to permit the mother, or in some cases the father, to work, to undertake an occupational training course if an adult training allowance was paid, or to carry out research if a grant was paid. Babysitting expenses for other purposes such as those paid in order to attend school or university will not normally qualify.' The rest is substantially unchanged (p. 16).

33E. Alimony or Separation Allowance Paid: Substantially unchanged (p. 17).

37. Married Exemption: Essentially unchanged, but with the following addition: 'Thus you may not claim a married exemption for a common-law spouse' (p. 18).

38. Equivalent-to-Married Exemption: Essentially unchanged, but with the addition: 'You may not claim this exemption for a common-law spouse' (p. 18).

39. Children and Other Dependants: Substantially unchanged.
Nieces and Nephews: Substantially unchanged.
Other Dependants: 'A claim ... may be made ... for the support of a person who supported you when you were a child. A deduction from income may be made for the support of your dependants who did not reside in Canada provided proof of support is submitted ...' (p. 19).

1977

7. Taxable Family Allowance Payments: Substantially unchanged (p. 11).

17. Other Income: Includes alimony or separation allowance (p. 19).

26. Child-Care Expenses: Substantially unchanged (p. 22).

27E. Alimony or Separation Allowance Paid: Substantially unchanged (p. 23).

31. Married Exemption: Substantially unchanged (p. 24).

32. Equivalent-to-Married Exemption: Unchanged (p. 24).

33. Children and Other Dependants: Substantially unchanged.
Nieces and Nephews: Unchanged.
Other Dependants: Unchanged (p. 25).

1978

17A. Alimony or Separation Allowance: 'If you were divorced or separated by written agreement, periodic payments received from your estranged spouse must be reported' (p. 6).

28E. Alimony or Separation Allowance Paid: Substantially unchanged (p. 10).

32. Married Exemption: Substantially unchanged (p. 11).

33. Equivalent-to-Married Exemption: Unchanged (p. 11).

34. Children and Other Dependants: Substantially unchanged (p. 11).

1979

17A. Alimony or Separation Allowance: Unchanged (p. 7).

26. Child-Care Expenses: Substantially unchanged (p. 9.

28. Alimony or Separation Allowance Paid: Essentially unchanged (p. 10).

32. Married Exemption: Substantially unchanged (p. 11).

33. Equivalent-to-Married Exemption: Unchanged (p. 11).

34. Children and Other Dependants: Substantially unchanged for children, nieces, nephews, other dependants, and non-resident dependants (p. 11).

57. Child Tax Credit: 'This credit is $218 per eligible child minus 5% of the amount of family income over $19,620. This credit may only be claimed by the person, usually the mother, who was entitled to receive the Family Allowance for an eligible child ... The other parent may claim a personal exemption for the child ...' (p. 15).

1980

26. Child-Care Expenses: Substantially unchanged (p. 8).

28E. Alimony or Separation Allowance Paid: Substantially unchanged (p. 10).

32. Married Exemption: Substantially unchanged (p. 11).

33. Equivalent-to-Married Exemption: Unchanged (p. 11).

34. Children and Other Dependants: Division changed to under 18, 18 or over, over 21.
Nieces and Nephews and Other Dependants: Substantially unchanged, although reworded: 'the word "parent" ... includes someone who supported you when you were a child' (p. 11).

57. Child Tax Credit:

Only the person who is entitled to receive Family Allowances for an eligible child may claim this credit. Usually the mother receives Family Allowances and claims the credit. In some cases the father may receive the Family Allowance and claim the credit. This might occur through death, divorce, etc.

The other parent, usually the father, may claim a personal exemption for the child ... If so, that parent must report the Family Allowances paid for the child ... Thus the mother may claim the child tax credit and the father may claim the child for a personal exemption (p. 15).

1981

17A. Alimony or Separation Allowance: Substantially unchanged (p. 7).

Child-Care Expenses: Unchanged (p. 9).

32. Married Exemption: Unchanged (p. 11).

33. Equivalent-to-Married Exemption: Unchanged (p. 11).

34. Children and Other Dependants: Substantially unchanged (p. 14).

57. Child Tax Credit: Substantially unchanged (p. 15).

1982

17A. Alimony or Separation Allowance: 'If you were divorced or separated, report periodic payments received from your estranged spouse under a written agreement. Periodic maintenance payments received from a former common-law spouse under court order must also be reported under certain circumstances ...' (p. 5).

26. Child-Care Expenses: Substantially unchanged (p. 8).

28D. Alimony or Separation Allowance Paid: Beginning unchanged, but: 'The former comments will also apply to payments made to a former common-law spouse ... ' (p. 9).

32. Married Exemption: Unchanged! 'You may not claim the married or equivalent to married exemption for a common-law spouse' (p. 10).

33. Equivalent-to-Married Exemption: Unchanged (p. 10).

34. Children and Other Dependants: Substantially unchanged (p. 10).

35. Non-resident Dependants:

Beginning in 1982, claims for non-resident dependants are subject to new restrictions. You may only claim your spouse and children living outside Canada as non-resident dependants provided that they are dependent upon you for their support. Claims for any other relatives are no longer available ...

Payments you intend as support do not necessarily entitle you to an exemption. Your spouse and/or children must actually be dependent on you for support. Those with enough income or assistance from other sources outside Canada for a reasonable standard of living in their own country are not considered dependent on a Canadian taxpayer for support.

A child must wholly depend on you for support ... (p. 10).

59. Child Tax Credit: Substantially unchanged (pp. 14–15).

1983

18A. Alimony or Separation Allowance: Substantially unchanged (p. 6).

37. Child-Care Expenses:

If, at the end of 1983, you were not residing with a supporting person, and did not before March 1, 1984, resume residing with a supporting person from whom you separated during 1983 ... you may claim child care expenses for the entire year, without taking anyone else's income into account.

If a supporting person resided with you at the end of 1983, or if a supporting person from whom you separated in 1983 resumed residing with you before March 1, 1984, both of you must estimate your net income for the year.... *In most cases, whichever of you has the lower net income must claim the child care expenses.*

... If you married in the year, include child care expenses paid by your spouse prior to the date of marriage. If you otherwise commenced residing with an individual who had children, include all payments made at any time in the year for children of whom you are the parent, or for whom you are claiming a personal exemption.

There are some specific exceptions to the rule that you can claim child care expenses only if your net income was lower than the supporting person's ... you were separated or the supporting person was in full-time attendance at a designated educational institution, infirm, or in an institution ...

Payments to certain individuals ... may not be claimed as child care expenses. For the purpose of this claim a 'relative' could be a child (including an adopted child), brother, or sister of yourself or of your spouse ... (p. 10).

42. Married Exemption: Substantially unchanged (p. 12).

44. Additional Personal Exemptions: Equivalent-to-Married Exemption: Substantially unchanged (p. 13).
Nieces and Nephews: Substantially unchanged.
Other Dependants: Substantially unchanged (p. 13).

78. Child Tax Credit: Substantially unchanged, except:

Other supporting person—in 1983, the income of a person other than your spouse may have to be added to yours when calculating your claim. If at the end of the year you were living with, but not married to the other parent of an eligible child, the other parent's income must be entered ... This applies even if the other parent is not claiming a personal exemption for the child. In addition, the income of any person (other than yourself or your spouse) who is claiming a personal exemption for an eligible child must be included ... whether that person was living with you or not ... (p. 17).

1984

130A. Alimony or Separation Allowance:

If you were divorced or separated, report periodic payments received from your former or estranged spouse under a decree, order, judgement or written agreement.

For agreements made after 1983, certain payments that are deemed to be an allowance payable on a periodic basis and payments made (and acknowledged in the agreement) before the agreement, decree, order or judgement is signed but not before the beginning of the previous calendar year are income in the hands of the recipient.

For payments to qualify as 'deemed periodic payments', the following conditions must be met:

1. The expense was incurred at the time when the payor and the taxpayer were separated and living apart.
2. The expense was incurred for the maintenance of a child in the custody of the recipient and the child was not residing with, visiting or otherwise in charge of the payor at the time the expense was incurred.
3. The court order or written agreement provides that these payments will be treated as taxable income of the recipient.

Amounts paid for tangible property are never considered to be 'deemed periodic payments' except (a) outlays for the purchase of improvement of the recipient's residence that do not exceed in the year 20% of the original cost of such property or (b) outlays for tangible property on account of a medical or educational expense (p. 7).

214. Child-Care Expenses: Substantially unchanged (p. 10).

222D. Alimony or Separation Allowance Paid: No substantial change.

Non-resident Dependants: Substantially unchanged (p. 13).

230. Married Exemption: No substantial change (p. 13).

231. Exemption for Wholly Dependent Children: Nieces, Nephews and Grandchildren: 'A claim for a wholly dependent niece or nephew living in Canada or a grandchild is allowed if they qualify as wholly dependent children' (p. 13).

233. Equivalent-to-Married Exemption: No change (p. 13).

450. Child Tax Credit: No substantial change (p. 18).

1985

130A. Alimony or Separation Allowance: No substantial change.

214. Child-Care Expenses:

'Child care expenses' are amounts for child care services to enable you, or a 'supporting person' (if the child resided with you or this supporting person at the time the expense was incurred) to earn income from employment, self-employment, training courses, research or similar work. Child care expenses *do not* include payments made during a period when either you or a 'supporting person' were unemployed …

If another individual does fall within the definition of 'supporting person', both you and this individual must calculate your net income for the year … Generally, whoever has the lower net income must claim the child care expenses (p. 10). [Otherwise substantially unchanged.]

222D. Alimony or Separation Allowance Paid: No substantial change (p. 11).

Non-resident Dependants: No substantial change (p. 12).

230. Married Exemption: No substantial change (p. 13).

231. Exemption for Dependent Children: 'Where two or more individuals are making a claim for the same dependant, it is their responsibility to decide what portion of the *maximum allowable deduction* each will claim. Any reasonable allocation will be accepted provided the total of all claims in respect of that dependant *does not* exceed the *maximum allowable deduction* for the year …' (p. 13).

233. Equivalent-to-Married Exemption: Substantially unchanged (p. 13).

450. Child Tax Credit: Substantially unchanged (p. 18).

1986

128. Alimony or Separation Allowance Income: First part substantially unchanged, but:

A maintenance payment received as a result of the breakdown of a common-law relationship is included in your income (and deductible by the payor …) only

(a) in respect of an order, made after December 11, 1979, or made earlier if both parties agree in writing, in accordance with the Family Law Reform Act of the Province of Ontario …

(b) the amount is paid as an allowance for the maintenance of you and/or your children,

(c) the payments are part of a series payable on a periodic basis … (p. 11).

214. Child-Care Expenses: Some modification, in particular:

Common-law situations—A common-law spouse is a 'supporting

person' where the individual lived in the common-law relationship at any time in 1986 and at any time in the first 60 days of 1987 if, in addition, the common-law spouse is

(a) the parent of the child, or
(b) claiming the child as a dependant ... (p. 14).

220. Alimony or Separation Allowance Paid: Several elaborations, and: 'The maintenance payments for a common-law spouse and/or children of the relationship are deductible only if the payments are made pursuant to an order under the Family Law Reform Act of Ontario and meet additional criteria ...' (p. 15).

Non-resident Dependants: No substantial change (p. 17).

230. Married Exemption: No substantial change.

231. Exemption for Dependent Children: No substantial change (pp. 17–18).

233. Equivalent-to-Married Exemption: No substantial change (p. 18).

450. Child Tax Credit: No substantial change (p. 26) Note under:

Other supporting person—If at the end of the year you were living with (but not married to) the other parent of an eligible child, the other parent is a supporting person. This applies even if the other parent is not claiming a personal exemption for the child. In addition, any person (other than yourself or your spouse) who is claiming a personal exemption for an eligible child is a supporting person, whether or not that person was living with you (p.26).

1987

128. Alimony or Separation Allowance Income: Great change in style, but not in substance. First time that descriptive examples are used to illustrate principles.

Example: Sandra and Mark separated in March 1987 and were separated for the remainder of 1987. They wrote their own separation agreement. Sandra has custody of their two children and Mark is paying her $500 a month for their maintenance. Because Sandra and Mark have a written separation agreement, the payments must be included in Sandra's income and are deductible by Mark.

Example: Ron and Jane separated in May 1986, and Jane paid Ron maintenance of $250 a month. They signed their separation agreement in February 1988. The agreement acknowledges the payments that were made to Ron since May 1986. However, Ron only has to report the payments received in 1987 and subsequent years. The payments he received from May to December 1986 do not have to be reported as income and are not deductible by Jane (p. 12).

'A maintenance payment received as a result of the breakdown of a common-law relationship is included in your income (and deductible by the payer ...)' under parallel conditions as for legal couples (p. 12).

214. Child-Care Expenses: A lot of textual changes, use of personal examples, but no substantive changes (p. 16).

Child care expense payments—Child care expense payments are those paid to any resident of Canada, except those paid to

• the mother or father of the child;
• a supporting person of the child;
• a person for whom either you, or a supporting person of the child, claimed a personal exemption;
• a person under 21 who is related to you or your spouse. For this purpose, a 'related person' could be a child (including an adopted child), brother, or sister of you or your spouse, but does not include a niece or nephew.

Example: Lynn and Paul married and have an eight-year-old daughter. They paid Lynn's 19-year-old sister to care for their daughter while they were at work. Neither Lynn nor Paul may claim these payments as child care expenses because the money was paid to a related person who is under 21.

Note: Child care expenses do not include payments made during a period when either you or a supporting person were unemployed.

Marriage in 1987: If you married in 1987, include child care expenses paid by you and your spouse for the entire year (including expenses prior to the date of marriage).

Example: In 1987, Janet, a widow with two children under 14 years of age, married Bob. He has a three-year-old son. Before their marriage, Janet paid $1,200 for child care for her children, and Bob paid $800 for child care for his son. During the rest of the year, they paid a total of $1,800. Janet's net income for the year was $30,000 and Bob's was $22,000. Since Bob has the lower net income, only he may claim any allowable child care expenses for 1987 ...

Common-law in 1987: If you lived common-law with an individual who had a child, include all payments made at any time in the year for children of whom you are the parent, or for whom you are claiming a personal exemption.

Example: Rick and Diane are living common-law. Three children under 14 years of age are living with them. Diane's net income for the year is higher than Rick's. Her *earned* income is $21,000 while Rick's is $15,000. Diane is the mother of the three children and she claims them as dependants. They paid $1,500 child care expenses for each child.

• If Rick is the father of the children, only he may claim the allowable child care expenses for the year because they are his eligible children and he has the lower net income ...

• If Rick is *not* the father of the children, Diane is entitled to claim any allowable child care expenses for the year because Rick is not a 'supporting person' as defined earlier, and the children are not his eligible children for purposes of claiming the child care deduction ...

• If Rick is the father of one child, only he may claim the child care expense deduction for that child while Diane may claim the deduction for the other two children. Rick includes $1,500 child care payments ... and Diane includes $3,000 ... child care payments ...

Note: If Rick claims any of the children as dependants on his tax return, whether or not he is the father, Rick is a 'supporting person' of the child claimed as a dependant. Therefore, only Rick may claim the $1,500 child care expenses for that child since he has the lower net income.

Limitations on Amounts That May Be Claimed as a Deduction:

• Limitation 'B'—Your claim for child care expenses is limited to 2/3 of your 'earned income'... .
• Limitation 'C'—You may claim up to $2,000 for each child to a maximum of $8,000... .
• Limitation 'D'—Only complete this ... if *your net income is higher* than the other supporting person's net income.

Example: Bill and Judy are married and have two children under 14. Both Bill and Judy work full time and leave the children with a baby-sitter. Judy was in the hospital for six weeks. Their child care expenses were $130 a week for 49 weeks. Bill and Judy were on vacation for the other three weeks in 1987. Bill's net income is higher than Judy's. His earned income was $24,000 and Judy's was $18,000.

Bill claims for the six weeks that Judy was in the hospital, and Judy for the rest of the time (p. 17).

220. Alimony or Separation Allowance Paid: Substantially unchanged (p. 19).

220C. Common-law Relationships: Substantially unchanged (p. 19).

Personal Exemptions: Common-law Situations: 'If you are living common-law and your common-law spouse's *children* depend on you for support, you may claim a personal exemption for them provided they qualify as dependants. Personal exemptions may not be claimed for a common-law spouse' (p. 21).

Non-resident Dependants: Substantially unchanged (p. 22).

230. Married Exemption: Substantially unchanged (p. 22).

231. Exemption for Dependent Children: A lot of textual changes, but substantially unchanged (p. 22).

450. Child Tax Credit: Many textual changes, but substantially unchanged (p. 33).

1988

118. Taxable Family Allowance Payments:

If you were *married*, the spouse with the higher net income for the year … must report the family allowance received by you or your spouse.

If you were *separated* for a period of *less than 90 days* starting in 1988, the spouse with the higher net income for the year … must report the family allowance received by you or your spouse.

Example: Janet and Rob separated on June 5 but got back together in August of the same year. Since they were not separated for a period of 90 days or more starting in the year, Rob must report the family allowance for the year because his net income for the year is higher than Janet's net income.

If you are *separated* for a period of *90 days or more* starting in 1988,

• the family allowance payment for *all months at the end of which you and your spouse were separated* must be reported by the recipient, and
• the family allowance payments for *each other month* must be reported by the spouse with the higher net income for the year.

Example: Tony and Maria separated in September and did not get back together in 1988. As they were separated for a period of 90 days or more starting in 1988, Maria must report the family allowance she received for September to the end of the year. Tony must report the family allowance payments for January to August as his net income for the year was higher than Maria's net income.

If you claim the 'equivalent-to-married amount' for a dependant, you must report the family allowance payments for the whole year in respect of that dependant, even if you did not receive the payments.

Example: Jane and Derek are living common-law. Derek supports Jane and her two children and Jane received the family allowance. Since Derek claims the equivalent-to-married amount for one of the children, he must report the family allowance Jane received for that child. Jane would report the family allowance for the other child and claim the amounts for dependent children for that child.

In all other situations, you must report the family allowance you received (p. 8).

128. Alimony or Separation Allowance Income: Great textual changes (pp. 12–14) and in addition the following change:

As a result of a recent court decision, payments made to you by your estranged spouse, where you had no discretion as to the use of the payment, may have to be included in your income and may be deductible by the payer depending on the date of your order or agreement.

Example: René received a monthly maintenance allowance plus an additional $200 per month. His agreement stated that he must use the additional $200 to pay the property taxes on his dwelling. In this case, the $200 is considered to be an allowance paid to him for a specific purpose. Even though René has no discretion as to the use of the payment, he may have to include the amount in his income depending on the date of his order or agreement ...

(C) Common-law Relationships: If you received maintenance payments as a result of the breakdown of your common-law relationship, you are only required to include them in your income and the payer may *only* deduct the payments if

• the amounts are paid as an allowance for your maintenance and/or the maintenance of your children,
• you and the payer were living apart when the payments were made and throughout the remainder of the year,

• the payments were an allowance payable on a periodic basis, *and* [were in accordance with some law] … *and* the payer is of the opposite sex *and* is the natural parent of your child *or* lived with you in a conjugal relationship before the date of the order (pp. 13–14).

214. Child-Care Expenses: Greatly revised text, but otherwise substantially the same (p. 17).

220. Alimony or Separation Allowance Paid: Substantially unchanged (p. 19).

Non-resident Dependants: Substantially unchanged (p. 24).

303. Married Amount: Substantially unchanged (p. 25).

304. Amounts for Dependent Children: Substantially unchanged (p. 250).

305. Additional Personal Amounts: Equivalent-to-Married Amount:

You may claim this amount if you were single, divorced, separated or widowed or you were living common-law *and* you supported a relative who

• was resident in Canada (except in the case of your child),
• lived with you in 1988 in a self-contained domestic establishment that you maintained,
• was related to you by blood, marriage or adoption, and
• was born in 1970 or later and was under 18 when you were single, divorced, separated, widowed, or living common-law, *or*
• was born before 1970 and was mentally or physically infirm or was your parent or grandparent.

Example: George lives common-law with Darlene and their 8-year-old son. George supports them both. Although George may not claim the equivalent-to-married amount for Darlene, he would be entitled to claim the equivalent-to-married amount for their son.

… only one claim for the equivalent-to-married amount is allowable for each dwelling.

Example: Nancy and Ken are living common-law and have four children. Ken claims the equivalent-to-married amount for one of the children and he reports all the family allowance received for that child. Nancy may only claim the 'amounts for dependent children' for the other three children and she must report the rest of the family allowance received … (p. 27).

Child Tax Credit: No substantial change (p. 28–9).

1989

118. Family Allowance Payments: No substantial change (p. 9).

128. Alimony or Separation Allowance Income: No substantial change (p. 13–14).

214. Child-Care Expenses: No substantial change (pp. 17–18).

215. Attendant Care Expenses: You are entitled under certain conditions to claim expenses paid for attendant care if 'the expenses were paid to a person 18 years old or older who is not related to you …' (p. 18).

220. Alimony or Separation Allowance Paid: Substantially unchanged (p. 19–20).

Non-resident Dependants: Substantially unchanged (p. 26).

303. Married Amount: Substantially unchanged (p. 26).

304. Amounts for Dependent Children: Substantially unchanged (p. 26).

305. Equivalent-to-Married Amount: Substantially unchanged (p. 27).

444. Child Tax Credit: Substantially unchanged (p. 39).

1990

118. Family Allowance Payments: No substantial change (p. 10).

128. Alimony or Separation Allowance Income: No substantial changes.

214. Child-Care Expenses: No substantial change (p. 19).

215. Attendant Care Expenses: No substantive change (pp. 19–20).

220. Alimony or Separation Allowance Paid: No substantial change (p. 21).

303. Married Amount: Substantially unchanged (p. 27).

304. Amounts for Dependent Children: Substantially unchanged (p. 27).

305. Equivalent-to-Married Amount: Substantially unchanged (p. 29).

444. Child Tax Credit: Substantially unchanged (p. 40).

1991

118. Family Allowance Payments: Substantially unchanged.

128. Alimony or Separation Allowance Income: Basically unchanged (pp. 15–17).

214. Child-Care Expenses: Substantially unchanged (p. 21).

215. Attendant Care Expenses: Substantially unchanged (pp. 21–2).

220. Alimony or Separation Allowance Paid: Substantially unchanged (p. 23).

Non-resident Dependants: Not substantially changed (p. 28).

303. Married Amount: Not substantially changed (p. 29).

304. Amounts for Dependent Children: Substantially unchanged (p. 29–30).

305. Equivalent-to-Married Amount: Substantially unchanged (p. 30).

444. Child Tax Credit: Change in wording, but substantially unchanged (p. 41).

1992

118. Family Allowance Payments: Substantially unchanged (p. 12).

128. Alimony or Separation Allowance Income: Basically unchanged (pp. 16–18).

214. Child-Care Expenses: No longer mentions reasons for which child care was incurred. Simply states: 'You can claim child care expenses for a child born in 1978 or later that is your child, your spouse's child or a child for whom you are claiming a personal amount ... You can also claim these expenses for a child born before 1978 if the child was a dependent on you or your spouse and had a mental or physical infirmity or impairment ...' (p. 22).

215. Attendant Care Expenses: No substantial change (p. 29).

220. Alimony or Separation Allowance Paid: Substantially unchanged (p. 24).

Non-resident Dependants: No substantial change (p. 29).

303. Married Amount: Substantially unchanged (p. 29).

304. Amounts for Dependent Children: Substantially unchanged (p. 30).

305. Equivalent-to-Married Amount: Basically unchanged (p. 31).

444. Child Tax Credit: Basically unchanged (p. 41).

1993

128. Alimony or Maintenance Income: Basically unchanged (p. 16).

214. Child-Care Expenses: Back to the previously spelled out restrictions:

You may be entitled to claim child care expenses if you or your spouse paid someone to look after your children so that you or your spouse could:

- earn income from employment or self-employment;
- take an occupational training course … ; or
- carry on research or similar work for which a grant is received … (p. 20).

215. Attendant Care Expenses: No substantial change (p. 20–1).

220. Alimony or Maintenance Paid: Substantially unchanged (p. 21).

303. Spousal Amount: 'If you are married or have a common-law spouse …, you may be able to claim part or all of the … spousal amount' (p. 26).

305. Equivalent-to-Spouse Amount: Common-law dropped from the eligibility criteria.

You may be able to claim all or part of the … equivalent-to-spouse amount if, at any time in the year, you were single, divorced, separated, or widowed and, at that time, you supported a relative who was:

- residing in Canada (except your child);
- living with you in a home that you maintained;
- related to you by blood, marriage, or adoption; *and*
- under 18 … (p. 26).

306. Additional Personal Amounts:

You can claim an amount for your or your spouse's dependent child or grandchild if that child or grandchild was born in 1975 or earlier and is mentally or physically infirm.

You can also claim an amount for a person living in Canada at any time in the year who meets *all* of the following conditions. The person must have been:

- dependent on you, or on you and others;
- your or your spouse's parent, grandparent, brother, sister, aunt, uncle, niece, or nephew;
- born in 1975 or earlier; and
- mentally or physically infirm ...

Note: A parent includes someone on whom you were completely dependent and who had custody and control of you while you were under 19 years of age (p. 27).

1994

128. Alimony or Maintenance Income: No substantial changes.

214. Child-Care Expenses: No substantial changes (p. 19).

215. Attendant Care Expenses: No substantial change (p. 20).

220. Alimony or Maintenance Paid: No substantial changes (p. 20).

303. Spousal Amount: No substantial changes. (pp. 25–6) Spouse is defined as follows:

Spouse: The term spouse used throughout this guide applies to a legally married spouse and a common-law spouse. A common-law spouse is a person of the opposite sex who, at that particular time, is living with you in a common-law relationship, and

- is the natural or adoptive parent (legal or in fact) of your child; or
- had been living with you in such a relationship for at least 12 continuous months, or had previously lived with you in such a relationship for at least 12 continuous months (when you calculate the 12 continuous months, include any period of separation of less than 90 days).

Once either of these two situations applies, we consider you to have a common-law spouse, except for any period that you were separated for 90 days or more because of a breakdown in the relationship.

Example 1: on May 1, 1991, Susan and Serge, who have no children, began to live together in a common-law relationship. On July 15, 1992, they separated because of a breakdown in their relationship. On February 29, 1994, they began to live together again. We consider Susan and Serge to be spouses as of February 27, 1994, the date they reconciled. This is because they once lived together in a common-law relationship for 12 continuous months.

Example 2: David and Renata, who have no children, have been living together in a common-law relationship since April 13, 1993. However, for the months of July 1993 and October 1993 they lived apart because of a breakdown in their relationship. We consider David and Renata to be spouses as of April 13, 1994. When calculating the 12 continuous months requirement, they have to include the two months they lived apart because each period of separation was less than 90 days (p. 8).

305. Equivalent-to-Spouse Amount: No substantial changes (p. 26).

Demographic Trends

Table 1
Crude Divorce Rates, Selected Countries

Country	1968	1980	1990
Canada	0.55	2.58	2.94
US	2.93	5.22	4.70
UK	0.93	2.99	2.88
Germany (Fed. Republic)	1.03	1.56	1.94
Germany (Dem. Republic)	1.68	2.68	3.01[1]
France	0.73	1.71	1.86
Japan	0.87	1.21	1.27
Netherlands	0.64	1.82	1.90
Sweden	1.42	2.39	2.26

[1]For 1989.

Source: United Nations, *Demographic Yearbook* (New York: United Nations, 1971, 1983, 1992). This table has been constructed for me by Lionne Carley.

Table 2
Proportion of Births to Unmarried Women, Selected Countries

Country	1970	1980	1989
Canada	10%	13%	23%
US	11%	18%	27%
UK	8%	12%	26%
France	7%	11%	28%
Japan	1%	1%	1%

Source: M. Belle and K. McQuillan, 'Births Outside Marriage', *Canadian Social Trends* 33 (Summer 1994):14–17.

Table 3
Percentage Births to Unmarried Women, Canada

Year	Per cent Born to Married Women	Per cent Born to Unmarried Women
1974	94.1	6.0
1975	91.0	9.0
1976	89.8	10.2
1977	88.5	11.0
1978	88.4	11.6
1979	87.9	12.1
1980	87.0	13.0
1981	85.9	14.1
1982	84.5	15.5
1983	83.8	16.2
1984	83.2	16.8
1985	82.0	18.0
1986	81.1	18.9
1987	79.8	20.2
1988	78.3	21.7
1989	76.8	23.1
1990	75.6	24.4
1991	73.0	27.0

Note: The percentages have been computed by adding single, separated, divorced, and widowed women together as unmarried. 'Unknown' are left out of the computation.
    Percentages of more or less than 100 per cent are due to rounding.

Source: Computed from Statistics Canada, *Births 1991*, cat. 84-210 (Ottawa: Minister of Industry, Science and Technology, 1993a): Table 21, p. 35.

Table 4
Custody of Children Involved in Divorces, 1978–1990, Canada

Custody given to:							Number of
	Mother	Father	Joint	Other	N/A	Total	Divorces with Children
1978	78.7	15.6		0.3	5.4	100	59,436
1979	78.8	15.8		0.2	5.3	100	57,856
1980	78.2	16.0		0.2	5.5	100	59,600
1981	77.9	15.8		0.3	6.0	100	62,434
1982	77.1	15.6		0.2	9.1	100	65,441
1983	74.9	15.7		0.2	10.0	100	64,221
1984	74.3	15.5		0.2	11.8	100	60,063
1985	72.8	15.2		0.3	11.2	100	56,336
1986	71.9	15.3	1.2	0.4	4.0	100	60,450
1987	74.7	13.6	7.4	0.2	1.0	100	53,699
1988	75.8	12.9	10.1	0.3	0.4	100	50,249
1989	74.1	12.8	12.4	0.2	0.2	100	50,333
1990	73.2	12.3	14.1	0.2		100	48,525

Source: Statistics Canada, *A Portrait of Families in Canada* (Ottawa: Minister of Industry, Science and Technology, 1993b):17, Table 1.3.

Diagnostic Questions for Identifying Sexism in Research[1]

1. SEXIST TITLES

1.1 Does the title evoke the image of applicability to both sexes? If yes, is it applicable to both sexes?
1.2 Does the title contain a sexist concept?
1.3 Does it contain sexist language?
If the answer is 'yes' to any of the questions, either the title or the content need to be changed.

2. SEXIST LANGUAGE

2.1 Are any male or female terms used for generic purposes?
If yes, use sex-specific terms only for sex-specific purposes.
2.2 Are any generic terms employed when, in fact, the author is speaking only about one sex?
If yes, use generic terms only for generic purposes.
2.3 Are females and males in parallel situations described by non-parallel terms?
If yes, use parallel terms.
2.4 When both sexes are mentioned together in particular phrases, does one sex consistently precede the other?
If yes, alternate in some manner.
2.5 Are the two sexes consistently discussed in different grammatical modes?
If yes, identify the passive or active portion that is missing and incorporate to the degree possible.

3. SEXIST CONCEPTS

3.1 Is the ego constructed from only a male or female perspective?
If yes, change either concept or content.
3.2 Does the concept refer to a relational quality expressed from the viewpoint of one sex only?
If yes, express from the viewpoint of both sexes, either by creating a conceptual pair or a superordinate concept.
3.3 Does the concept demean one sex?
If yes, replace with a non-demeaning concept.

3.4 Is there a difference between the theoretical and the empirical referent of a concept?

If yes, match the theoretical and empirical referent.

3.5 Is the concept premised on an attribute that is present in both sexes but is operationally defined in such a manner that it will categorize females and males differently?

If yes, categorize females and males equally if they display equal attributes.

3.6 Does the concept refer, in a sex-linked manner, to a situation, trait, or behaviour that exists for both sexes?

If yes, change the concept so that it expresses human attributes in non-sex-specific terms.

3.7 Does a conceptual pair correspond largely to a sexual division in an unjustified value-laden manner?

If yes, reformulate so that equal value is assigned to male- and female-dominated attributes.

3.8 Is the concept premised on the notion that certain *human* behaviours, traits, or attributes are appropriate for one sex only?

If yes, change the concept so that it is descriptive, not prescriptive.

3.9 Does the concept attribute individual properties, attributes, or behaviours to families or households?

If yes, substitute concepts that identify individual properties, attributes, or behaviours as such.

4. SEXISM IN THE RESEARCH DESIGN

4.1 Is the frame of reference androcentric? Test by substituting 'woman' or 'girl' for generic terms such as 'individual', 'person', 'patient', 'child'.

If the result is nonsensical, explore the females' situation and incorporate, or revamp the study as pertaining to one sex only. The latter is not appropriate when the study deals with an issue that by necessity involves both sexes.

4.2 Is the frame of reference slightly gynocentric?[2]

If yes, give attention to the role of males.

4.3 Are men consistently treated as actors and women as acted upon?

If yes, explore the role of women as actors and of men as acted upon.

4.4 Is male behaviour taken as the norm and female behaviour as the deviation that needs to be explained?

If yes, either expand the framework by assessing male behaviour against female behaviour or establish a genuinely sex-unrelated behaviour as the norm. The latter is not feasible if the behaviour in question is strongly sex-differentiated.

4.5 In cases in which victims and perpetrators are involved, are women blamed—with or without justification? Are women or men perpetrators? Are perpetrators held personally responsible for their deeds? Is the role of male participants in the overall process adequately considered? Are overall structural factors adequately taken into account?

Perpetrators need to be held responsible for their actions, the role of males needs to be considered as carefully as that of the female participants, and overall structural factors need to be taken into account.

4.6 Does the phenomenon under consideration affect both sexes? If so, does the literature give adequate attention to the roles of both sexes? (In particular, in studies concerning family roles and reproduction, has the role of men been given adequate attention? In *all other* studies, has the role of women been given adequate attention?)

Include the excluded sex in your study design. However, where a field of study has largely excluded one sex, a one-sex study of the excluded sex may be highly appropriate. At issue is the overall balance of the collective research effort.

4.7 Are both sexes asked the same questions?

If not, ensure that they are.

4.8 Is the same research instrument used for both females and males? If not, is the use of a differential instrument justified by physical differences between the sexes?

If different instruments are used without compelling reason, develop an instrument that is applicable to both sexes; if different instruments are necessary, justify them in detail.

4.9 Does the research instrument divide the sexes into two discrete groups when, in fact, they have overlapping characteristics?

If yes, develop a new instrument that does not dichotomize overlapping distribution of traits.

4.10 Of the major variables examined in the study, are they equally relevant to women and men? Is there an imbalance of variables pertaining more to one sex than the other?

If so, correct imbalance by including variables that affect the underrepresented sex.

4.11 Is the sex of the relevant participants in the research process reported and controlled for?

If not, report and control where possible and necessary. Where not possible, potential distorting effects of the sex of the participants need to be acknowledged and discussed.

4.12 When dealing with family issues, is it possible that the event (attribute, traits, experience, behaviour) under consideration may be different for different family members?

If yes, then using the family as the smallest unit of analysis is inappropriate. Individual actors within the unit need to be identified and studied separately to observe potential different effects. This may involve a drastic revision of the research design.

4.13 Are explicit or implicit comparisons made between the sexes? If so, are the sex groups being compared equivalent on all those variables that are likely to influence the outcome under investigation?

If no, create comparable groups. Where this is impossible for practical reasons, carefully list and discuss the variables that differentiate the two groups.

5. SEXISM IN METHODS

5.1 Has the research instrument been validated on one sex only but is used on both sexes?

If so, use only for the sex on which it has been validated or validate for both sexes.

5.2 Is the sex composition of the sample adequately reported?

If not, do so.

5.3 Does the question posed use sexist language or concepts (see above)?

If so, replace with non-sexist language and concepts.

5.4 Does the question take one sex as the norm for the other, thus restricting the range of possible answers?

If so, reformulate the question to allow for the theoretically possible range.

5.5 Is the question implicitly or explicitly premised on the behaviours of one sex and therefore fails to ask equivalent things for the other sex?

If so, reformulate to probe for the existence of such behaviours in both sexes.

5.6 Does this particular method categorize males and females into discrete groups on the basis of attributes that can be found in both sexes?

Categorize non-discrete traits in non-discrete ways.

5.7 When opinions are asked of one sex about the other (including in indirect form, such as by using historical information), are they treated as opinions of one sex about the other rather than as fact?

If no, reinterpret other-sex opinions as statements of opinions and no more.

5.8 Are identical coding procedures used for females and males?

If no, make coding procedures identical.

6. SEXISM IN DATA INTERPRETATION

6.1 Are the implications of findings for both females and males explicitly considered?

If not, do so.

6.2 Are biases in the data collection process explicitly acknowledged and their implications discussed?

If not, do so.

6.3 Is there any justification for female subjugation or male dominance? Is any form of bodily mutilation, death, or other abrogation of human rights justified in the name of a supposedly higher value?

If yes, describe and analyse such practices, but under no circumstances excuse or justify them.

6.4 Is there a clear victim? If so, is the victim blamed for her (occasionally his) victimization?

If so, identify the circumstances (or individuals) that led to victim-blaming and eliminate the blame from the interpretation.

6.5 Is only one sex considered? If so, are conclusions drawn in general terms?

Make conclusions sex-specific where only one sex is considered, or change the research design and consider both sexes.

6.6 Are data collected on both sexes? If so, are they analysed by sex? Is the difference or lack thereof between the sexes considered?

If not, do so.

6.7 Does the particular situation or event under consideration have potentially different implications for the two sexes? Have these been explicitly considered and discussed?

If not, do so.

6.8 Are sex roles (or sex identities) seen as normatively appropriate?

If yes, acknowledge sex roles (and sex identities) as socially important and historically grown, but make it clear that they are neither necessary, natural, nor normatively desirable.

7. Sexism in Policy Evaluations and Recommendations

7.1 Does this policy affect both sexes? Is the position of the sexes comparable with respect to the important factors that inform and are governed by this policy? Is the effect of this policy positive for both sexes?

If the policy affects both sexes but has differential effects, it is biased. This does not necessarily mean it should be abandoned. If it is meant to right an old unfair situation, there may be reasons for maintaining it. Or if it is disadvantageous for one sex, but nevertheless highly desirable for other reasons (e.g., environmental considerations), it may be more appropriate to develop compensatory policies. If there is no justification for a biased policy, or if compensatory policies cannot be enacted, it should be re-evaluated in terms of its impact on both sexes.

7.2 Are the same circumstances evaluated differently on the basis of sex?

If so, re-evaluate so that the sexes are treated in the same manner.

7.3 Is there a division that corresponds largely to a division by sex and for which differential treatment is recommended?

Make the sexual division apparent and treat the sexes equally.

Notes

Introduction

[1]A healthy baby boy was born recently in France from an egg that was given a microinjection with a spermatid from the semen of a man previously considered sterile (*Toronto Star*, 24 August 1995, A19).

[2]See Eichler (1996).

[3]In *Thibaudeau v. Canada*, the judges use spousal and parental terms interchangeably to discuss the tax rights and obligations of ex-spouses who are joint parents. The majority of judges refer to the ex-spouses as the 'couple' and the 'family unit'. See Chapter 8 for a detailed discussion of this problem. Here I wish to make the point that we need to develop a more precise language that adequately reflects rather than hides the existing fractures.

[4]*Leshner v. Ontario* (1992), 16 C.H.R.R. D/184; *Canada (Attorney General) v. Mossop* [1993] 1 S.C.R. 436; *Egan v. Canada*, S.C.C., 1995, file #23636.

[5]*Miron v. Trudel* [1995] 2 S.C.R. 418.

[6]*Thibaudeau v. Canada* [1995] 2 S.C.R. 267.

[7]*Symes v. Canada* [1993] 4 S.C.R. 695.

[8]See Skrypnek and Fast (forthcoming) for a helpful overview of issues. See Pulkingham (1989) for an interpretation of where the crisis stems from. See McDaniel (1990) for a feminist approach.

[9]Jacobs and Davies (1991).

[10]Burke (1995:32–3) sums up the situation as follows:

> Childhood is under siege in Central and Eastern Europe. Rapidly falling birth rates and soaring mortality rates have reduced the number of children in the region. Environmental pollution continues unchecked. The health and nutritional status of mothers is poor. Children are exposed to high rates of illness and disability. Murder, suicide, violent crime and premature death are rampant. Children are being abandoned, forced to live on the street, or orphaned. Public policies are increasing the burden on families, contributing to high rates of poverty and unemployment. The whole social infrastructure is unravelling.

[11]See Crysdale (1991); Elder et al. (1992:25) noted that 'Husbands became angry and hostile towards wives in response to greater economic pressure and budgetary reductions. In hard-pressed families, financial woes made men more irritable and explosive.' See also Fagin and Little (1984) and Harman (1995). Kelly and Ramsey (1991:393) argue that

'Children need one or more adults to provide consistent material support and emotional nurturance, and it is clear that parenting is an extremely difficult role to fulfil in urban ghettos.' See further National Forum on Family Security (1993).

[12]The problem is not a scarcity of jobs but our definition of what constitutes a regular job. A strong argument can be made that we could have full employment with adequate compensation if we were to distribute the available work differently by shortening the work week. See O'Hara (1993) for a compelling exposition on this issue.

[13]See Chapter 8 for a discussion of this point.

[14]National Forum on Family Security (1993:16–17).

[15]For a discussion of two opposing definitions, see Chapter 2.

Chapter 1

[1]'Ideal' does not mean good, but expresses the fact that these models present exaggeratedly clear (because they are simplified) types.

[2]Compare McKinney (1966:6, 63) on the use of ideal types.

[3]A note on terminology is needed regarding the usage of the nouns 'sex' and 'gender'. In the mid-1970s, sociologists attempted to make a theoretical distinction between sex and gender. Sex was to denote the physical differences between the sexes, and gender the social differences that are related to the physical differences. Unfortunately, gender soon became the 'politically correct' term, and was—and continues to be—used in an entirely inappropriate manner. Today many questionnaires even ask 'What is your gender: male or female?' In other words, 'gender' is used when 'sex' would be appropriate, thus hopelessly obfuscating an otherwise important distinction. I use the terms largely interchangeably, conforming reluctantly to what seems to be the currently preferred expression within a given context.

[4]See Eichler (1988a) for a detailed discussion of the first five biases in which the ageist bias is treated as a subaspect of the conservative bias. I decided to split it from the conservative bias in order to be better record what activates the conservative bias.

[5]This bias was first described in 1983. At that time, I defined it partially as 'the tendency to either largely ignore recent changes, or to treat them as ephemeral, rather than comprehending them as central and fundamental. This results in using analytic frameworks which are totally inadequate for newly emergent situations. An example of this type of thinking would be the tendency to regard remarriage families as basically the same as families based on first marriages, and to try and analyze them in terms which were developed for this type of family' (Eichler 1988a:2). Today few authors would deny the pervasiveness, importance, and depth of the changes in the past twenty-five years. Hence the nature of this particular bias has shifted somewhat. The views as described are now mostly applied to the families of the past. The next step is then usually to make

unfavourable comparisons with present-day families, and to blame those who make up today's families.

[6]A recent review of 'family' caregiving argued that 'the caregiving family is a smokescreen behind which stands a solitary figure, usually female' (Keating et al. 1994:271).

[7]This is an extremely limited description of an important bias. See Appendix 3 for a detailed operationalization of the sexist bias.

[8]I have made every effort to avoid all of the biases. However, the ageist bias is so pervasive in the literature that it is impossible to avoid.

[9]See Johnston (1983) and Monture (1989).

[10]See Chapter 3 for an extended discussion of same-sex couples. See Ryder (1990) for a good overview of some of the issues. See also Herman (1990).

[11]O'Brien and Weir (1995).

[12]For a good description of the legal changes concerning family law in Italy, see Saraceno (1990).

[13]This meant that property was passed on only to the 'legitimate' heirs, and mistresses had no right to legal status.

[14]See Snell (1991:10, Table 1).

[15]See Pike (1975:124).

[16]For 1930 figures, see Urquhart and Buckley (1983, series B65-74); for 1993 figures, see Dumas et al. (1995:17).

[17]Remarriage of widowers to widows 'was historically important when death reduced the adult population, but it lost most of its prominence and now concerns almost exclusively old people. Only 25% of remarriage involving widowers occurs before age 50, and remarriage of widowers accounts for only 3% of marriages. In 50% of cases, widowers remarry widows' (Dumas and Peron 1992:89).

[18]Of course, this still happens today (see Muzzin, Brown, and Hornosty 1995 for a recent example), but at least it is no longer legal.

[19]The *Persons* case involved five Alberta women who tested the constitutionality of female personhood by petitioning for an Order-in-Council to have the Supreme Court of Canada rule on the question. In 1928, the Supreme Court ruled that Canadian women were *not* persons in the sense of the *British North American Act* and were therefore not eligible to be appointed to the Senate (the request of having a woman appointed being the impetus behind this case). The five women—Emily Murphy, Nellie McClung, Louise McKinney, Irene Parlby, and Henrietta Muir Edwards—appealed to Her Majesty's Privy Council in London, which concluded that women *were* persons. For a more detailed description of the case, see Eichler (1987).

[20]In 1955, the following were the eligibility criteria for mother's allowances in the various provinces: in all provinces, widows and mothers with disabled husbands were eligible for the mother's allowance. Deserted mothers were eligible in all provinces except Nova Scotia.

However, wives with husbands in penal institutions were eligible only in Newfoundland, PEI, Quebec, Saskatchewan, and BC; divorced and separated mothers only in Newfoundland, Ontario, Saskatchewan, and BC; and unmarried mothers only in Newfoundland, Manitoba, Saskatchewan, Alberta, and BC, but not in the other provinces (Department of National Health and Welfare, memorandum #1, Social Security Division, 1955, as cited in Haddad 1986:49).

[21]The double standard still exists today (see Robinson et al. 1991). However, it is considerably less drastic than it used to be.

[22]Snell (1991:25).

[23]The fact that the extended family has predominantly resided in more than one household, both historically as well as at present, is not relevant in this context for any of the models. The focus here is only on parents and their *dependent* children.

[24]See chapters 6 and 7 for a detailed discussion of this question.

[25]For instance, the *Ontario Family Law Reform Act* states: 'The purpose of this section is to recognize that child care, household management and financial provision are the joint responsibilities of the spouses and that *inherent in the marital relationship there is equal contribution*, whether financial or otherwise, by the spouses to the assumption of these responsibilities ...' (emphasis added). See Chapter 5 for a discussion of this assumption.

[26]See Chapter 3 for a discussion of both the progress as well as the lack of progress that has been made in this regard.

[27]Inkeles (1981), Popenoe (1994).

[28]Glendon (1981).

[29]Fineman (1995) provides a trenchant critique of aspects of this model without using this particular terminology.

[30]Gairdner (1992:59).

[31]See Chapter 7 for a discussion on non-kin familial relationships.

[32]Jaffe (1972:469).

[33]This is no longer true in personal injury cases. See Fast and Munro (1994).

[34]The most important of these is arguably Waring (1988), which provides a thorough critique and pulls together many of the earlier critiques. She also provides a highly informative historical explanation as to *why* we ended up with the United Nations System of National Accounts on which this particular type of national accounting is based. This is a problem shared by most nations of the world.

[35]Statistics Canada (1994b).

[36]Statistics Canada uses two different approaches to estimate this amount. One is the opportunity cost (divided into net and gross opportunity costs). This measure is premised on the notion that the time spent on household work could have been used for paid work. The figure expresses how much money could have been earned had the time been

used in that manner. Since this measure expresses the value of housework in terms of what is *not* done rather than in terms of what *is* done, I do not find this a meaningful concept for my purposes and hence do not use it (it is useful for other purposes). Their other approach is to measure the replacement cost by estimating the value of housework activities and comparing them to the hourly earnings of people who do similar activities in their paid jobs.

[37]Housework is defined as 'those economic services produced in the household and outside the market, but which could be produced by a third person hired on the market without changing their utility to members of the household' (Statistics Canada 1994b:35).

[38]Ibid., 40.

[39]This applies in insurance cases, as well as in the division of property under family law.

[40]This is phrased more generally because the logic applies to all situations in which a person who is incapable of caring for himself or herself (regardless of age) is cared for by another person. This will be developed further in chapters 6 and 7.

[41]The Canada Pension Plan/Quebec Pension Plan give some credit to the raising of children in the 'drop-out' provision, which allows a parent to count up to seven years spent rearing a child as if she was in the labour force, provided she was in the labour force before and after the drop-out period (see Cassels [1995]). I am not arguing that the state should pay for the benefits mentioned in all instances. Instead, I have proposed elsewhere that if the work performed is socially useful, it should be paid for by society. If it is privately useful, it should be paid for by the people who benefit from it. See Eichler (1988a).

[42]In 1991, an American economist suggested to me, in the context of an international conference on poverty, that it is sexist to look only at the income of mothers in Aid to Families with Dependent Children (AFDC), the US version of family welfare benefits. It is sexist, he argued, because the woman who is the head of the lone-parent family on AFDC is such a terrific worker who creates all this wealth through her unpaid work. We really need to add an imputed amount to the income of these families, he maintained. The effect of doing this, of course, would be to reduce the number of families in poverty, thus creating a rationale for further reducing benefits. By a magic trick, poverty has thus disappeared. Even worse, were we to use the Canadian figures for this type of exercise, the income of poor female-headed one-parent households would be lowered more than that of poor male-headed one-parent households, since as a group women create more value with their unpaid work than do men. See Maloney (1989) for just such a proposal. See Donnelly (1993) for a somewhat different view. Neither of the authors makes a distinction between socially and privately useful housework; see Chapter 7.

[43]R.S.C. 1985, c.1 (5th Supp.) [hereinafter the 'TTA'].

[44]Philipps and Young (1995:222).

[45]All quotes are taken from Appendix 1. See Appendix 1 for a detailed set of excerpts that provide the actual wording of the provisions summarized here with respect to their effect.

[46]There are some exceptions to this general rule, since spouses may transfer various deductions and other benefits to each other.

[47]This is not always the case: with respect to claiming the deductions for children or other dependants, this may also occur between households.

[48]This has been demonstrated repeatedly. See, for instance, Battle (1992), Finnie (1994), Zweibel (1993a), and many others.

[49]See Lewis and Åström (1992).

[50]See the 1987 provision for child-care expense payments.

[51]This is in line with a Kuhnian analysis. Kuhn (1971) suggests that a paradigm is revised so often in the face of anomalies that it eventually becomes too cumbersome to be useful. An almost page-long definition of 'spouse' exemplifies this type of cumbersomeness, I would suggest. Clearly we have reached some sort of limit here.

Chapter 2

[1]Baker et al. (1990), Bould (1993), Conway (1990), Eichler (1988a), European Centre (1993), Fineman (1995), Gairdner (1992), Hudson and Galaway (1993), Nett (1988), Popenoe (1993), and Veevers (1991).

[2]Clive (1980), Deech (1980), Eekelaar and Katz (1980), Eichler (1985, 1993), Herman (1991), Hughes and Andrews (1985), Melton (1990–1), Robson (1994), Thomlison and Foote (1991), Wilson (1985).

[3]The federal Parliament that was dissolved in 1993 had a caucus on family issues that met regularly to influence the government with respect to family-oriented matters.

[4]See Eichler (1988a:409–28) and Fineman (1995) for a summary of some of these struggles. In a poll on families during the International Year of the Family, Angus Reid found that 68 per cent of parents and 63 per cent of the entire population they sampled agreed with the statement that 'Canada's families are in crisis' (Angus Reid Group 1994:75).

[5]Cf., Popenoe (1994) and Fineman (1995) for two opposing viewpoints on this issue.

[6]I had some trouble settling on a name for the second group of people. In legal circles, the type of analysis undertaken by what I have called egalitarians is considered a functionalist approach, whereby people are recognized as family members because they subserve a familial function. An alternative to calling them egalitarians would be to call them functionalists. This is, in fact, what I did in an earlier version of this work written for the Department of Justice. However, in sociological terms, a func-

tionalist approach has a very distinct meaning that is related to the work of specific sociologists, many of whom would *not* agree with this definition of the family. This is why I settled on calling them egalitarians. Where the term 'functional' is used in this context in this book, it is used in its legal rather than sociological meaning.

[7]This term will be defined below.

[8]The Vanier Institute of the Family (1994:10) defines a family as follows:

> Family is defined as any combination of two or more people who are bound together over time by ties of mutual consent, birth and/or adoption/placement and who, together, assume responsibility for variant combinations of some of the following:
> • physical maintenance and care of group members;
> • addition of new members through procreation or adoption;
> • socialization of children;
> • social control of members;
> • production, consumption and distribution of goods and services; and
> • affective nurturance—love.

For the purpose of establishing who can look after a person who needs care, Bould (1993:138) defines a family as 'the informal unit where those who cannot take care of themselves find care in time of need'.

[9]The revolution contrasts with the fact that families are and always have been evolving and changing, and that previous generations have perceived family crises. See Eichler (1996).

[10]See Parsons, Shils, and Olds (1951), Parsons (1955), Bales and Slater (1955), Zelditch, Jr (1955).

[11]For a detailed critique of this entire approach, see Eichler (1980:29–48).

[12]Gairdner (1992:86).

[13]Certain modern religious tracts still put forward this antiquated version of marriage. A recent book by Opus Dei, an ultraconservative Roman Catholic group, for instance, argues that

> … men and women are simply not the same.
> A woman may complain about things that look ridiculous to a man. For example, she may feel hurt because her husband did not say anything about her new hairdo or because he did not notice the nice flower arrangement she had made …
> … A man can get also annoyed easily if his wife or children interrupt him in the middle of an interesting paragraph he happens to be reading at the moment or if *he sees that his decisions are not immediately implemented at home.*

... [Men] are more logical in their approach to things ... On the other hand, women ... tend to use their hearts more (Abad and Fenoy 1988:39–40, emphasis added).

[14]Bradbury (1993:220).

[15]Indeed, this is the title of a book; see Gairdner (1992).

[16]It should be noted that not everyone who otherwise adopts an egalitarian perspective takes this last step.

[17]*Reality*, the newsletter of the antifeminist organization REAL Women, provides a monthly forum for the expression of such views, for instance.

[18]For a discussion of equality, its meanings, problems, and an alternative approach, see Chapter 7.

[19]Some recent works include Barret and McIntosh (1982), Mackie (1995), Maloney (1989), and Seccombe (1993).

[20]In 1991, 4.9 per cent of all households were non-family households with two or more persons. Families of lesbian and gay couples would be included in this figure, which would, however, include many other categories. It therefore seems safe to estimate that same-sex couples (and potentially their children) constitute a very small fraction of all Canadian households; see Jorgensen (1995).

[21]Newer historical data show that this is not the first time demographic trends have converged. Fertility in the last quarter of the nineteenth century and first quarter of the twentieth century also fell (albeit from dramatically different starting-points) in the United States, England and Wales, Sweden, France, Denmark, Finland, Norway, Luxembourg, Germany, Austria, Hungary, Australia, and the Netherlands; see Haines (1990).

[22]See Glendon (1981).

[23]See Baker (1994) for a review of a number of important themes in this debate.

[24]See Appendix 1 for much more detail on this matter.

[25]Burch and Matthews (1987:495). See also Eichler (1984) and Inkeles (1981).

[26]Italy, 1.3; followed by Spain with 1.4; Austria, Germany, Greece, and Portugal with 1.5; Belgium, Luxembourg, and Switzerland with 1.6; Denmark, Japan, and the Netherlands with 1.7; Canada, Finland, France, and Hungary with 1.8; Australia, Bulgaria, Norway, and the United Kingdom with 1.9; Czechoslovakia, Sweden, and the US with 2.0 (United Nations 1993:207).

[27]Malta, New Zealand, and Poland (United Nations 1993:207).

[28]Iceland, Ireland, and Rumania with 2.2; Albania with 2.8; and Israel with 2.9 (United Nations 1993:207).

[29]See Table 1 in Appendix 2.

[30]See Table 2 in Appendix 2.

[31]Gordon and McLanahan (1991). In addition to death and desertion, there was also temporary separation due to immigration or migration in which one family member (usually the husband/father) migrated first and the wife and children (if any) followed. However, this affected a *relatively* small proportion of families. At the time of the 1910 census, under 2 per cent of the entire population of foreign-born women, and under 6 per cent of the men, claimed to be married, although their spouses were absent. See Robles and Watkins (1993).

[32]See Appendix 2, Table 4 for the number of Canadian divorces involving children over time, as well as custody assignments.

[33]Statistics Canada in McKie and Thompson (1990:128). Before 1730, 1.25 per cent of all births registered were illegitimate; see Dumas and Peron (1992).

[34]See Appendix 2, Table 3 for figures.

[35]Computed from Statistics Canada (1993a:11).

[36]For instance, if we break down the overall figure of 27.0 per cent of births to unmarried women in 1991 (see Table 1) into its component parts, we find that 25.2 per cent are to never-married women, 1.5 per cent to divorced women, and 0.1 per cent each to separated and widowed women.

[37]Belle and McQuillan (1994:17) note that Quebec in 1991 had the highest number of births to unmarried mothers (41 per cent, almost double that of other provinces), and also had the highest proportion of couples living common law (14 per cent as compared to 6 per cent for the rest of Canada). In other provinces, there are also parallel trends between the two phenomena.

[38]Personal information from Paul Reid, Statistics Canada.

[39]For a fuller discussion of this case, see Chapter 8.

[40]Vanier Institute of the Family (1994:61).

[41]The correspondence is not one on one because a few of these parents may be dead, or one man or woman can have children with more than one partner and not be coresident with the children.

[42]In the 1980s, more than 40 per cent of all marriages contracted in the US were remarriages for one or both spouses (Wilson and Clarke 1992).

[43]This ignores other factors, such as commuting couples who maintain two principal residences. We do not know how many couples fall within this category. Other incongruities may exist because one spouse is in a penal institution or some other institution.

[44]In 1991, 48 per cent of all Canadian families were married with children, 29 per cent were married without children, 13 per cent were single-parent families, 6 per cent were common-law couples without children, and 4 per cent were common-law couples with children (Vanier Institute of the Family 1994:30). We also know that 7 per cent of all families raising children were blended families (Ibid., 61). However, these percent-

ages have a shifting base (all families versus families raising children) and do not take into account that for every one-parent family, as well as for every blended family, there is (in the vast majority of cases) another parent alive (usually a father) who does not live with his biological children, and if there was more than one father to different children of the same mother, this figure increases even more. We therefore need to roughly double the number of lone-parent and blended families in order to estimate the degree of incongruence. Some of the non-resident parents live with other families who may appear to be non-blended, but in which a biological child of one of the partners lives in some other family unit. Others may live as individuals, thus shifting the basis again. In any case, it is clear that the proportion is high.

[45]To be exact, 77,249.

[46]This is an estimate. Statistics Canada breaks down the figures only until '5 or more' children, and combines 'no children and unknown' into one category. Depending on how large the unknown category is, this may therefore be a serious underestimate of the number of children involved. If we add up the known children and only count five for the ones that have five or more, we arrive at 48,202 children.

[47]Computed from Statistics Canada 1992:23.

[48]When custody is split, one or more children may live with one parent and the others with the other parent or a third party.

[49]Although the life cycle model as cited here was much more of an adequate description of the majority of families than it is today, nevertheless even at that time it only presented the majority picture and omitted the minority variations.

[50]Adapted from Duvall and Miller (1985:26).

[51]Campaign 2000 (1994:19) defines a life cycle perspective as one that

> ... includes all families through their entire life courses. Its foremost objective is to prevent problems, rather than alleviate them after they occur. Economically, it focuses on families with modest and median incomes as well as on poor families. These families are most vulnerable to life cycle events that lead to poverty. Because the strategy of a life cycle approach is preventive, it makes the most efficient use of public dollars. Child development and health promotion research has proven that preventive approaches are more cost-effective than remedial ones. The life cycle approach builds on this research.

Used in this manner, the life cycle perspective is both useful and of direct policy relevance. It is also useful for following individuals over their life cycle as they interact with others across generations; see Cheal (1983, 1987).

[52]Another problem with assuming a normal (or natural cycle) is the idea that people start having children at a propitious time. This is often *not* the case. A national British study documents that men were more likely to become fathers as teens when their families experienced greater economic hardship than when they were in a position to support the child they had generated (Dearden et al. 1994).

[53]See Eichler (1988a, Chapter 1) for a discussion of some of these complexities. Of course, the literature recognizes that there have always been some exceptions. At issue is the utility of this approach if it is simplistically applied to a numerical majority today. I am suggesting that this is inappropriate.

[54]See the discussion on productive work in Chapter 1.

[55]See Cohen (1988).

[56]There were some day nurseries that were started in the nineteenth century and continued into the twentieth century; see Lalonde-Graton (1985), who describes the day care operated by Les Soeurs Grises de Montreal, and Montreal Day Nursery (1960), which discusses the history of the Montreal Day Nursery. In Ontario, the first day nursery was founded in 1892, but formal government involvement only began with the Second World War. When the war ended, so did the provision of day care, although in Ontario the *Ontario Day Nursery Act* replaced the Dominion-Provincial Agreement, which had provided government day care subsidies. See Krashinsky (1977), Friendly et al. (1991), and McLeod (1975).

[57]This included such women as Dr Helen MacMurchy, who received her medical degree in 1901 and went on to a distinguished career in medicine and government (McConnachie 1983), Dr E. Cora Hind, who was one of Canada's best agricultural reporters (Haig 1967), Agnes Macphail, the first woman elected to the Canadian Parliament (French 1967), Alice Wilson, who became Canada's first female geologist (Montagnes 1967), and others.

[58]Urquhart and Buckley (1983), Series D107-122.

[59]Computed from Urquhart and Buckley (1983), Series D86-106.

[60]Pierson (1986:22-51).

[61]The total fertility rate in 1941 (during the Second World War) was 2,832, in 1951 (after the end of the war) it was 3,503, in 1961 (during the baby boom) it was 3,840. By 1971 it began to drop to 2,187. See Boyd, Eichler, Hofley (1976:32, Table 2.8).

[62]See Eichler (1988a:54, Table 2.5).

[63]Statistics Canada (1993b:21).

[64]Ibid., p. 21.

[65]Grindstaff (1986).

[66]See Glendon (1981) and Weitzman (1985).

[67]Edwards (1981).

[68]The picture for Canada is complicated. Cheal (1993a) notes that in his sample of couples in Winnipeg, most couples have a joint bank account. However, he also notes that the majority of husbands have an additional personal account: 58 per cent of husbands in breadwinner couples, 57 per cent of men in provider/coprovider couples, and 57 per cent of men in dual-career couples have a personal account. By contrast, only 18 per cent of homemakers, 39 per cent of women in dual-career couples, and 50 per cent of coproviders have a personal account. There are thus a substantial minority of cases in which husbands have, besides a joint bank account, a personal bank account, while wives do *not* have a personal account. This suggests that some of the spending power is kept in male hands even when there is a joint account.

[69]Pahl (1989).

[70]Bradbury (1993:216).

[71]Light and Pierson (1990:289).

[72]Vanier Institute of the Family (1994:75).

[73]National Council of Welfare (1995a:7, Table 2).

[74]In 1993, the poverty rate of women in all age categories exceeded that of men, with the greatest differences among the young and the old. See National Council of Welfare (1995a:33, graph O). The overall ratio of female to male poverty rates was 1.33 in 1993; see Table 17 in National Council of Welfare (1995a:69).

[75]National Council of Welfare (1995a:8, Table 3). For an explanation of the type of circumstances in which these children live, see pp. 60–1.

[76]Economic Council of Canada (1992). Cheal (forthcoming) found the highest degree of financial stress among lone parents in a Winnipeg sample.

[77]Statistics Canada (1995:94, Table 7.6).

[78]Statistics Canada and most data-collecting institutions, as well as scholars, tend to equate a husband-wife family with a two-parent family if there are dependent children present. I find this practice highly problematic because it hides the degree of incongruity between family and household memberships, and I therefore consistently use the term husband-wife family (with or without dependent children). It is more cumbersome, but more accurate.

[79]National Council of Welfare (1995a:44–5).

[80]This difference has been consistent over time. For figures from 1980 to 1993, see Statistics Canada (1995:94, Table 7.6). In 1993, the percentage of male-headed lone-parent families that were poor increased substantially from 20.9 per cent in 1992 to 31.3 per cent. The incidence of poverty among female-headed lone-parent families, by contrast, was 59.6 per cent. The different incidence of poverty shows itself in a multitude of ways. For instance, in 1993, 79.2 per cent of all husband-wife families owned their home, compared to 57.8 per cent of lone-parent male-

headed families and 30.5 per cent of lone-parent female-headed families (Ibid., 30, Table 3.1).

[81]National Council of Welfare (1995a:31, graph N). The absolute numbers of people involved are larger than these figures suggest for two reasons: first, there are, by definition, two poor adults in a husband-wife family compared to a lone-parent family and, second, poor husband-wife families had an average of 2.0 children, while poor lone-parent families had an average of 1.84 children; see National Council of Welfare (1995a:36).

[82]National Council of Welfare (1995a:62, graph Y).

[83]For example, Popenoe (1994).

[84]Campaign 2000 (1994:Table B).

[85]Ibid., Table C.

[86]Aitken and Mitchell (1995). For some experiential data in how it affects young couples, see Child Poverty Action Group et al. (1994b).

[87]*Young* v. *Young* (1994), 49 R.F.L. (3d), McLachlin J., p. 148.

[88]Fineman (1988: 737–9) puts the date around the middle of the nineteenth century. By contrast, Goldstein and Fenster (1994:39–40) suggest that 'over a period of about 50 years beginning about 1920, the courts tended—in an almost 180-degree reversal of the traditional preference for the father as the custodial parent—to award custody to the mother ...'

[89]*Divorce Act*, R.S.C. 1985, (2nd Supp.) c. 3.

[90]The relevant section of the *Divorce Act* reads as follows:

16(8) In making an order under this section, the court shall take into consideration only the best interests of the child of the marriage as determined by reference to the condition, means, needs and other circumstances of the child.

[91]Fineman (1995:82–3). See also Crean (1988).

[92]Even in the case of joint custody, the emphasis may be more on rights than obligations of both spouses. Delorey (1989:38) has argued that 'fathers who favour joint custody are actually seeking more rights and control without a corresponding increase in responsibility for their children.' While this may not be true in all instances, she makes a powerful argument that given the difference between joint physical and legal custody, 'joint *legal* custody gives legal decisionmaking power to parents without corresponding responsibility for physical care of children' (Delorey 1989:39). This, she suggests, is a means to control women and children rather than to care for children.

[93]See Table 4 in Appendix 2.

[94]This is perhaps most clearly expressed in laws pertaining to sexual assault. Until 1983, it was legally impossible for a man to rape his wife, even if the spouses had separated (Bala 1995). This was due to a concep-

tualization of wives as their husbands' sexual property even after divorce! See Clark and Lewis (1977).

[95]Weitzman (1985:78) has demonstrated that in 1968 in 61 per cent of the divorce cases in California, most of the value of the family home went to the wife, compared to 46 per cent of divorce cases nine years later. Equal division of the house may mean that the house is sold and the proceeds divided equally. 'The number of cases in which there was an explicit order to sell the home rose from about one in ten in 1968, to about *one in three* in 1977' (Weitzman 1985:78; emphasis in the original).

[96]I have not been able to find any studies that indicate the proportions of women and men who are able to maintain their family home after divorce or buy a new one, thus the number of women affected remains an unanswered question.

[97]Novac (1994:49). In general, women are more likely than men to rent; see ibid., 50.

[98]Subject to premarital contracts.

[99]Statistics Canada (1994a:18–19, Table 1).

Chapter 3

[1]This, of course, was a social ideal rather than the reality, or else there would not have been so many shotgun weddings.

[2]In fact, all the literature suggests that divorce is extremely difficult emotionally for both spouses, and has major economic consequences for the ex-wife; see Kitson and Morgan (1990) for an overview of the research. Nor is the legal process simple. It is simple only when viewed from a 100-year perspective.

[3]One of the behaviours that fall in between is marital non-cohabitation, i.e., legally married couples live in separate households for reasons other than marital discord. Rindfuss and Stephen (1990) suggest that this was the case for a small but significant minority during the census years 1960, 1970, and 1980, averaging from 5 per cent to 6 per cent among Whites aged eighteen to twenty-four, and consistently over 10 per cent for Blacks in that age range in the US. Reasons for this type of separation include military service, incarceration, and unemployment. The data do not allow us to identify commuting marriages because of career reasons (a cause of intermittent marital non-cohabitation).

[4]Denmark blazed the trail for this; see Pedersen (1991–2). See also Lesbian and Gay Legal Rights Service (1993). See Friedman (1987–8) for a strong argument for permitting marriage between same-sex partners.

[5]For instance, in earlier times, the income tax guides referred to spouses without specifying them as opposite-sex partners. Today they specify that same-sex partners are *not* included. Clarifications of this type only happen when boundaries are blurred.

[6]Van Kirk (1992:78).

[7]Ibid., p. 84.

[8]Ibid., 86.

[9]See Appendix 1.

[10]One US study found that of all the couples with children who divorced within a certain time period, 41 per cent returned to court for relitigation, and that this is probably a low estimate, since other couples of that cohort may return at a later date as well; see Koel et al. (1994).

[11]Ambert (1980), Sev'er (1992).

[12]I have focused on divorce involving parents of young children, since I will be dealing with parental roles in the next chapter, and this is one relevant aspect. However, it needs to be noted that of course childless couples divorce, and that divorce of parents with adult children has significant effects on the parent-adult child relationship (Aquilino 1994).

[13]Bradbury (1993:189).

[14]Ibid., 189.

[15]Ibid., 244.

[16]Ibid., 196.

[17]Snell (1991:234).

[18]Ibid., 229.

[19]Bradbury (1993:183).

[20]I refer to 'legal' marriage as a fully legal marriage because the literature makes it clear that most of the alternatives have partial legal and often full civic sanction.

[21]Levasseur (1995a:97). For a thorough review of the older research, see Newcomb (1983).

[22]Deech (1980:303).

[23]It is, of course, possible that one partner would like to marry and the other refuses, in which case cohabitation is the 'choice' of only one of the partners. Even so, it is problematic to impose marriagelike conditions on the unwilling partner.

[24]Deech (1980:302). Her argument is supported by a study of the Institute of Law Research and Reform (1984:65–7), which found that the fourth reason (out of thirteen reasons) people gave for living in a common-law relationship was '4. We didn't want the legal commitment that marriage involves', after '1. We were (are) in love', '2. For companionship', and '3. At least one of us was not legally free to marry'. Kotkin (1985) found that 'no divorce' was listed as one of the benefits of cohabitation by his respondents. Fels (1981:38–40) suggests that a rejection of marriage is one of the reasons why people cohabit.

[25]Deech (1980:302).

[26]LaNovara (1993:13).

[27]Ibid., 13.

[28]Ibid.

[29]Bumpass et al. (1991:914) note that increasing rates of cohabitation are

found in France, Sweden, and Australia. 'In the United States, the proportion of persons who lived with a partner before marrying for the first time increased from 11 per cent around 1970 ... to nearly half for recent first marriages ...'

[30]See S.C. 1974-75-76, c. 58, s. 1, cf., Sopinka, J. in *Egan* v. *Canada* [1995] 2 S.C.R. 513.

[31]See L'Heureux-Dubé J. in *Miron* v. *Trudel*, par. 97.

[32]*Miron* v. *Trudel* [1995] 2 S.C.R. 418.

[33]One-sixth of all never-married cohabiting couples had a child since they began living together (Bumpass et al. 1991:919).

[34]Ibid., 926.

[35]Alberta does not cover cohabitants by law at all (see *Domestic Relations Act*), although there have been several legislative proposals to this effect. BC defines a common-law relationship as one in which a man and a woman have lived together as husband and wife for not less than two years (*Family Relations Act*); Manitoba requires five years or one year and a child of the union (*Family Maintenance Act*); NB requires three years or a relationship of some permanence where there is a child born to the union (*Family Services Act*); Newfoundland requires one year and a child of the union (*Family Law Act*); NWT requires one year of a relationship of some permanence and a child of the union (*Maintenance Orders Enforcement Act*); NS requires one year (*Family Maintenance Act*); Ontario requires three years of a relationship of some permanence and a child of the union (*Family Law Act*); PEI does not recognize common-law couples in the *Family Law Reform Act*, but does so in the *Worker's Compensation Act* (no time limit established); Quebec does not define unmarried cohabitants as common law, but does recognize a 'societé du fait particulière' under certain conditions (Holland and Stalbecker-Poutney 1990:2–41); Saskatchewan requires three years of a relationship of some permanence and a child of the union (*Family Maintenance Act*); Yukon requires a relationship of some permanence, which has been interpreted from anywhere between one to five years (*Family Property and Support Act*).

[36]Levasseur (1995a:25–6).

[37]Levasseur (1995b:26).

[38]Straver (1981:59–60) found the following types among the unmarried couples living together in the Netherlands: (1) like a traditional marriage, (2) complete togetherness, (3) social independence tendencies, (4) social and economic independence tendencies, (5) sharing internally, independent *vis-à-vis* the government, (6) internally and externally independent, if possible, (7) consequently independent, whether living together or not, (8) conflicting goals between partners, (9) in a transitional stage. Ridley et al. (1978) distinguish between four different types: 'Linus Blanket', 'Emancipation', 'Convenience', and 'Testing'.

[39]In particular, anal intercourse.

[40]Until 1969, it was a crime for two adult men to engage in sexual intercourse; see Bala (1995).

[41]However, many differences remain. The Coalition for Lesbian and Gay Rights in Ontario (1992) lists modifications to thirty-six provincial statutes that they would like to see amended to include same-sex couples.

[42]Bill 167.

[43]In 1984, the European Parliament urged member states to abolish any laws that make homosexual acts between consenting adults liable to punishment, and to apply the same age of consent as for heterosexual acts. While the latter has not yet been achieved in all member states, many discriminatory laws have been repealed: in Belgium, France, Germany, Greece, Luxembourg, Scotland, Spain, and others. See Waaldijk (1993:81–2). Antidiscrimination protection for lesbians and gay men is enforced in Denmark, France, Netherlands, Norway, and Sweden (Tatchell 1992:80).

[44]Allen and Demo (1995:113) define lesbian and gay families 'by the presence of two or more people who share a same-sex orientation (e.g., a couple) or by the presence of a least one lesbian or gay adult rearing a child.'

[45]The notion of procreative sex within the family is usually accompanied by a sexual double standard, which allows men access to other forms of sexuality, while denying the same to women. It is therefore more a way of restricting and regulating female sexuality than a descriptive statement of actual sexual behaviours of married men and women.

[46]In 1993, a judge denied a gay couple the right to marry on just these grounds; see *Layland* v. *Ontario* (*Minister of Consumer and Commercial Relations*) 104 D.L.R. (4th), p. 214.

[47]See *Egan* v. *Canada*, S.C.C., (1995) file #23636 for a good example of this reasoning. See Chapter 7 for a detailed discussion of this case.

[48]Parliamentary Subcommittee on Equality Rights (1985:26).

[49]Cited in Morin (1977:629).

[50]See Weston (1991:46).

[51]But even in Ireland there have been no prosecutions since 1974, except where minors were involved or the acts were committed in public or without consent; see Waaldijk (1993:84). However, public indecency laws are used more often against homosexual rather than heterosexual acts performed in public; see Waaldijk (1993:88–9).

[52]Weston (1991:44).

[53]Weston (1991:48) argues that there is a one-in-four chance that lesbians and gays will be accepted by their families if they come out to them, suggesting that there is a three-in-four chance that they might be rejected. However, she extrapolates this figure from the results of a poll in the *Los Angeles Times* in which 73 per cent of respondents viewed homosexual sex

as 'wrong' (Ibid., 47). There is no way of knowing, short of an independent study, whether people change their judgements when they find out that members of their family are lesbian or gay. Nor is it clear that lesbian and gay couples are regarded in that light. Hare (1994) found that 80 per cent of the twenty-eight lesbian couples she interviewed had disclosed the nature of their relationship to their parents, but even more (98 per cent) had done so to non-gay friends, suggesting that they expected somewhat more acceptance from their friends than from their family.

[54]Homosexual youths, both female and male, are two to three times more likely to attempt suicide than heterosexual youths. Of all those adolescents who have committed suicide, 30 per cent are homosexual. Over 75 per cent of suicide attempters cited conflict over their sexual orientation as the prime reason; see Kroll and Warneke (1995).

[55]Cf., Emmert (1993:382).

[56]Ibid., 382.

[57]Most US case laws concerning gays in the military deal with highly decorated individuals who clearly performed their duties well. In the Canadian military, one can be disciplined for inappropriate sexual conduct, but no distinction is made—at least in theory—between homosexual and heterosexual transgressions.

[58]*Canada (Attorney General)* v. *Mossop*, [1993] 1 S.C.R. 436.

[59]*Vogel* v. *Manitoba* (1992) 90 D.L.R. (4th) 84.

[60]For a partial listing of US municipalities that provide employment benefits for same-sex partners, see Lambda Legal Defense and Education Fund, Inc. (n.d. [1992?]). For a partial list of Canadian employers who recognize lesbian and gay couples for the purpose of various fringe benefits, see Young (1994).

[61]*Leshner* v. *The Queen in Right of Ontario*, 92 C.L.L.C. [17,035].

[62]See Rusk (1993) for an overview of Canadian cases.

[63]In re *Kowalski* (1991) 478 N.W. (2d) 790 (Minn. App.).

[64]*Consent to Treatment Act*, S.O. 1992, c. 31, s. 1(2) & 17(1)(4).

[65]See Bala (1995:22).

[66]In *Canada (Attorney General)* v. *Mossop*, [1993] 1 S.C.R. 436, the Supreme Court denied bereavement leave to Mossop when the father of his long-time lover, Popert, died; see also Herman (1991) and Freeman (1994) for comment.

[67]Hare (1994:32).

[68]Waaldijk (1993:98).

[69]'Over the past decade, family immigration has represented about 60 per cent of total immigration to Canada' (Vanier Institute of the Family 1993:16).

[70]Rusk (1993:175). See Hathaway (1994) for a thoughtful discussion of this issue.

[71]In particular, Denmark, the Netherlands, and Germany (see Waaldijk 1993:100–1). In addition, Swedish lesbian and gay lovers who live together enjoy the same rights as cohabiting heterosexual couples. Dutch same-sex partners who confirm their relationship by legal contract are eligible for some of the rights granted to married heterosexual people. In Italy, there is a *de facto* legal recognition of same-sex couples at the level of municipal administration; see Tatchell (1992:81).

[72]Australia allows a person to sponsor someone for permanent residency in Australia if

> The applicant and the sponsor ... [are] in a relationship that is acknowledged by both parties and which involves:
> a. residing together; and
> b. being closely interdependent; and
> c. having a continuing commitment to mutual emotional and financial support ... [and some other requirements].

Canadian gay rights activists object to the criterion of joint residency because there are many places where residing together is not safe for same-sex couples; cf., Lesbian and Gay Immigration Task Force (1993).

[73]Lesbian and Gay Immigration Task Force (1992:18) and Blair (1993).

[74]*Braschi* v. *Stahl Associates*, 74 N.Y.(2d) 201; 543 N.E.(2d) 49; 544 N.Y.S.(2d) 784.

[75]Waaldijk (1993:99–100).

[76]At present, eight provincial jurisdictions include sexual orientation as a prohibited ground for discrimination.

[77]Dooley (1990:395). This is also a problem in most European countries. Waaldijk (1993:102). For extensive references, see Majury (1994).

[78]See Dooley (1990) for a detailed argument concerning the three approaches.

[79]Dooley (1990:423); see also Arnup (1989). For a review of British cases, see Bradley (1987).

[80]Between 1981 and 1990 the number of children adopted dropped from 5,376 to 2,836. Moreover, almost half of these were private rather than public adoptions (Vanier Institute of the Family 1994:60). We can assume that a good number of these private adoptions are step adoptions, meaning that these children are not available for general adoptions.

[81]At present, it is still impossible in member states of the European Community; cf., Waaldijk (1993:104).

[82]*K. and B.; F. and K.; B. and K.; C.L.P. and C.H.*, (24 May 1995), (Ont. Ct) [unreported].

[83]Currently, support entitlements must be based on constructive trust criteria, since the provincial family laws do not recognize same-sex partners as spouses. However, at present there are ongoing cases that are trying to challenge this notion; *M.* v. *H.* in Ontario, and *Forrest* in BC.

[84]Cf., Gavigan (1994).

[85]Robson (1994:991–2).

[86]*Egan* v. *Canada*, S.C.C., 1995 file #23636, recognized it as a protected ground under s. 15 of the *Charter*.

[87]Seven provinces and one territory provide protection through their human rights codes: Quebec (1977), Ontario (1986), Manitoba (1987), Yukon (1987), Nova Scotia (1991), New Brunswick (1992), British Columbia (1992), and Saskatchewan (1993). It was also ordered 'read into' the *Canadian Human Rights Act* by the Court of Appeal in Ontario.

[88]Over 600 employers in 1995 because of low associated business costs. Information from Lisa Hitch.

[89]For an extensive overview of the status of gay and lesbian families and the debate around them see Ryder (1990). Ryder concludes: 'There is intense debate in lesbian and gay communities about the desirability of gaining admission to the traditional institutions of heterosexuality … What is clear is that there will be neither freedom nor equality of sexual identity until the walls of heterosexual privilege are dismantled, and lesbians and gay men no longer suffer the assaults of heterosexuality's natural pretensions' (Ryder 1990:97).

[90]See Eichler (1988a:chapter 1) for an exposition on this topic.

[91]For a very clearly expressed stance along these lines, see Robson (1994:987). See Schneider (1986) for an empirical finding that suggests the division of labour is different between lesbian and heterosexual couples. Peplau (1991) refutes the myth that homosexual couples adopt the roles of 'husband and wife'.

[92]Robson (1994:986–7. For a critical review of Robson's work, see Herman (1994).

[93]See Warneke (1995:19).

[94]Registered domestic partnerships are one way to address this issue. In 1989, Denmark allowed lesbians and gay men to register their partnerships, and other jurisdictions (Sweden, the Netherlands, France) may follow (see Lambda Legal Defense and Education Fund, Inc. 1992:7; Waaldijk 1993:96–7).

[95]Popenoe (1993:531).

[96]The literature on this issue is voluminous and very consistent. The following references represent only a sample of recent work, and themselves provide many more references: for Australia, Bittman and Lovejoy (1993) and Dempsey (1988); for Bulgaria, Niemi and Anachkova (1992); for Canada, Duxbury et al. (1994), Fast and Munro (1991), Michelson (1985); for Finland, Babarczy et al. (1991), Niemi et al. (1991), Niemi and Anachkova (1992); for Latvia, Babarczy et al. (1991); for Java, Sanchez (1994); for Latvia, Niemi et al. (1991); for Lithuania, Niemi et al. (1991); for the Philippines, Sanchez (1994); for Russia, Niemi et al. (1991); for South Korea, Sanchez (1994); for the Sudan, Sanchez (1994); for Taiwan,

Sanchez (1994); for the UK, Warde and Hetherington (1993); for the US, Aldous (1995), Blair and Lichter (1991), Chang and White-Means (1991), Dwyer and Seccombe (1991), Gallagher (1994), Greenstein (1995), Hilton and Haldeman (1991), Loomis and Booth (1995), Manke et al. (1994), Marks and McLanahan (1993), Sanchez (1994), and Ward (1993). See also Ward (1990).

[97] Stafford et al. (1977), Shelton and John (1993).

[98] Ishii-Kuntz and Coltrane (1992:226, Table 2).

[99] Warde and Hetherington (1993:33).

[100] Ishii-Kuntz and Coltrane (1992) note that children's contributions to housework vary with the contributions fathers make in first marriages versus stepfamilies. In dual-earner households, children perform less housework than do children in single-earner households. 'In our sample, the two types of stepparent households were most likely dual-earners, and these were the families with the largest contribution to housework by children. Children's contributions could theoretically substitute for the father's contribution ... but we found just the opposite. Controlling for all major hypothesized causal variables, when children do more housework, so do fathers ... the opposite tendency was found for remarried biological parents, where small contributions by children were accompanied by the highest levels of housework by husbands' (Ishii-Kuntz and Coltrane 1992:230–1). However, nothing changes the basic overall gender imbalance that is observed everywhere.

[101] See Tuttle (1994:122).

[102] Ferree (1990).

[103] Warde and Hetherington (1993:42).

[104] Dempsey (1988:434).

[105] See Gannage (1986).

[106] Hochschild (1989).

[107] A US study of mothers who care for children with disabilities found that families with such children 'tend to follow the most traditional pattern of family life with a breadwinning husband and a full-time wife and mother ... The study suggests that although the majority of women have managed to enter the public arena of paid work, education, and other activities outside the home, these new and expanded boundaries of women's lives are very fragile. As soon as there is an increased demand for traditional women's work within the home—such as caring for a child with a disability—the boundaries shift and women come under tremendous pressure to leave the public arena and go back into the home' (Traustadottir 1991:225).

This general conclusion is confirmed by a Polish study, which found that the economic crisis in 1990 and before in Poland often caused a decrease in time devoted to paid work and a corresponding increase in household work. 'The disturbing trend of the substitution of time by goods and services pertained mostly to women' (Gucwa-Lesny 1995:127).

[108]Duxbury et al. (1994). With respect to small business owners, Loscocco and Leicht (1993:885) found that family intrudes on married women's business success, but promotes that of men; single women show the same pattern as men.

[109]See Bittman and Lovejoy (1993), Dempsey (1988), Warde and Hetherington (1993).

[110]See Thompson (1991).

[111]Bittman and Lovejoy (1993:302).

[112]Harrison and Laliberté (1994:180–6).

[113]Ibid., 180.

[114]Ibid., 181.

[115]Whyte (1956).

[116]Papanek (1973).

[117]When researchers try to locate couples with an egalitarian division of labour, they would usually advertise or otherwise try to initiate contact with a highly specialized group of people. For instance, over an *eight-month period* Blaisure and Allen (1995) recruited twenty-three couples who were self-identified feminists. They placed advertisements in the regional weekly and monthly newspapers of NOW, local newspapers, made announcements at a regional NOW meeting, announced the study in graduate classes at the university, and used snowballing. Of the twenty-three couples they eventually identified, thirteen had to be eliminated for various reasons. Of the ten remaining couples, six demonstrated a distinctly unequal division of labour.

[118]LaRossa (1977).

[119]For a summary of some of the issues, see Thompson (1993).

[120]Gilligan (1982).

[121]See Thompson (1993:561–2).

[122]Ibid.

[123]See Rubin (1985), Thompson (1993:562–3).

[124]Thompson (1993:563).

[125]There are incidents of husband battering, as well as of abuse within lesbian relationships; see Ristock (1994). I have called this section wife battering to call attention to its gendered nature. There is a trend to subsume it under 'family violence' or 'family abuse', which hides the fact that an overwhelmingly number of victims are women, and men are the perpetrators. I have included common-law wives under this heading, since physical violence is more likely to occur in common-law relationships than in legal marriages; see Stets (1991).

[126]See DeKeseredy and Kelly (1993) on woman abuse in dating relationships; see Canadian Panel on Violence (1993) for a comprehensive examination of the extent and nature of violence.

[127]Statistics Canada (1993c).

[128]Rodgers (1994:4, 8). The figures in the US are comparable: between 1973 and 1991, two-thirds of the women victims experienced violence at the hands of people they knew: 28 per cent from intimates such as husbands or boyfriends, 35 per cent from acquaintances, 5 per cent from other relatives, and only 31 per cent from strangers. 'The rate of violence committed by intimates was nearly 10 times greater for females than for males' (Bachman 1994:1).

[129]Wilson and Daly (1994). During this period, 1,435 women versus 451 men were slain by their spouses, i.e., 3.2 women for every man. To this must be added that 'in cases of wives killing husbands, there is often evidence that the husband was the initial aggressor, with much the same motives as in uxoricide, and that her lethal action was "defensive" ...' (Ibid., 6–7). Looking at the most extreme of these cases, namely familicide (the killing of spouse and children in the same incident) sixty-five such familicides involving 172 victims took place during this period, of which 94 per cent were committed by men.

[130]The female/male ratio of spousal homicide victimization is similar in Australia, Denmark, and the United Kingdom. In the US, by contrast, only 1.3 wives are slain for each husband killed by his wife (Ibid.).

[131]Roberts (1994:3). Of these cases, only 6 per cent were reported to the police!

[132]Bass and Davis (1988:33–54), Blume (1990), Browne and Finkelhor (1986), Canadian Panel on Violence (1993), Herman (1981:96–108), Jenu and Gazan (1989), Maltz (1992), Sleeth and Barnsley (1989), Statistics Canada (1993b), Wachtel (1988).

[133]Arlett et al. (1988:3–4), Russell (1986).

[134]Arlett et al. (1988:11–12).

[135]Herman (1992:113).

[136]The law defines spouse in a particular way, which does not always agree with the conventional social definition of this term, thus further confusing matters.

[137]*McLeod* v. the *A.G. of Canada and the Minister of National Health and Welfare*, filed at the Court of Queen's Bench of Alberta, Edmonton, 14 Nov. 1991.

Chapter 4

[1]This leaves aside more complicated issues such as the status of grandparents, aunts, uncles, cousins, etc. In such situations, kin relationships as defined by blood, marriage, or adoptive ties are often greatly modified through actual social interaction patterns, particularly when the two biological parents are not living together. For instance, are the children of the son's second wife his parents' grandchildren (there is no blood relationship involved) or not? Are they still the grandchildren of the wife's

first husband's parents, even though no contact is maintained? In order to keep things manageable, I have bracketed all such issues here.

[2]About half of all fathers lose contact with their children after divorce within a relatively short time.

[3]This is a typical consequence of the monolithic bias in operation; see Eichler (1988a).

[4]Ambert 1994:534.

[5]Ibid., 530.

[6]While women may still be refused jobs on these grounds, at least this is no longer legally sanctioned.

[7]There are now a number of legal cases in the US in which sperm donors—who were never recognized as social fathers to begin with—have been recognized as fathers. This is a special instance of a reinstated father. See Arnup (1994) for a discussion of these cases.

[8]See Eichler and McCall (1993) for a category system for fathers, which takes all of these factors into account.

[9]There is another form of post-mortem parenthood when a parent continues to actively influence a child's life beyond his or her death, for instance, via a legacy, survivor's entitlement, etc. Although important, I will also disregard this form of post-mortem parenthood here to keep things manageable.

[10]The first human embryos have already been cloned, although they were destroyed at a very early stage, and with the new reproductive and genetic technologies, more than two people may be involved in creating a child.

[11]Bane (1979:279) has calculated that between 1901 and 1910, 28.9 per cent of all children in the US experienced a marital disruption before the age of eighteen, most of these due to the death of the mother or the father.

[12]With the omissions noted earlier for clarity.

[13]This is somewhat simplified. Fathers might be partial fathers even at that time because their children were temporarily or permanently under the care of the Crown. However, this was then (as now) the case only for a very small proportion of fathers.

[14]Intact is often taken to mean well functioning. However, the composition of a family tells us nothing about how this family functions, whether well or badly. Presumably, all those families that undergo divorce experience at least some period before divorce during which they do *not* function well, hence the eventual divorce. Other families may have a high level of conflict and/or abuse, yet remain 'intact'. Neither of these can be described as well-functioning families.

[15]The official numbers may underestimate the number of illegitimate children somewhat, taking into account those men who had deserted their first wife and founded a second family, without the second wife (and

her children) being aware of the existence of a first wife and the first set of children. In such cases, both sets of children might have been regarded as legitimate.

[16]Goode hypothesized for the 1950s—at a time when the patriarchal model was still in full swing—that 'Although the wife will have fairly serious charges to make against her husband, we believe that in our generation it is more often the husband who first wishes to escape from marriage' (Goode 1956:135). In order to force a divorce, then, 'The husband must make himself so obnoxious that his wife is willing to ask for and even insist upon a divorce' (Ibid., 135–6). It is insufficient to simply look at who formally sues for divorce if one wishes to determine who desired a divorce first and perhaps most strongly.

[17]There might be a few exceptions to this generalization, but by and large it seems safe to assume that most divorced or separated men decided at some point that a union dissolution was preferable to a continued union.

[18]James G. McLeod on *Young* V. *Young* (1994), 49 R.F.L. (3d), p. 132.

[19]Cited in Fine and Kurdek (1992).

[20]Ishii-Kuntz and Coltrane (1992:225).

[21]See Department of Justice (1990), Furstenberg et al. (1983), Hetherington et al. (1978), Kruk (1993).

[22]However, for some evidence to the contrary, see Arditti and Keith (1993:708), who found that 'Highly involved fathers were those who lived nearby, reported higher levels of father-child closeness before the divorce, and had joint custody arrangements.'

[23]Kruk (1993:51–2).

[24]Ibid., (66–7).

[25]Others who might be involved are potential step-parents on both sides, potential step siblings, other relatives such as grandparents, and some social agencies such as schools that deal with a child on an ongoing basis and need to know to whom to send report cards, for instance, or into whose custody a child may be released, etc.

[26]See Maccoby, Depner, and Mnookin (1990) for evidence to this effect and a review of previous research. See Hawkins and Eggebeen (1993) for a national US study on the effect of the absence or presence of either the biological father or some other coresident adult male on small children. They conclude that 'this study suggests that it may be misleading to speak of negative consequences for young children of no father or father figure in the household, at least after an initial period of adjustment. Indeed, the results of this study hardly challenge the position being taken by a handful of researchers that the stability of the No Male pattern may be an adaptive, even preferable situation for disrupted children …' (Hawkins and Eggebeen 1993:968). They continue: 'Similarly, the position that adult men are important to young children's well-being, but

social fathers are effective father substitutes, is not supported by this research, either' (Ibid., 969).

Gringlas and Weintraub (1995:47) examined the different outcomes for children of solo mothers versus married mothers and concluded that the intervening variable is maternal stress: 'it appears that children reared in solo-parent families may be in a more vulnerable position when coping with preadolescence and with their mother's life circumstances ... Across the board, children from solo-parent/high-stress level families demonstrated the highest incidence of behaviour problems ... Conversely, and most interestingly, were the findings with regard to solo-parent children from low-stress households. On all measures, these solo-parent children were rated no differently than the two-parent family children, where maternal stress levels did not yield within group differences.'

[27]See Table 4 in Appendix 2.

[28]Girdner (1989:137).

[29]Ibid., 138.

[30]For a comprehensive study see Maccoby, Depner, and Mnookin (1990).

[31]Cf., Chapter 3 on the division of labour.

[32]Drakich (1989:87).

[33]Atkinson and Blackwelder (1993) provide a careful discussion and interpretation of their findings:

> We suggest that, during the twenties, the conceptualization of parenting began to change from a very gendered view, with mothers and parents regarded as equivalent, to a less gendered perspective. While it would be tempting to use these data to infer that interest in fathering has therefore increased, to do so risks committing an ecological fallacy. It is just as likely that people began to use the term *parenting* when they were actually referring to the behaviors of mothers and simply found that parenting was a more acceptable term. The data on division of labor in child care supports this interpretation. Even so, this change in language indicates a less gendered view of the world. Perhaps more likely, the increased use of the term *parenting* may indicate that most people think that fathers and mothers should be engaging in the same behavior regardless of what they actually do (Atkinson and Blackwelder 1993:984; emphasis in the original).

[34]See Drakich (1989:79–81).

[35]LaRossa and Reitzes (1993).

[36]This section draws heavily on work done by Lianne Carley.

[37]See Bertoia and Drakich (1993).

[38]Fine (1994).

[39]Crean (1988:117).

[40]See Bertoia and Drakich (1993). Indeed, one group, In Search of Justice, wants to completely eliminate alimony and child support. Strangely enough, Ross Virgin, its leader since 1974, has never been married himself, nor is he a father (of any type). See Crean (1988:105–12) and Habib (1995).

[41]See the following examples; *Wilbur* v. *MacMurray* (1991) 38 R.F.L. (3d) 122 N.B.R. (2d) 79, 306 A.P.R. 79 (Q.B.); *Harrison* v. *Harrison* (1987) 10 R.F.L. (3d) 1, 51 Man.R. (2d) 16 (Q.B.); *Casement* v. *Casement* (1987) 9 R.F.L. (3d) 169, 53 Alta L.R. (2d) 256, 81 A.R. 76 (Q.B.); *Brownwell* v. *Brownwell* (1987) 9 R.F.L. (3d), 82 N.B.R. (2d) 91, 208, A.P.R. 91 (Q.B.).

[42]For the US, see Chesler (1986), Polikoff (1983), Weitzman (1985); for Canada, see Crean (1988), McKie et al. (1983), Richardson (1988). For a balanced discussion of the issue, see Bertoia and Drakich (1993).

[43]A review of legal practice in the US notes that 'Few judges impose protective limitations on visitation in the context of domestic violence, and fewer limit access to supervised visitation ... Furthermore, judges almost never deny abusive parents access to their children ... bias also operates' (Hofford et al. 1995:216–17). See Crean (1988) for details and examples of Canadian cases.

[44]Frankel-Howard (1992:76).

[45]See Boyd (1989) for a discussion of some of these aspects.

[46]Bertoia and Drakich (1993:612). See also Delorey (1989), Drakich (1989), Dulac (1989), and Fineman (1989). For a first-hand report of how fathers' rights groups can play havoc with the personal life of one woman and her children, see Gordon (1989).

[47]See Mitchell (1993:146–60).

[48]Levasseur (1995b:25–6).

[49]A right to support is a relatively recent development.

[50]It is not clear what this means in terms of where the children actually live. Once a custody disposition has been made, and the couple do not come back before the court, the assumption usually is that the child resides with the custodial parent. That may, in fact, not be true. There is considerable postdivorce mobility for children; see Eichler (1988a).

[51]Cf., Fillion (1993).

[52]I will provide a personal anecdote here. While I was writing this section, on 27 July 1995 then Health Minister Diane Marleau provided the first official federal response to the Royal Commission on New Reproductive Technologies, which filed its report in November 1993 (Royal Commission on New Reproductive Technologies 1993). She called for a voluntary moratorium on nine practices, including buying and selling eggs, sperm, and embryos, and donating eggs in exchange for *in vitro* fertilization services (Greenspon 1995; Valpy 1995). A reporter called me for comment. When I indicated that I opposed egg donation because it split the genetic and gestational aspects of motherhood, her

disappointed comment was 'That's all? That's the basis on which you dislike this?' She ended the discussion soon after. For her—and I believe for many others—this profound shift in reproduction has become so normalized that she was not expecting anyone to question whether we *should* do something that we are obviously capable of doing.

[53]Sanchez (1994:399) credits Nancy Folbre with this statement.

[54]Although fathers 'help out' with their children, they rarely take responsibility for the planning and management of child care. The few studies on this issue find that fathers rendered *parental assistance*, but failed to take *parental responsibility*; see Leslie et al. (1991).

[55]This has been shown for the Netherlands (van Wel 1994:839), where both daughters and sons were found to have a closer bond with the mother than with the father, although it was closer for the girls than the boys and the difference between the tie with mother and father was particularly pronounced for the girls.

Women in the US are significantly more likely than men to help primary kin (parents or children). One study found a difference of ten hours or more per month in this regard (Gallagher 1994:573).

[56]Fineman (1995:735).

[57]The *Child and Family Services Act* (1984) of Ontario specifies in s. 37 (2) that

A child is in need of protection where …:

(c) the child has been sexually molested or sexually exploited, by the person having charge of the child or by another person where the person having charge *knows or should know* of the possibility of sexual molestation or sexual exploitation and fails to protect the child;

(d) there is substantial risk that the child will be sexually molested or sexually exploited as described in clause (c) [emphasis added].

The person who is usually held responsible for a child is the mother, who therefore 'should have known' that the child was molested. The first woman has now been convicted in Canada for failing to protect her child against abuse by her father; see *J.(L.A.)* v. *J.(H. and J.(J.)* (1993), 13 O.R. (3d) 306 (Gen. div.). See Grace and Vella (1994) for a critique and comment on the judgement.

[58]By far, more abuse is committed by men who are known to the child (as father, stepfather, uncle, older brother, cousin, or neighbour) than by women.

[59]Carter (1990).

[60]Ibid., 215.

[61]Krane (1994:219; emphasis in the original).

[62]Ambert (1994:539).

[63]Fineman (1995).

[64]Rothman (1989).

[65]Ambert (1994:532).

[66]This term is used here in its sociological rather than legal sense.

[67]Royal Commission on New Reproductive Technologies (1993:582).

[68]Ibid.

[69]Ibid., p. 587.

[70]Ibid., p. 677.

[71]Ibid., p. 685.

[72]The increasing number of cocustodial parents does not translate into joint physical custody.

[73]See Chapter 8 for a discussion of child-support levels and awards.

Chapter 5

[1]Pateman (1992:28).

[2]This is not to deny that there are extremely important differences in the degree of inequality between different societies at one point in time and in the same society over time. Even in fiction, however, there are very few *positive* examples of societies based on equality. There are, by contrast, a number of dystopias in which everyone is equal, living a joyless, highly regulated, and bureaucratized life. For three classic examples, see Orwell ([1949] 1962), Rand ([1946] 1961), and Zamyatin ([1972] 1983). For a largely unsuccessful search for positive visions, see Eichler (1981).

[3]The legal doctrine of 'separate-but-equal' is a version of equality according to which 'those who are similarly situated should be similarly treated', and as such it can look back to a lengthy heritage of attempting to decrease discrimination, especially on the basis of race; see Bacchi (1991). By contrast, sociologists regard this notion as the basis of race apartheid as, for instance, practised in South Africa before the election of a democratic government. By extension, one can use a parallel term of 'gender apartheid' to describe specific societies, e.g., the Victorian Age in the Euro-American context (see Cook and Mitchinson 1976 and Vicinus 1973) as well as some contemporary countries, such as fundamentalist Islamic nations. Separate-but-equal is thus the epitome of *in*equality. Same term, different meanings.

[4]See Charlesworth (1992) for a discussion of this approach.

[5]Bacchi (1991:71).

[6]This formulation assumes that pregnancy is a disability to begin with— surely a most ironic miscategorization, given that it is the manifestation of the most important biological ability, not disability—although it may result in temporary incapacity to perform some functions.

[7]*Bliss* v. *Attorney-General of Canada*, [1978] 92 D.L.R. (3d) 422.

[8]*Ibid.* Decisions in other cases years later overthrew this understanding of equality.

[9]Sevenhuijsen (1991:92–3).

[10]Ibid., 88.

[11]These types were originally constructed to identify various problems of sexism in research and policy analysis (Eichler 1988b, 1992). They are not meant to be descriptive of the various forms of sexism in different societies—a quite different categorization would be required for that task. The types as defined here are vastly simplified (all subtypes have been omitted). Two types (overgeneralization and sex appropriateness) have been omitted since they are less relevant (although not irrelevant) in this context. However, a diagnostic tool to identify sexism based on all types and subtypes is included in Appendix 3.

[12]Justice Heureux-Dubé provides a good example of familism in her reasons for judgement in *Thibaudeau* v. *Canada*, [1995] 2 s.c.r. 627, par. 10: 'There is no doubt ... that an unequal burden arose in the old Marital Property Acts of the nineteenth century, under which, upon marriage, the wife's assets automatically became those of the man. Yet if the only unit of analysis were taken to be the "couple", we would be precluded from looking at the effects of these provisions on each member of the couple ...'

By looking at the individuals rather than at the couple, L'Heureux-Dubé as well as McLachlin came up with the opposite deposition in the *Thibaudeau* case, as did the men (who were the majority), all of whom took the couple as the unit of analysis. These forms of sexism have extremely serious consequences.

[13]Susan Boyd provides many examples of double standards in custody decisions in which fathers sought (usually successfully) custody of their children; see Boyd (1989).

[14]For instance, Fineman (1995:41–2) states: 'The argument is that legal theory must recognize the reality of existing systemic and persistent inequality and move beyond the simplistic equality paradigm ... equality has proven insufficient as a concept with which to both assess and address the position of women under law ... The argument is not that the concept is useless, but rather that equality should no longer be the overarching goal ... the metaobjective that drives all other considerations.' Flax (1992:194) argues for justice as an alternative goal because 'I cannot imagine equality apart from some measure of sameness.' 'Feminists have begun to question whether "equality" can mean anything other than assimilation to a pre-existing and problematic "male" norm' (Ibid., 196).

[15]See Forbes (1991:18–19).

[16]One commentator (Geller 1991:389) has characterized this model as follows: 'The "equal opportunity" principle as espoused by liberal feminists assumes that the gender-neutral model of equality addresses the needs of all women. Those who support this model believe it will achieve equal status for men and women. The liberal models of equality, however, only allows women the "equality" to be like men ... Under the liberal par-

adigm, women who can, or who want to, accept the world as it is and fit within it will be allowed to do so.'

[17]For one recent example, see Harvey et al. (1990).

[18]By Littleton (1993).

[19]Ibid., 120.

[20]Ibid., 111–12.

[21]Ibid., 120.

[22]See Siim (1991).

[23]Ibid., 178.

[24]Parvikko (1991:44).

[25]Siim (1991:179; emphasis in the original).

[26]Sometimes these questions can be combined by asking whether or not there should be any differences between legal marriages and common-law unions. I believe this is a mistake because there is no necessary symmetry between entitlements from the state and individuals' obligations towards each other. See Chapter 7 for a discussion of this issue.

[27]There is one exception to this statement. There is considerable evidence that common-law unions are less stable than legal marriages. About '40 per cent of unions in the United States break up without the couple getting married, and this tends to occur rather quickly. By about one and one-half years, half of cohabiting couples have either married or broken up ...' (Bumpass et al. 1991:917). 'Only about 1 out of 10 remain cohabiting after five years without either marrying or breaking up. Nonetheless, this does not mean that there are few cohabitants of long duration at any point in time. Longer cohabitants tend to "accumulate" in the population ... 20 per cent of cohabiting couples have lived together five or more years' (Ibid., 919).

From the state's perspective, a waiting period of between one and three years after a couple first begin living together might therefore be advantageous to weed out the short-lived unions before conferring benefits.

[28]Ristock (1991:74) notes that abuse in lesbian relationships may include physical abuse (hitting, punching, choking), sexual abuse (forced sexual acts, sexual assaults with objects), psychological abuse (repetitive and excessive criticizing, humiliation, degradation, threats), economic abuse (controlling finances, creating debt), and destruction of personal items.

[29]Gairdner (1992:86) argues that the biological difference between the sexes requires that men be tamed by women—a feat women achieve via the nuclear family. The nuclear family is therefore 'a means for taming male sexual and physical aggression'. Popenoe (1994:98) suggests that unattached men are the source of many societal ills, and that every society must be wary of them.

[30]One very large-scale, representative US study found that cohabiting couples were more likely to divorce than legally married couples and reported significantly lower levels of happiness than married couples.

They also show poorer intergenerational relations. Concerning the reasons for this finding, the author concludes:

> Together, these results suggest that much, if not most, of the difference in relationship quality found to be associated with cohabitation, as opposed to marriage, is actually due to different levels of commitment and differences in the quality of relationships with parents. Cohabitation, that is, appears to take its toll on relationship quality because cohabitors have poorer relations with their parents and have lower levels of commitment—and these foster poorer assessment of the relationship ...
>
> ... cohabitation and marriage do not differ as much in terms of the ordinary, everyday partnerships as they do with respect to long-term concerns and relationships with people beyond the immediate dyad (Nock 1995:72–3).

Presumably, then, greater social support would alleviate the problems, while reduced support would increase them. If the state wants stable, happy relationships among its citizens, it should therefore support all types of unions.

[31]Institute of Law Research and Reform (1984:65–7). There is the troublesome issue that one partner may wish to marry, while the other does not. The choice may therefore represent the 'choice' of only one of the two parties involved. Since marriage is supposed to be a quintessentially consensual union in our society, it requires the agreement of both parties. This may put women, who tend to be the economically weaker partner in the majority of cases, in a disadvantaged position, but I do not believe that the answer to this very real dilemma lies in imposing a marriagelike condition on every common-law couple, some of whom may indeed wish to avoid just this. Instead, the solution must be sought outside the family by equalizing the economic situation of women and men. I realize that this is a long-term proposition of little help to individuals at present, but I believe it is problematic to try to solve what are social problems (the disadvantaged economic and social position of women) through essentially private means (ensuring their economic well-being through attachment to one particular man).

[32]One answer to this question is that the lifestyle enjoyed during the relationship as well as the dependency maintained entitles the dependant to ongoing support. This argument needs to be put into the broader context of how to deal with dependent relationships in general. See Chapter 7 for a discussion of this issue.

[33]We do not know exactly how many men are either not ordered to pay support or default (partially or totally) on their payments. See Finnie et al. (1994) for a detailed discussion of the problems in available data sets. However, we do know that the vast majority of men do not pay any type

of support. In 1993, only 16 per cent of all lone-parent, mother-led families received any support payments whatsoever; see National Council of Welfare (1995a:54, Table 14).

[34]Justice Fleury's rationale in *Primeau* v. *Primeau* (1986), 2 R.F.L. (3d) 113 (Ont. H.C.) provides a good example of this problem. In this case, the couple were married for just over four years. There were two children that the wife brought into the marriage from a previous union. The issue was whether the second husband was responsible for paying support for the second child, Brandi. The second husband's relationship with Brandi is described as follows:

> The petitioner was the main breadwinner and supplied the funds to purchase all of the child's clothing as well as most of her other needs. To quote the petitioner: 'she never wanted for anything.' He participated in disciplinary matters and conceded that he would yell at her when she misbehaved and that he would send her to her room occasionally. He would hug her before she retired for the night, he would play with her, swim with her, take her places such as Crystal Beach, the Zoo, Canada's Wonderland, etc. He attended a school Christmas concert on at least one occasion and attended outings organized as family picnics, hayrides, etc. He would buy gifts for her including a trail bike which he showed her how to ride. The entire family would regularly participate in such activities as pool parties and barbecues and when family reunions would take place at the petitioner's parents' home, Brandi would be treated as though part of the petitioner's family for all to observe. The petitioner even carried a picture of Brandi in his wallet. In spite of all this, the petitioner insists that he did not stand in 'loco parentis'. He refers to the fact that Brandi did not call him 'dad' but, rather, used his first name, he also alleges that Brandi never confided in him that she was afraid of him. I find these allegations very weak indeed and I do not accept his evidence in that respect.

Fleury argues: 'A parent-child relationship is not one that can be terminated unilaterally by the parent or the child. The same result should follow in either the case of the natural parent or the "deemed" parent.' However, there actually *was* a biological father of the child, and indeed the wife resumed living with her ex-husband, who was Brandi's natural father, for some five months after her separation from the second husband.

> Counsel for the petitioner elicited in cross-examination an admission from the respondent that Brandi's natural father resumed 'acting as Brandi's father' during the period of their cohabitation. I was urged to conclude that because of this renewed interest on the part

of Brandi's natural father it would be unseemly to insist on the parental obligations imposed by law on the petitioner. I see no reason for agreeing with this position … There was no evidence before me of any ability on the part of the natural father to provide maintenance for his daughter except for the terms of a decree nisi pronounced some years earlier. Although it is arguable that natural parents should be made to bear the primary burden of supporting their children, the Parliament of Canada has not seen fit to impose such a distinction between 'parents' and it is not up to me to add such a requirement when applying the Divorce Act.

He therefore made a maintenance order of $100 per week.

[35] Finnie in Finnie et al. (1994:80).

[36] Arditti and Keith found that joint-custody fathers pay lower amounts of child support than non-custodial fathers, but custody satisfaction is positively related to child-support outcomes, and joint-custody fathers tend to be more satisfied, thus mitigating this relationship. However, 'neither visitation frequency nor quality have any bearing on child support payment, a finding that supports several other studies that failed to find a relationship between greater father involvement and child support payment …' (1993:710).

[37] Department of Justice (1990:107).

[38] The same study notes: 'Careful analysis of the interviews where women did express dissatisfaction suggest that the major difficulty they were experiencing was that their ex-husband was not sharing equally in parenting the children. Simply, there is a gap between what men and women perceive as an adequate level of parenting …' (Ibid., 107).

[39] A parallel situation occurs today when fathers who do not pay child support still have liberal access to their children.

[40] In early 1996, the federal government committed itself to changing this regulation. This new regime will start in May 1997.

[41] Cf., note 18.

[42] In the wake of this decision, two other cases, *Gernat* v. *Gernat* and *Luckhurst* v. *Luckhurst*, have already adopted the reasoning put forward by Justice Abella. What makes the latter case particularly interesting is that the father had cocustody, although the children had been living continually with Ms Luckhurst since the separation. It was the substance and not the formal aspect of the arrangement that made the difference in allowing the move; see Schmitz (1995:4).

[43] *MacGyver* v. *Richards* (1995), F.L.R. (4th) pp. 445–7.

[44] *Gordon* v. *Gertz* [1996] S.C.J. #15 file #2422.

[45] There are, of course, some instances in which it *is* appropriate to take the household as the administrative unit, for instance, with respect to water or electricity consumption. When it comes to income-tested ben-

efits, the matter is more complicated. Canada has, at present, income-tested programs that operate either on an individual basis (e.g., unemployment insurance) or on a couple basis (e.g., social welfare or the guaranteed income supplement). While welfare should probably remain income-tested on a couple basis, I could see substantial benefits in converting all other income-tested benefits to an individual basis, since failing to do so will penalize people for living together.

[46]See Eichler (1988a:115–18).

[47]This vignette was elaborated on in 1992 with the help of Sally Huemmert in preparation for a day-long consultation with the premier's group, which prepared Alberta's Family Policy Grid. It reflects actual policies and actual rates of benefits or pay for the conditions specified at the time in Alberta. It is modelled after an actual case in Ontario; see Eichler (1988a:134).

[48]A US study of child care among welfare recipients concluded that 'approaches to encouraging in-home care by relatives, when this is possible, might lead to more durable arrangements. Policies that subsidize care provided by relatives in the child's home, for example, might result in more long-lasting arrangements for a portion of mothers' (Wolf and Sonenstein 1991:534).

[49]Lewis and Åström (1992:64).

[50]See Chapter 2.

[51]See Chapter 1 for a discussion of the value of productive work.

[52]See the discussion on the division of labour in Chapter 3.

[53]*Ontario Family Law Reform Act*, R.S.O. 1986, c. 4, s. 5(7). Similar or identical formulations are found in other provincial laws: cf., PEI *Family Law Reform Act*, S.P.E.I. 1978, c. 6, s. 5(7); the Civil Code of Quebec, S.Q. 1980, c. 39, art. 445; the *Matrimonial Property Act* of Saskatchewan, s.s. 1997, c. M-6.1, s. 20; the Yukon *Family Property and Support Act*, R.S.Y. 1986, c. 63, s. 5.

[54]Compare with Chapter 3.

[55]See Ontario Law Reform Commission (1993:45).

[56]As the European Ministers Responsible for Social Affairs have noted:

> Only a few countries, such as Denmark and the Netherlands, have introduced minimum state pensions for women. This amounts to a partial recognition of their unpaid family work and compensates in part for the typical rupture in female job biographies. The definition of women as housewives who care for their husband and children and in return are—at least partially—maintained by the husband's income, is still inherent to most social security systems. It renders impossible an independent economic subsistence for the majority of women and furthermore leads to the impoverishment of

many women (feminization of poverty) (European Centre 1993:160).

[57]See Chapter 6.

[58]This is evident in the recent welfare reforms in the US, which aim to get welfare mothers to work under the (mistaken) assumption that this will enable them to get off welfare. A study of 288 women in Baltimore (Harris 1991) who had their first child at age eighteen or younger over a seventeen-year period demonstrated that welfare mothers shared the desire and willingness to earn their living, and that an early start in the labour force kept them dependent on welfare for a significantly *longer* period than finishing high school and being able to find jobs that paid well enough to enable them to be self-sufficient. Child-care constraints prolonged welfare dependency. 'Women with preschool children to care for faced 43 per cent lower odds of leaving welfare while working than did working mothers with older children' (Harris 1991:512). Ontario introduced 'workfare' in 1996.

[59]Of course this is only *one* contributing factor. Others include outright discrimination and occupational segregation by sex with women predominantly in the so-called secondary labour market in which jobs have low security, low pay, low fringe benefits, while men are predominantly in the primary labour market with higher security, better fringe benefits, and higher pay as well as other factors.

[60]Bould (1993:139) defines family as 'the informal unit where those who cannot take care of themselves can find care in time of need. If someone has no family or if the family fails to function informally in this way, then that person must be able to take care of himself or herself or the state takes over the responsibility.'

[61]Please note that I am talking about spousal support, not child support. While the figures remain the same if we include child support, the moral obligation to contribute to the economic well-being of one's children should not be negotiable.

[62]See Eichler (1990).

Chapter 6

[1]Popenoe argues that nations with a collectivist ethos will economically surpass nations like the United States, which is 'culturally deconstructing into a sea of individualistic chaos' (1994:103). With respect to those nations that are stronger on collectivism, 'One thinks of nations like Japan, Taiwan, Singapore, and Korea, but it is also likely that—partly because of their relatively stronger collectivism—most European nations will come to overshadow the economic achievements of the United States' (Ibid., 88–9).

[2]Ibid., 98.

[3]Ibid., 103.

[4]See Fineman (1995:14), Stacey (1993), Glenn (1993), and Cowan (1993). However, there are critics who disagree with at least part of his description of the demise of the family. One of the points Popenoe and others make is that there is only a small proportion of households of married couples with minor children. Popenoe attributes this fact primarily to an increase in divorce, births outside of marriage, and a decline in fertility and marriage. 'The decline in the percentage of households containing a married couple with their minor children, however, is due as much to the changing age structure of the population together with the ability of most elderly, both married and single, to afford a home of their own' (Bould 1993:136).

[5]There are many contrary views to this. See, for example, Bernardes (1993:36) who asks: 'How could those who enthusiastically praise the nuclear family face the consequences of their praise in the frequently reported guilt and shame felt by victims of abuse … It is arguable that the nuclear family is such an unrealistic myth that even presenting it as a viable goal has done harm in generating unrealistic expectations …'

[6]Popenoe (1994:96).

[7]Ibid., 101.

[8]Ibid.

[9]Ibid., 102.

[10]Ibid., 103.

[11]Ibid., 104.

[12]Ibid., 103.

[13]Ibid., 96.

[14]Kertzer (1992:15).

[15]Fuchs (1992:8). 'The scale on which mothers abandoned newborns in the European past is only now beginning to be appreciated in the general scholarly community' (Kertzer 1992:13) Babies were a commodity. 'Child abandonment was a system of exchange whereby poor women who could not keep their babies gave, or loaned, them to other poor women who needed the extra income [as wetnurses] or eventual labor that the foundling provided' (Fuchs 1992:11–12). However, for the vast majority of babies, this was a death sentence (Ibid.). See also Tilly (1992) and Ransel (1992).

[16]See Chapter 2.

[17]Arguably, women and children may be *more* locked into an unhappy marriage than men, as used to be the case in the past. Since the idea behind this approach is that children should be raised by their parents, and since this has and still does usually mean a much greater time investment by the mother than by the father, this would decrease women's participation in the labour force and lead to attendant economic disadvantages. In turn, lone-parent families (having been defined as the problem

that needs to be overcome) would not receive much (if any) public assistance, thus making women and children much more dependent on the men to whom they are attached.

[18]For a review of older studies on the differential effects of divorce versus unhappy marriages, see Eichler (1988a:212–21). A recent US study, using a national sample and looking at the long-term effects of divorce, examined whether it is the effects of divorce that are harmful or the processes that antedate separation and divorce and that eventually lead to divorce. The authors note:

> Many of the same processes that are often thought to be initiated when marriages dissolve actually antedate the separation event. Our analysis suggests that exposure to these conditions may compromise children's economic, social, and psychological well-being in later life whether or not a separation takes place. Thus it appears that the added contribution of divorce and its aftermath to children's problems in later life is not nearly as great as might be inferred from findings that do not take adequate account of family conditions prior to separation (Furstenberg and Teitler 1994:187).

[19]See Chapter 2. A US study of welfare recipients concluded that 'encouraging young Black mothers to marry is probably not a useful strategy in improving the long-run economic status of these women … preventing births to adolescent mothers and providing mechanisms to help young mothers help themselves by completing more education and acquiring work experience in upwardly mobile jobs would appear to be more effective in preventing the problems associated with early childbearing' (Rudd et al. 1990:350–1).

[20]Stacey (1993:546).

[21]Ibid., 547.

[22]Popenoe also argues that 'State agencies increasingly have the family under surveillance, seeking compliance for increasingly restrictive state laws covering such issues as child abuse and neglect, wife abuse, tax payments, and property maintenance.' This, he argues, is a 'denial of power to the family unit' (1993:537). It is only possible to come up with this conclusion if one identifies the power of the family unit with the power of the male patriarch—an instance of the sexist problem of familism. It is assumed that a particular characteristic—power in this case—is lodged within the unit, when in fact it is power for one person (the abuser) versus powerlessness for other person(s) (the abused).

[23]'However one looks at it, and unfortunate though it may be, the decline of economic interdependence between husband and wife (primarily the economic dependence of the wife) appears to have led, in the aggregate, to weaker marital units as measured by higher rates of divorce and separation …' (Ibid., 536). This decline of economic interdependence is due

to the increased labour force participation of wives and state welfare support.

[24]Popenoe (1994:100).

[25]Ibid. However, given the low contributions of most fathers to child care, this is not always true. Indeed, some single mothers report having more time for the children after divorce than before.

[26]Okin (1989:135).

[27]Ibid.

[28]Ibid., 175.

[29]Ibid., 176.

[30]Ibid., 179.

[31]Ibid.; emphasis in the original.

[32]Ibid., 180–1; emphasis in the original.

[33]Ibid., 183; emphasis in the original.

[34]Ibid., 135.

[35]See Chapter 5.

[36]This is considered further later.

[37]Orton and Rosenblatt have indeed found that public preventive programs in sex education in schools, family planning services in public health units, and other infrastructural support have a measurable impact on reducing teenage pregnancies (measured both in terms of births and abortions); see Orton and Rosenblatt (1986, 1991, and 1993).

[38]For an empirical example of such a case that went to the Supreme Court on just this issue, see *Leblanc* v. *Leblanc*, [1988] 1 S.C.R. 217, 12 R.F.L. (3d) 225, 81 N.R. 299.

The couple were first married in 1957 when the woman was pregnant with her first child. Within the first eight years of the marriage, seven children were born. The husband worked fairly regularly for the first four or five years of the marriage. Subsequently, he worked only at occasional odd jobs. He was an alcoholic and drank heavily. According to the children's testimony, he took virtually no part in their upbringing. Until 1965, the family lived mostly on welfare, although the wife worked from time to time. After her youngest child was born, Mrs Leblanc started working full-time at a take-out restaurant, working a 3 p.m. to 3 a.m. shift. She took out a loan and bought the restaurant. Ten years later she bought a house for the family, and eventually she bought land on which a cottage was built. The husband's contributions to all this were minimal to non-existent.

The trial judge divided the property unequally, awarding $6,000 to the husband and everything else to the wife. The husband appealed and sued for an equal share of the entire matrimonial property. The appeal judge held that the husband was entitled to an equal share. The wife appealed this decision, and in 1988 the Supreme Court of Canada upheld the original unequal division of assets.

This may be an extreme example. However, given the literature on the division of labour by sex, I am assuming that in the vast majority of the approximately one-fifth of all marriages in which the wife earns as much or more than her husband, the wife still does most of the housework and family care. Equal splitting of assets in such cases does not seem fair.

[39]See Dulude (1984), Edwards (1981), Pahl (1989).

[40]Fineman (1995:67).

[41]Ibid., 162.

[42]Ibid., 162–3.

[43]Ibid., 164.

[44]Ibid., 165.

[45]Ibid., 228.

[46]Ibid., 131–2.

[47]Ibid., 234.

[48]Ibid., 235.

Chapter 7

[1]For a practical tool to achieve this, see Appendix 3.

[2]See Cassels [1995].

[3]Even in fiction there are very few examples of two-sex societies that are not stratified by sex; cf., Eichler (1981).

[4]Marx 1961:263.

[5]These dimensions were first developed in Eichler (1988b). They are drawn from a vast amount of literature dealing with inequalities of all types.

[6]This is a deliberate double simplification. Families are organized by age and gender. I have omitted age—and hence the important stratification that occurs between children and adults and between middle-aged adults and older people in order to concentrate on gender. I have also largely bracketed the stratification that occurs on the basis of parental status. In so far as it interacts with gender (being a mother versus being a father), this will be considered somewhat. However, one could do the entire analysis around parental status. I have chosen not to do so in order to maintain the relevance of this approach for the three models under consideration.

[7]Bernard (1972).

[8]In the first overall longitudinal study of a total cohort born in a Swedish locality, Samuelsson and Dehlin's (1993) hypothesis that network resources of families are normally more beneficial to men than women was supported. 'Single men and divorced men, and also widowers have lower survival rates compared with women in these same categories. The finding that widowhood and divorce were "positive" survival factors for women would also appear to lie in agreement with this perspective' (Ibid., 290).

In examining a representative sample of Germans in the old German Federal Republic (before the integration of the previous German Democratic Republic), Klein (1993) found that being widowed increases the mortality risk of men by a factor of 1.5, and being divorced by a factor of 2.1. However, he found that women as well run a higher mortality risk by a factor of 1.7, although there is no difference between being widowed or divorced.

Looking at all Canadian deaths between 1951 and 1981, Trovato and Lauris (1989) found that overall, marriage was of greater benefit to men than to women in reducing mortality. Using the same data set and focusing on suicide, Trovato found that 'the change from a nonmarried state to a married state produces greater reduction in the risk of suicide for men than for women' (1991:437; see also p. 440).

[9]In 1990, the overall life expectancy was 69.2 years, and in 1993 it was 66 years. Broken down by sex, it was 63.8 years in 1990 and 59 years in 1993 for males. For females, it was 74.3 years in 1990 and 73 years in 1993. The figures are from the *National Report for the IV World Conference on the Status of Women* (in Russian), Moscow (1994:24). This information was translated and provided by Yevgenia Issraelyan.

[10]Bala (1995).

[11]For an analysis of the prevalence, nature, and seriousness of marital rape, see Russell (1982).

[12]See also Kaganas and Murray (1991) for an interesting discussion on the debate around this issue in South Africa.

[13]Until after the Second World War, abortion was restricted almost everywhere. Abortion laws were liberalized in most countries of eastern and central Europe in the 1950s, and in almost all highly industrialized countries during the 1960s and 1970s. Some Third World countries also relaxed their restrictions on abortion during this period, most notably China and India. Since the fall of the Berlin Wall, abortion laws have since become more restrictive in some of the previously socialist countries. See Childbirth by Choice Trust (1992), Boland (1993), David (1992), Funk (1993), Newman (1993), and Sachdev (1988).

[14]The new reproductive technologies may involve more people, even if the embryo is generated with the egg and sperm of the couple.

[15]Most people have an innate individual capacity to reproduce that may be (maliciously or otherwise) harmed or taken away. Even if we deny individuals the 'right' to reproduce, there may be a *capacity* to reproduce for single women who utilize sperm banks.

[16]For some of the public costs related to private cars, see Zuckerman (1991) and Zielinski (1995).

[17]Several options come to mind: license fees could be increased (rather than fares for public transit), the tax on gas could be increased, tolls could

be charged for driving in the city for those who are neither disabled nor make deliveries, etc.

[18]This does not mean that men are less in need of emotionally sustaining relationships, but merely that this need may be less person specific, i.e., as long as they have *someone* with whom they have a relationship, this may suffice.

[19]*Egan* v. *Canada*, s.c.c., 1995, file #23636 Lamer, C.J. and La Forest, Gonthier and Major JJ., p. 4.

[20]Some of the women and children live in common-law unions and therefore must be deducted from the total.

[21]*Egan and Nesbit* v. *the Queen*, 1995, par. 25.

[22]This is being nibbled away by the new reproductive technologies, but in terms of sheer numbers the world over, we could still consider this as the only unit as far as congruence between biological and social parenthood is concerned. It is also the only unit in which most of the child care is provided by the mother (see the notes on the division of labour in chapters 3 and 4). Fineman (1995), of course, bases her policy proposals on just this argument.

[23]However, parental rights of the non-coresident parent will be negatively affected, because otherwise the custodial parent cannot adequately carry out her (or his) parental role as well as live her (or his) life unimpeded by decisions by a former spouse. See the reasoning of Justice Abella in *MacGyver* v. *Richards* (1995), 11 R.F.L. (4th), Ont. C.A.

[24]If a step-parent voluntarily continues to pay, there is, of course, no issue. If a step-parent wishes to continue social contact with the children, and if the children wish for the same, this should be encouraged in principle if such contact is beneficial for the children—whether or not the step-parent also pays support. In fact, this is what happens with many biological parents (mostly fathers) today. Only around 16 per cent pay support, but around 50 per cent maintain some contact with the children, meaning that there is a substantial minority who maintain some contact but do not pay support.

[25]The former family allowance has since been folded into the Child Tax Credit, which is income-tested on a family basis and hence shifts the balance towards further treating the family/household as the unit of administration.

[26]Maloney (1989:187).

[27]Ibid., 191. I do not agree with all of Maloney's proposals. In particular, I disagree with her stance on imputed income—taxation of housework performed by the woman (see pp. 192–203). In particular, she fails to take into account the dual nature of unpaid work performed at home: socially useful work (care for inevitable dependants) versus privately useful work (services and care for physically and mentally fit adults).

[28]See Eichler (1988a:140–64).

[29]Full-time is also a problematic word. Full-time jobs usually mean working eight hours a day for five days a week. That leaves two days with twenty-four hours each and sixteen hours per weekday and night still open. If one person needs round-the-clock care, we are actually talking about three full-time jobs, plus three part-time weekend jobs, not one.

[30]There are, of course, any number of variations and combinations. If care is partially rendered by another person or institution, such as a day care centre or a homemaker service, the caregiver can take on part-time work for pay, or full-time work for pay if alternative help is rendered on a full-time basis.

[31]Rubin (1985).

[32]I am not suggesting that in individual instances all family members will be expected or wanted to participate, but there is a social construction that legitimates such participation as 'normal'.

[33]Rubin (1985:191).

[34]Ibid., 64.

[35]Ibid., 106.

[36]Ibid., 142–3.

[37]From the 'Economic and Emotional Caring and Sharing Relationships Study: Field Notes', June 1994, by Meg Luxton, Atkinson College, York University, 4700 Keele Street, North York, Ontario.

[38]For example, people are eligible for the guaranteed income supplement on the basis of their own incomes or, in the case of a couple, their joint incomes, even if they have adult children who are well off. The federal income tax allows people to deduct support for people on whom they were either 'wholly dependent' or 'dependent' (depending on the year in question) while they were a child (variously identified as up to age eighteen or nineteen); see Appendix 1 for a detailed summary. Under these regulations, John could not claim any of his dependants, nor would the former dependants be able to claim him were they to support him if he was in need, since he provided partial, not exclusive help.

[39]This is in line with the principles elaborated by the Federal/Provincial/Territorial Family Law Committee (1995:3), which include the following (there are a total of eight principles):

1. Parents have legal responsibility for the financial support of children.
2. Child support legislation should not distinguish between parents or children on the basis of sex.
3. The determination of child support should be made without regard to the marital status of parents.

[40]Angus Reid Group (1994:52–3).

Chapter 8

[1]Particularly in Alberta and Ontario.

[2]In 1994, there were an estimated 1,163,000 children on welfare, representing 38 per cent of all welfare recipients (National Council of Welfare 1995b:4).

[3]Campaign 2000 (1994:22). For another set of highly useful and compatible proposals, see the National Council of Welfare (1994:49–50).

[4]The report of the Ontario Social Assistance Review Committee (1988) pulls many of these arguments together.

[5]Aitken and Mitchell (1995).

[6]Canadian Council for Social Development (1995:3).

[7]As Campaign 2000 (1994:5–6) has noted: 'A divided society is costly, both socially and economically. The 1991 World Development Report by the World Bank established that income inequality can cause slower economic growth. On the other hand, a cohesive, harmonious society fosters a healthy economy. Healthy communities help their members develop their capacities and achieve well-being. This contributes to economic regeneration and avoids the wasteful costs of despair and disorder.'

[8]It is important to realize that the debt was accumulated in the past. Since 1986, Canada's expenditures (minus debt charges) have been lower than the total revenue. The debt charges maintain both the deficit and the debt. We should therefore ask who benefited from the consumption in the past before we decide where to allocate responsibility. It certainly was not children born today who generated the debt. For figures from 1970 to 1992, see Campaign 2000 (1994:Table G).

[9]The Canadian budget reduced spending for the Canada Health and Social Transfer by 9.4 per cent from 1995–6 to 1996–7, and by a further 6.7 per cent in 1997–8. (National Council of Welfare 1995b:10).

[10]The Child Poverty Action Group et al. (1994a:8) note that the amount of federal taxes deferred by corporations due to fast write-offs for capital investment totalled about $3 billion in 1972, and almost $40 billion by the early 1990s—roughly equivalent to the nation's debt servicing charges.

[11]The Social Council for Social Development proposes to cap RRSP contributions at $7,500 per year per person, for a savings of $1 billion in the first year and more in subsequent years. They suggest that capital gains should be taxed at 100 per cent rather than at 75 per cent (as at present), for about another billion dollars of savings. The Dividend Tax Credit could be reshaped for a saving of $230 million. The meals and entertainment expense could be abolished. A 5 per cent inheritance tax would raise $3.3 billion annually. These changes combined would save about $6 billion in the first year and more in subsequent years. This would allow us to keep our social safety net intact; see Canadian Council for Social Development (1995).

The National Council of Welfare makes the following set of suggestions: tax capital gains at their full value, $1.7 billion; tax dividends at their full value, $1.0 billion; tax lottery and gambling winnings, $1.2 billion; eliminate extra allowances for tax depreciation for corporations, $1.2 billion; give tax credits for RRSP contributions instead of tax deductions, $1.1 billion; give tax credits for contributions to registered pension plans instead of tax deductions, $0.6 billion; tax wealth transfer, $1.9 billion; for a total of $8.7 billion; see National Council of Welfare (1994:37, Table 4).

The total poverty gap in 1993 was $14.5 billion (National Council of Welfare 1995a:47). If we wanted to eradicate poverty for everyone, this is the amount of savings we would have to generate altogether.

[12]It must be noted that compared to most other OECD countries, Canada's tax revenues as a proportion of GDP are low. In 1989, the following countries had a proportion of higher tax revenues (in descending order): Sweden, Denmark, Netherlands, Norway, Belgium, France, Luxembourg, Austria, New Zealand, Germany, Finland, Italy, Ireland, and the United Kingdom. Canada's tax revenues as a proportion of GDP were higher than the following countries (in descending order): Portugal, Spain, Iceland, Greece, Switzerland, Japan, Australia, the United States, and Turkey; see Economic Council of Canada (1992:10).

[13]National Council of Welfare (1994:50).

[14]For example, the Child Poverty Action Group et al. (1994a:6–8), have proposed to encourage more private sector job creation by returning foreign investment thresholds for pension/retirement plans to the 1989 levels (10 per cent instead of the current 20 per cent), thereby rerouting about $25 billion back each year for investment in Canada. Canada could play a leadership role in calling for the introducing of a Tobin tax, proposed by Nobel-prize winning economist James Tobin. This involves a 1 per cent transaction charge on all currency trading. This would discourage short-term speculation, reduce exchange rate volatility and generate revenue for governments. Every day almost $1 trillion is exchanged in financial paper across national borders. Further, the tax holiday enjoyed by corporations and richer individuals needs to cease.

[15]This is quite similar to and compatible with the policy goals identified by the Canadian Council for Social Development:

- reducing economic inequities between individuals and regions
- providing equal access to opportunities, so that a person's future is not limited by social and economic environments
- providing means of self-support and the ability to influence decisions that affect one's life
- providing collective support for those unable to support themselves

- sharing responsibility for our collective well-being; all Canadians should be included in our social and economic fabric
- establishing a system that maintains income security and stability, one that *prevents* poverty rather than simply *responds* to it

[16]Vanier Institute of the Family (1993:1–18).

[17]*Thibaudeau* v. *Canada* [1995] 2 S.C.R. 627.

[18]This is an impressionistic statement, based on closely following the debate, but not on actually counting letters.

[19]House of Commons Debates (17 July 1942) at 43600-61.

[20]As McLachlin comments: Parliament 'focused solely on improving the financial situation of the non-custodial parent and ignored the tax position of the custodial parent. It contained no provision to ensure that the custodial parent receiving payments for children would not see her personal tax burden increased, much less share the advantageous tax treatment enjoyed by the non-custodial parent' (*Thibaudeau* v. *Canada* [1995] 2 S.C.R. 627, par. 174).

[21]*Thibaudeau* v. *Canada* [1995] 2 S.C.R. 627, par. 158.

[22]See Appendix 3 for a description of the sexist bias. One subform is familism—treating the family as the smallest analytical unit when in fact it is individuals within families who are differentially affected by something—in this instance, by provisions of the *Income Tax Act*.

[23]*Thibaudeau* v. *Canada*, L'Heureux-Dubé, par. 36, emphasis added.

[24]Ibid., par. 9.

[25]Ibid., par. 60. Of course, all arguments are vastly more complex than represented here. I have pulled out those characteristics relevant in this context.

[26]*Thibaudeau* v. *Canada*, McLachlin, par. 183.

[27]Ibid.

[28]Ibid.

[29]In fact, in 20 per cent of the cases, the custodial parent is the higher-income earner. This figure includes, of course, custodial fathers.

[30]L'Heureux-Dubé cites a savings of $330 million (par. 12), while McLachlin cites $203 million (par. 194), both using sources supplied by the government. The Federal/Provincial/Territorial Family Law Committee puts the savings at $300 million.

[31]This is in line with the recommendation of the Federal/Provincial/Territorial Family Law Committee (1995:50), which recommends either improving the current deduction/inclusion scheme or 'changing the system to a no deduction/no inclusion system *combined* with preserving the value of the $300 M subsidy and targeting it to children'.

[32]Finance Canada Distribution Centre (1996:8).

[33]See Pask (1989), Pask and McCall (1989), Finnie (1994), Pask (1993), Department of Justice (1990), L'Heureux-Dubé (1993), Pilon (1993),

Zweibel (1993a and 1993b), Weitzman (1985), and McLanahan and Garfinkel (1993).

[34]National Council of Welfare (1995a:54, Table 14). It is, of course, not only lone-support mothers who are entitled to child-support payments. The non-custodial parent's obligation to pay should not cease if the custodial parent forms a new union. An American study, using a representative sample of sole-support mothers found that most of them remarry while still eligible for and/or receiving child support from their first husband (Folk et al. 1992). Further, lone-support fathers should be equally entitled to support; see Meyer and Garasky (1993).

[35]National Council of Welfare (1995a:54, Table 14).

[36]Pask and McCall (1989:95–106), Pask (1989:169), Finnie (1994:42–3).

[37]Pask and McCall (1989:106–11), Pask (1989:169), Finnie (1994:45–7).

[38]Pask and McCall (1989:111–16), Pask (1989:170).

[39]This is the model recommended by the Federal/Provincial/Territorial Family Law Committee (1995:9). They refer to it as the 40/30 Equivalence Scale. They explain this model as follows:

> An equivalence scale basically responds to the question 'How much does a family with children need to be as well off as a couple without children?' A family with children may have a higher income than a childless couple but its needs are also greater. The difference in income when the standards of living of families with and without children are equivalent can be expressed as a ratio. The series of all ratios produced across all types of families at different income levels can be translated into an equivalence scale. These scales are usually expressed in 'adult equivalent units' with a single individual having the reference value of 1.0 and with a couple with children having reference values greater than 1.0.
>
> The 40/30 equivalence scale is proposed in the absence of a definitive and perfect method for determining expenditures on children which is totally reliable and without criticism … Under this equivalence scale, a couple is presumed to need 40 per cent more money to maintain the same standard of living as an individual living alone (the 40 in the 40/30), while the first child adds another 30 per cent to the family's costs (the 30 in the 40/30). In other words, a couple with a child requires 170 per cent of the income of a person living alone to be as well off. The child's costs in a two parent family would be 30 divided by 170 or 17.6 per cent of the family's total income. These rates are the same for all income levels.

This is also the recommendation that Finnie (1994) eventually arrives at after careful consideration and critique of the other methods. For a critique of his arguments, see Zweibel (1994). It is the model that the federal government has decided to adopt.

[40]Harrison (1991).

[41]But a formula approach *is* likely to increase the level of payments; see Garfinkel et al. (1991).

[42]The current median monthly amounts are $184.92 per child for families with one child, $122.75 per child for families with two children, and $100.17 per child for families with three children (computed from figures provided by Jim Sturrock). Under the present system, the recipients had to pay tax on these amounts, while under the new system they will not pay tax on child-support payments received.

[43]The Federal/Provincial/Territorial Family Law Committee identified the median income for a custodial parent as $15,600 and for a non-custodial parent as $24,996 (these figures were provided by Jim Sturrock of the Department of Justice). Looking at the new guidelines, a non-custodial parent in Ontario will have to pay $235 per month per child if there is one child, $189 per month per child if there are two children, and $161.33 per month per child if there are three children. The amounts drop further with more children. Half the families will therefore receive these amounts or less (since half of the non-custodial parents earn $25,000 or less).

[44]Canada was one of the seventy-one countries that met at the 1990 World Summit for Children and committed itself to eradicating poverty among children; see Department of Justice (1993).

[45]McLanahan and Garfinkel (1993:28–9).

[46]This scheme could apply whether the lone-parent family was the result of separation, divorce, or childbirth outside of marriage.

[47]The Ontario Conservative government announced in August 1995 that it would reinstate unannounced home inspections of welfare recipients that had been discontinued under the previous social democratic government. It also announced that common-law spouses would be made responsible for the economic support of the other household members. This in effect reintroduces the infamous search for the 'man in the house'. Under the previous government, welfare recipients were entitled to their benefits for three years after forming a new common-law relationship. This allowed women to form new relationships without expecting the man to immediately take over financial responsibility for them and the children.

[48]This is regardless of the reason for the existence of a lone-parent family.

[49]Human Resources Development (1994:49, Table 3.4a).

[50]The maximum amounts in 1993 were $1,020 per child, but only $75 for the third and each subsequent child (Human Resources Development 1994:39).

[51]The annual value of basic child benefits for a median-income family with two children ages seven and eleven in 1992 were (in Canadian dollars and in descending order) as follows: Norway, $3,867; Austria, $3,770;

Belgium, $3,755; Sweden, $3,605; United Kingdom, $2,938; Netherlands, $2,509; Denmark, $2,178; Finland, $2,140; France, $1,606; United States, $1,486; Canada, $965; see Campaign 2000 (1994:table E).

[52]*Symes* v. *Canada* [1993] 4 S.C.R. 695.

[53]*Symes* v. *Canada* [1993] 4 S.C.R. 695, p. 775 (c).

[54]*Symes* v. *Canada* [1993] 4 S.C.R. 695, p. 739 (a).

[55]*Symes* v. *Canada* [1993] 4 S.C.R. p. 740 (f) and p. 741 (a).

[56]*Symes* v. *Canada* [1993] 4 S.C.R. 773 (i) 774 (d).

[57]*Symes* v. *Canada* [1993] 4 S.C.R. 798 (a) + (e).

[58]*Symes* v. *Canada* [1993] 4 S.C.R. 695, p. 819 (b).

[59]*Symes* v. *Canada* [1993] 4 S.C.R. 695, p. 823 (g).

[60]An American study looked at what would happen if the American tax deduction for children was replaced with an annual children's allowance, and found that it would result in a modest reduction of poverty, as well as savings to the state; see Meyer, Phillips, and Maritato (1991).

[61]If the partner had not adopted the child, the couple would be treated like a heterosexual common-law couple whose child was the biological child of only one of the partners.

[62]If the work week was shortened (which would make sense given that we have an oversupply of labour) the public contribution to child care could be reduced accordingly.

[63]See Friendly (1994) for a comprehensive discussion of child-care policies.

[64]With a universal child-care plan, we would generate about 30,000 jobs, according to a federal official who spoke to me after the universal child-care plan was scrapped.

[65]One American city, Fremont, proposed to provide child care with a $12 surcharge on all residential dwelling units. The measure failed when it was put to a referendum because those who supported it failed to make their case to the voters. However, it seems like an idea that could be explored further; see Yeager and Strober (1992).

[66]There are already a range of child-care facilities at workplaces across the country Mayfield (1990:45–50). Employers can pool their resources to run shared child-care facilities. This could be especially attractive to small employers. We could also consider a compulsory contribution towards child-care facilities for employers that generate a certain proportion of child-care places depending on the number of their employees. Since companies profit from the fact that potential future workers are being raised, they could be asked to share a portion of the cost involved in raising them. See also Starrels (1992) and Kingston (1990). The overall contribution of employers to child care at present is extremely modest, to say the least. A US study found that only 2 per cent of businesses and government agencies sponsored child-care centres for their employees' children, and an additional 3 per cent subsidized such expenses; cited

in Aldous (1990:357). A Canadian survey of nearly 400 companies found that fewer than 5 per cent provided support in the form of on-site childcare facilities or subsidies for off-site care; cited in Skrypnek and Fast (forthcoming).

[67]There have, over time, been many proposals for various types of guaranteed annual incomes and just as many critiques. Most proposals foresee a guaranteed annual income on a *family* basis. This would put the familism-individualism flip-flop into full swing. However, it remains a very attractive, rational, and effective idea if applied to *individuals*.

[68]It would not be exactly the same since the conversion to a refundable credit would eliminate the current regressive nature, thus increasing the total income of lower-income households and decreasing it for higher-income households, which would be appropriate.

[69]See Pahl (1989) and Edwards (1981).

[70]Of course, this person could be a man. I am simply using the term that would apply in the majority of cases.

[71]It would also reallocate monies from households that do not provide care for seniors or disabled people to those that do have such responsibilities.

[72]There are, for course, many other potential benefits that would make the workplace more family-friendly. For a discussion of flextime, see Christensen and Staines (1990). For a good overview of various policies, see Skrypnek and Fast (forthcoming). For a short overview, see Aldous (1990). For a historical view, see Starrels (1992).

[73]Freeman (1994:64–5).

[74]Lewis and Åström (1992:69).

[75]Pleck, as quoted in Hyde et al. (1993:617).

[76]Haas (1990:407).

[77]When it comes to parental leave for fathers, an American attitudinal study found that, interestingly, the women were stronger supporters of parental leave for men than were men; see Hyde et al. (1993:627).

[78]O'Connell (1994:113) notes that internationally, 'Maternity leave provisions, whether liberal or restricted, benefit only comparatively few women. In many countries, provision is rife with discrimination: for example, exclusion of part-time workers and of those in small workplaces. Most women in part-time, temporary or informal sector work do not benefit from maternity legislation. Domestic workers in most countries have no protection. Farmers and agricultural workers throughout Africa, Asia and Latin America usually work until the day of delivery and, except in rare cases, return to work immediately afterwards. All women in the informal sector, and home-workers, are likewise unprotected.'

[79]Evans and Pupo (1993:418). The United States lag behind most European countries in this respect (see Raabe 1990), and Canada falls somewhere between these two points.

Appendix 3

[1]This is a slightly revised version of the appendix that appears in Eichler (1992).

[2]No true gynocentric framework can emerge in a society that continues to be profoundly sexist. However, certain questions, particularly those concerning reproduction and family matters, are usually studied by focusing on women only. This is simply a reverse form of sexism from that involved in an androcentric frame of reference.

References

Abad, J., and E. Fenoy. 1988. *Marriage: A Path to Sanctity*. Manilla: Sinagtala Publ.

Abella, R.S. 1984. *Equality in Employment: A Royal Commission Report*. Ottawa: Minister of Supply and Services Canada.

Aitken, F., and A. Mitchell. 1995. 'The Relationship between Poverty and Child Health: Long-Range Implications'. *Canadian Review of Social Policy* 35:19–36.

Aldous, J. 1990. 'Specification and Speculation Concerning the Politics of Workplace Family Policies'. *Journal of Family Issues* 11, no. 4:355–67.

_____. 1995. 'New Views on Grandparents in Intergenerational Context'. *Journal of Family Issues* 16, no. 1:104–22.

Allen, K.R., and D.H. Demo. 1995. 'The Families of Lesbians and Gay Men: A New Frontier in Family Research'. *Journal of Marriage and the Family* 57:111–27.

Ambert, A.M. 1980. *Divorce in Canada*. Don Mills: Academic Press Canada.

_____. 1994. 'An International Perspective on Parenting: Social Change and Social Constructs'. *Journal of Marriage and the Family* 56:529–43.

Angus Reid Group. 1994. *The State of the Family in Canada*. Ottawa: Angus Reid Group.

Aquilino, W.S. 1994. 'Later Life Parental Divorce and Widowhood: Impact on Young Adults' Assessment of Parent-Child Relations'. *Journal of Marriage and the Family* 56:908–22.

Arditti, J.A., and T.Z. Keith. 1993. 'Visitation Frequency, Child Support Payment, and the Father-Child Relationship Postdivorce'. *Journal of Marriage and the Family* 55:699–712.

Arlett, C., et al. 1988. *The Long-Term Effects of Child Sexual Abuse*. Ottawa: Health Canada, Family Violence Prevention Division.

Arnup, K. 1989. '"Mothers Just Like Others": Lesbians, Divorce, and Child Custody in Canada'. *Canadian Journal of Women and the Law* 3, no. 1:18–32.

_____. 1994. 'Finding Fathers: Artificial Insemination, Lesbians, and the Law'. *Canadian Journal of Women and the Law* 7, no. 1:97–115.

Atkinson, M.P., and S.P. Blackwelder. 1993. 'Fathering in the 20th Century'. *Journal of Marriage and the Family* 55:975–86.

Babarczy, A., et al. 1991. *Time Use Trends in Finland and in Hungary.* Helsinki: Central Statistical Office of Finland.

Bacchi, C. 1991. 'Pregnancy, the Law and the Meaning of Equality'. In *Equality Politics and Gender*, edited by E. Meehan and S. Sevenhuijsen, 71–87. London: Sage.

Bachman, R. 1994. *Violence Against Women: A National Crime Victimization Survey Report.* [n.p.]: US Department of Justice.

Baker, M., ed. 1994. *Canada's Changing Families: Challenges of Public Policy.* Ottawa: The Vanier Institute of the Family.

_____, et al. 1990. *Families: Changing Trends in Canada*, 2nd ed. Toronto: McGraw-Hill Ryerson Ltd.

Bala, N. 1995. *Legal Principles for Families, Children & Youth: A Discussion Paper.* Ottawa: Department of Justice.

Bales, R.F., and P.E. Slater. 1955. 'Role Differentiation in Small Decision-Making Groups'. In *Family, Socialization and Interaction Process*, edited by T. Parsons and R.F. Bales, 259–306. Glencoe: Free Press.

Bane, M.J. 1979. 'Marital Disruption and the Lives of Children'. In *Divorce and Separation: Context, Causes and Consequences*, edited by G. Levinger and O.C. Moles, 276–86. New York: Basic Books.

Barret, M., and M. McIntosh. 1982. *The Anti-social Family.* London: Verso.

Bass, E., and L. Davis. 1988. *The Courage to Heal: A Guide for Women Survivors of Sexual Abuse.* New York: Harper and Row.

Battle, K. 1992. 'Critique of 1992 Budget's New Child Tax Benefit', mimeo. Ottawa: Caledon Institute of Social Policy.

Belle, M., and K. McQuillan. 1994. 'Births Outside Marriage'. *Canadian Social Trends*, cat. 11–008E, no. 33 (Summer):14–17.

Bernard, J. 1972. *The Future of Marriage.* New York: Bantam.

Bernardes, J. 1993. 'Responsibility in Studying Postmodern Families'. *Journal of Family Issues* 14, no. 1:35–49.

Bertoia, C., and J. Drakich. 1993. 'The Fathers' Rights Movement: Contradictions in Rhetoric and Practise'. *Journal of Family Issues* 14, no. 4:592–615.

Bittman, M., and F. Lovejoy. 1993. 'Domestic Power: Negotiating an Unequal Division of Labour within a Framework of Equality'. *Australian and New Zealand Journal of Sociology* 29, no. 3:302–21.

Blair, S. 1993. 'New Zealand Immigration Law and Gay and Lesbian Couples'. *Australian Gay and Lesbian Law Journal* 3:30–8.

Blair, S.L., and D.T. Lichter. 1991. 'Measuring the Division of Household Labor: Gender Segregation of Housework among American Couples'. *Journal of Family Issues* 12, no. 31:91–113.

Blaisure, K.R., and K.R. Allen. 1995. 'Feminists and the Ideology and

Practice of Marital Equality'. *Journal of Marriage and the Family* 56:5–19.

Blume, E.S. 1990. *Secret Survivors: Uncovering Incest and Its Aftereffects in Women.* New York: Ballantine Books.

Boland, R. 1993. 'Abortion Law in Europe in 1991–1992'. *Journal of Law, Medicine and Ethics* 21, no. 1:72–93.

Bould, S. 1993. 'Familial Caretaking: A Middle-Range Definition of Family in the Context of Social Policy'. *Journal of Family Issues* 14, no. 31:133–51.

Bourne, P. 1993. 'Women, Law and the Justice System'. In *Canadian Women's Issues: Strong Voices*, edited by R.R. Pierson et al., 321–48. Toronto: Lorimer.

Boyd, M., M. Eichler, and J.R. Hofley. 1976. 'Family: Functions, Formation and Fertility'. In *Opportunity for Choice: A Goal for Women in Canada*, edited by G.C.A. Cook, 13–52. Ottawa: Statistics Canada in association with the C.D. Howe Research Institute.

Boyd, S.B. 1989. 'Child Custody, Ideologies, and Employment'. *Canadian Journal of Women and the Law* 3, no. 1:111–33.

Bradbury, B. 1993. *Working Families: Age, Gender, and Daily Survival in Industrializing Montreal.* Toronto: McClelland and Stewart.

Bradley, D. 1987. 'Homosexuality and Child Custody in English Law'. *International Journal of Law and the Family* 1:155–205.

Browne, A., and D. Finkelhor. 1986. 'Impact of Child Sexual Abuse: A Review of the Research'. *Psychological Bulletin* 99, no. 1:66–77.

Bumpass, L.L., et al. 1991. 'The Role of Cohabitation in Declining Rates of Marriage'. *Journal of Marriage and the Family* 53:913–27.

Burch, T.K., and B.J. Matthews. 1987. 'Household Formation in Developed Societies'. *Population and Development Review* 13, no. 3:495–511.

Burke, M.A. 1995. 'Child Institutionalization and Child Protection in Central and Eastern Europe', Innocenti Occasional Papers, Economic Policy Series, #52. Florence: UNICEF.

Campaign 2000. 1994. 'Investing in the Next Generation: Policy Perspectives on Children and Nationhood', discussion paper, Toronto.

Canada. 1992. 'The Child Benefit'. A white paper on Canada's new integrated Child Tax Benefit.

Canadian Council for Social Development. 1995. *Social Policy Beyond the Budget.* Ottawa: Canadian Council for Social Development.

Canadian Panel on Violence. 1993. *Changing the Landscape: Ending Violence, Achieving Equality.* Ottawa: Minister of Supply and Services.

Carter, B.J. 1990. 'But You *Should* Have Known: Child Sexual Abuse and the Non-Offending Mother'. Unpublished Ph.D. thesis, Faculty of Social Work, University of Toronto.

Cassels, J. [1995]. 'Pension Credits for Unpaid Work: A Discussion Paper'. Unpublished paper, University of Victoria.

Chang, C.F., and S.I. White-Means. 1991. 'The Men Who Care: An Analysis of Male Primary Caregivers Who Care for Frail Elderly at Home'. *Journal of Applied Gerontology* 3:343–58.

Charlesworth, H. 1992. 'A Law of One's Own? Feminist Perspectives on Equality and the Law'. MEANJIN 51, no. 1:67–76.

Cheal, D.J. 1983. 'Intergenerational Family Transfers'. *Journal of Marriage and the Family* 45 (November):805–14.

_____. 1987. 'Intergenerational Transfers and Life Course Management: Towards a Socio-economic Perspective'. In *Rethinking the Life Cycle*, edited by A. Bryman et al., 141–54. London: MacMillan.

_____. 1993a. 'Changing Household Financial Strategies: Canadian Couples Today'. *Human Ecology* 21, no. 2:197–213.

_____. 1993b. 'Intergenerational Family Transfers'. *Journal of Marriage and the Family* 45:805–13.

_____. Forthcoming. 'Rethinking Intergenerational Comparisons: Temporal Relations in the Anglo-Saxon Countries'. In *Actes de la Conférence Européenne 'Les personnages et la solidarité entre les générations'*, edited by C. Allias-Donfut. Paris: CNAV.

Chesler, P. 1986. *Mothers on Trial: The Battle for Children and Custody*. New York: McGraw-Hill.

Childbirth by Choice Trust. 1992. *Abortion in Law and History*. Toronto: Childbirth by Choice Trust.

Child Poverty Action Group, et al. 1994a. *Paying for Canada: Perspective on Public Finance and National Programs*. Toronto: Child Poverty Action Group.

_____. 1994b. *Voices of Young Families*. Toronto: Child Poverty Action Group.

Christensen, K.E., and G.L. Staines. 1990. 'Flextime: A Viable Solution to Work/Family Conflict?' *Journal of Family Issues* 11, no. 4:455–76.

Clark, L., and D. Lewis. 1977. *Rape: The Price of Coercive Sexuality*. Toronto: Women's Press.

Clive, E.M. 1980. 'Marriage: An Unnecessary Legal Concept?' In *Marriage and Cohabitation in Contemporary Societies: Areas of Legal, Social and Ethical Change*, edited by J.M. Eekelaar and S.N. Katz, 71–81. Toronto: Butterworth & Co.

Coalition for Lesbian and Gay Rights in Ontario. 1992. 'Happy Families:

The Recognition of Same-Sex Spousal Relationships', a brief for the Ontario legislature. Toronto: Coalition for Lesbian and Gay Rights in Ontario.

Cohen, M.G. 1988. *Women's Work, Markets, and Economic Development in Nineteenth-Century Ontario*. Toronto: University of Toronto Press.

Conway, J.F. 1990. *The Canadian Family in Crisis*. Toronto: James Lorimer & Company.

Cook, R., and W. Mitchinson, eds. 1976. *The Proper Sphere: Woman's Place in Canadian Society*. Toronto: Oxford University Press.

Cowan, P.A. 1993. 'The Sky *Is* Falling, But Popenoe's Analysis Won't Help Us Do Anything About It'. *Journal of Marriage and the Family* 55:548–53.

Crean, S. 1988. *In the Name of the Fathers*. Toronto: Amanita Enterprises.

Crysdale, S. 1991. *Families under Stress: Community, Work, and Economic Change*. Toronto: Thompson Educational Publishing.

David, H.P. 1992. 'Abortion in Europe, 1920–91: A Public Health Perspective'. *Studies in Family Planning*, 23, no. 1:1–22.

Deardon, K., et al. 1994. 'Family Structure, Function, and the Early Transition to Fatherhood in Great Britain: Identifying Antecedents Using Longitudinal Data'. *Journal of Marriage and the Family* 56:844–52.

Deech, R. 1980. 'The Case Against Legal Recognition of Cohabitation'. In *Marriage and Cohabitation in Contemporary Societies: Areas of Legal, Social and Ethical Change*, edited by J.M. Eekelaar and S.N. Katz, 300–12. Toronto: Butterworth & Co.

DeKeseredy, W., and K. Kelly. 1993. 'The Incidence and Prevalence of Woman Abuse in Canadian University and College Dating Relationships'. *Canadian Journal of Sociology* 18, no. 2:137–60.

Delorey, A.M. 1989. 'Joint Legal Custody: A Reversion to Patriarchal Power'. *Canadian Journal of Women and the Law* 3, no. 1:33–44.

Dempsey, K. 1988. 'Exploitation in the Domestic Division of Labour: An Australian Case Study'. *Australian and New Zealand Journal of Sociology* 24, no. 3:420–36.

Department of Justice. 1990. *Evaluation of the Divorce Act, Phase II: Monitoring and Evaluation*. Ottawa: Bureau of Review.

_____. 1993. *Brighter Futures Child Development Initiative*. Ottawa: Department of Justice.

Donnelly, M. 1993. 'The Disparate Impact of Pension Reform on Women'. *Canadian Journal of Women and the Law* 6, no. 2:419–54.

Dooley, D.S. 1990. 'Immoral Because They're Bad, Bad Because They're Wrong: Sexual Orientation and Presumptions of Parental Unfitness in Custody Disputes'. *California Western Law Review* 26:395–424.

Drakich, J. 1989. 'In Search of the Better Parent: The Social Construction of Ideologies of Fatherhood'. *Canadian Journal of Women and the Law* 3, no. 1:69–87.

Dulac, G. 1989. 'Le lobby des pères divorce et paternité'. *Canadian Journal of Women and the Law* 3, no. 1:45–68.

Dulude, L. 1984. *Love, Marriage and Money ... an Analysis of Financial Relations Between the Spouses.* Ottawa: Canadian Advisory Council on the Status of Women.

Dumas, J. 1994. *Report on the Demographic Situation in Canada, 1993,* 91–209E. Ottawa: Statistics Canada.

_____, and Y. Peron. 1992. *Marriage and Conjugal Life in Canada.* Ottawa: Minister of Industry, Science and Technology.

_____, et al. 1995. *Report on the Demographic Situation in Canada.* Ottawa: Statistics Canada.

Duvall, E.M., and B.C. Miller. 1985. *Marriage and Family Development,* 6th ed. New York: Harper and Row.

Duxbury, L., et al. 1994. 'Work-Family Conflict: A Comparison by Gender, Family Type, and Perceived Control'. *Journal of Family Issues* 15, no. 3:449–66.

Dwyer, J.W., and K. Seccombe. 1991. 'Elder Care as Family Labor: The Influence of Gender and Family Position'. *Journal of Family Issues* 12, no. 2:229–47.

Economic Council of Canada. 1992. *The New Face of Poverty: Income Security Needs of Canadian Families.* Ottawa: Minister of Supply and Services.

Edwards, M. 1981. *Financial Arrangements within Families.* Canberra: National Women's Advisory Council.

Eekelaar, J.M., and S.N. Katz, eds. 1980. *Marriage and Cohabitation in Contemporary Societies: Legal, Social and Ethical Change.* Toronto: Butterworth & Co.

Eichler, M. 1980. *The Double Standard: A Feminist Critique of Feminist Social Science.* London: Croom Helm.

_____. 1981. 'Science Fiction as Desirable Feminist Scenarios'. *Women's Studies International Quarterly* 4, no. 1:51–64.

_____. 1984. 'The Familism-Individualism Flip-flop and Its Implications for Economic and Social Welfare Policies'. In *20th International CFR Seminar on Social Change and Family Policies,* Part 2: Key Papers, edited by Australian Institute of Family Studies, 431–72. Melbourne: Australian Institute of Family Studies.

_____. 1985. 'Family Policy in Canada: From Where to Where?' In

Justice Beyond Orwell, edited by R.S. Abella and M.L. Rothman, 353–63. Montreal: Les Editions Yvon Blais Inc.

_____. 1987. 'Social Policy Concerning Women'. In *Canadian Social Policy*, 2nd ed., edited by S.A. Yelaja, 139–56. Waterloo: Wilfrid Laurier University Press.

_____. 1988a. *Families in Canada Today: Recent Changes and Their Policy Consequences*, 2nd ed. Toronto: Gage Educational Publishing.

_____. 1988b. *Nonsexist Research Methods: A Practical Guide*. Boston: Allen and Unwin.

_____. 1990. 'The Limits of Family Law Reform, or the Privatization of Female and Child Poverty'. *Canadian Family Law Quarterly* 7:59–84.

_____. 1992. 'Nonsexist Research: A Metatheoretical Approach'. *Indian Journal of Social Work* 53, no. 3:329–42.

_____. 1993. 'Grasping the Ungraspable: Socio-legal Definitions of the Family in the Context of Sexuality'. In *Transactions of the Royal Society of Canada*, series VI, vol. III, edited by Royal Society of Canada, 3–15.

_____. 1996. 'The Impact of New Reproductive and Genetic Technologies on Families'. In *Families: Changing Trend in Canada*, 3rd ed., edited by M. Baker, 104–18. Toronto: McGraw-Hill Ryerson.

_____, and M. McCall. 1993. 'Clarifying the Legal Dimensions of Fatherhood'. *Canadian Journal of Family Law* 2:197–232.

Elder, G.H., et al. 1992. 'Families under Economic Pressure'. *Journal of Family Issues* 13, no. 1:5–37.

Emmert, F. 1993. 'The Family Policy of the European Community'. In *Homosexuality: A European Community Issue: Essays on Lesbian and Gay Rights in European Law and Policy*, edited by K. Waaldijk and A. Clapham, 232–394. Dordrecht: Martinus Nijhoff Publ.

European Centre. 1993. *Welfare in a Civil Society*. Report for the Conference of European Ministers Responsible for Social Affairs, United Nations European Region, Bratislava, 28 June–2 July 1993. Vienna: European Centre.

Evans, P., and N. Pupo. 1993. 'Parental Leave: Assessing Women's Interests'. *Canadian Journal of Women and the Law* 6, no. 32:402–18.

Fagin, L., and M. Little. 1984. *The Forsaken Families: The Effects of Unemployment on Family Life*. Harmondsworth: Penguin.

Fast, J.E., and B. Munro. 1991. 'Value of Household and Farm Work: Evidence from Alberta Farm Family Data'. *Canadian Journal of Agricultural Economics* 39:137–50.

_____, and B. Munro. 1994. 'Toward Eliminating Gender Bias in Personal Injury Awards: Contributions from Family Economics'. *Alberta Law Review* 32, no. 1:1–15.

Federal/Provincial/Territorial Family Law Committee. 1995. *Report and Recommendations on Child Support*. Ottawa: Minister of Justice.

Fels, L. 1981. *Living Together: Unmarried Couples in Canada*. Toronto: Personal Library.

Ferree, M.M. 1990. 'Beyond Separate Spheres: Feminism and Family Research'. *Journal of Marriage and the Family* 52:866–84.

Fillion, K. 1993. 'Fertility Rights, Fertility Wrongs'. In *Misconceptions: The Social Construction of Choice and the New Reproductive and Genetic Technologies*, edited by G. Basen, M. Eichler, and A. Lippman, 33–55. Prescott: Voyageur.

Finance Canada Distribution Centre. 1996. *The New Child Support Package*. Ottawa: Finance Canada Distribution Centre.

Fine, M., and L.A. Kurdek. 1992. 'The Adjustment of Adolescents in Stepfather and Stepmother Families'. *Journal of Marriage and the Family* 54:725–36.

Fine, S. 1994. 'Enforcing Child Access a Delicate Business'. *Globe and Mail* (29 June):A1, A6.

Fineman, M. 1988. 'Dominant Discourse, Professional Language, and Legal Change in Child Custody Decisionmaking'. *Harvard Law Review* 101, no. 4:727–74.

_____. 1989. 'Custody Determination at Divorce: The Limits of Social Science Research and the Fallacy of the Liberal Ideology of Equality'. *Canadian Journal of Women and the Law* 3, no. 1:88–110.

_____. 1995. *The Nurtured Mother, the Sexual Family and Other Twentieth-Century Tragedies*. New York: Routledge.

Finnie, R. 1994. 'Child Support: The Guideline Option'. In *Child Support: The Guideline Options*, edited by R. Finnie et al., 9–130. Montreal: Institute for Research on Public Policy.

_____, et al. 1994. *Child Support: The Guideline Options*. Montreal: Institute for Research on Public Policy.

Flax, J. 1992. 'Beyond Equality: Gender, Justice and Difference'. In *Beyond Equality and Difference*, edited by G. Bock and S. James, 193–210. London: Routledge and Kegan Paul.

Folk, K.F., et al. 1992. 'Child Support and Remarriage: Implications for the Economic Well-Being of Children?' *Journal of Family Issues* 13, no. 2:142–57.

Forbes, I. 1991. 'Equal Opportunity: Radical, Liberal and Conservative Critiques'. In *Equality Politics and Gender*, edited by E. Meehan and S. Sevenhuijsen, 17–35. London: Sage.

Frankel-Howard, D. 1992. *Family Violence: A Review of Theoretical and Clinical Literature*, cat. H21–103/1989. Ottawa: Health and Welfare Canada, Policy, Communications and Information Branch, Minister of Supply and Services.

Freeman, J. 1994. 'Defining Family in Mossop v. DSS: The Challenge of Anti-Essentialism and Interactive Discrimination for Human Rights Litigation'. *University of Toronto Law Journal* 44:41–96.

French, D. 1967. 'Agnes Macphail'. In *The Clear Spirit: Twenty Canadian Women and Their Times*, edited by M.Q. Innis, 179–97. Toronto: University of Toronto Press.

Friedman, A. 1987–8. 'The Necessity for State Recognition of Same-Sex Marriage: Constitutional Requirements and Evolving Notions of Family'. *Berkeley Women's Law Journal* 3:134–70.

Friendly, M. 1994. *Child Care Policy in Canada: Putting the Pieces Together.* Don Mills: Addison-Wesley.

_____, et al. 1991. *Child Care for Canadian Children and Families.* Toronto: University of Toronto Press.

Fuchs, R. 1992. 'Child Abandonment in European History: A Symposium'. *Journal of Family History* 17, no. 1:7–13.

Funk, N. 1993. 'Feminism and Post-communism'. *Hypatia* 8, no. 4:85–112.

Furstenberg, F.F., Jr, and J.O. Teitler. 1994. 'Reconsidering the Effects of Marital Disruption: What Happens to Children of Divorce in Early Adulthood?' *Journal of Family Issues* 15, no. 32:173–90.

Furstenberg, F.F., et al. 1983. 'The Life Course of Children of Divorce'. *American Sociological Review* 48:656–68.

Gairdner, W.D. 1992. *The War Against the Family: A Parent Speaks Out on Political, Economic, and Social Policies That Threaten Us All.* Toronto: Stoddart.

Gallagher, S.K. 1994. 'Doing Their Share: Comparing Patterns of Help Given by Older and Younger Adults'. *Journal of Marriage and the Family* 56:567–78.

Gannage, C. 1986. *Double Day, Double Bind: Women Garment Workers.* Toronto: Women's Press.

Garfinkel, I., et al. 1991. 'Child Support Guidelines: Will They Make a Difference?' *Journal of Family Issues* 12, no. 34:404–29.

Gavigan, S.A.M. 1994. 'Paradise Lost, Paradox Revisited: The Implications of Familial Ideology for Feminist, Lesbian, and Gay Engagement to Law'. *Osgoode Hall Law Journal* 31, no. 3:1–35.

Geller, C. 1991. 'Equality in Employment for Women: The Role of Affirmative Action'. *Canadian Journal of Women and the Law* 4, no. 2:373–406.

Gilligan, C. 1982. *In a Different Voice.* Cambridge: Harvard University Press.

Girdner, L.K. 1989. 'Custody Mediation in the United States: Empowerment or Social Control?' *Canadian Journal of Women and the Law* 3, no. 1:134–54.

Glendon, M.A. 1981. *The New Family and the New Property*. Toronto: Butterworths.

Glenn, M.D. 1993. 'A Plea for Objective Assessment of the Notion of Family Decline'. *Journal of Marriage and the Family* 55:542–4.

Goldstein, J., and C.A. Fenster. 1994. 'Anglo-American Criteria for Resolving Child Custody Disputes from the Eighteenth Century to the Present: Reflections on the Role of Socio-cultural Change'. *Journal of Family History* 19, no. 1:35–56.

Goode, W. 1956. *Women in Divorce*. New York: Free Press.

Gordon, J. 1989. 'Multiple Meanings of Equality: A Case Study in Custody Litigation'. *Canadian Women and the Law* 3, no. 1:256–68.

Gordon, L., and S. McLanahan. 1991. 'Single Parenthood in 1900'. *Journal of Family History* 16, no. 2:97–116.

Grace, E.K.P., and S.M. Vella. 1994. 'Vesting Mothers with Power They Do Not Have: The Non-Offending Parent in Civil Assault Cases; J.(L.A.) v. J.(H.) and J.(J.)'. *Canadian Journal of Women and the Law* 7, no. 1:184–207.

Greenspon, E. 1995. 'Ottawa Backs Off Test-tube Issues'. *Globe and Mail* (28 July):A1, A9.

Greenstein, T.N. 1995. 'Gender Ideology, Marital Disruption, and the Employment of Married Women'. *Journal of Marriage and the Family* 57:31–42.

Grindstaff, C.F. 1986. 'Adolescent Marriage and Childbearing: The Long-Term Economic Outcome, Canada in the 1980s'. Unpublished paper, University of Western Ontario.

Gringlas, M., and M. Weintraub. 1995. 'The More Things Change ... Single Parenting Revisited'. *Journal of Family Issues* 16, no. 1:29–52.

Gucwa-Lesny, E. 1995. 'Which Role the More Difficult: The Situation of Women in the Household'. In *Women: The Past and the New Roles*, Bulletin 1, 125–37. Warsaw: Centre for Europe, Warsaw University, Information and Documentation Unit on the Council of Europe.

Haas, L. 1990. 'Gender Equality and Social Policy: Implications of a Study of Parental Leave in Sweden'. *Journal of Family Issues* 11, no. 4:401–23.

Habib, M. 1995. 'Court Gives Custodial Parents Right to Move'. *Montreal Gazette* (3 April):A14.

Haddad, J. 1986. 'Women and the Welfare State: The Introduction of Mothers' Allowances in Ontario in the 1920s', Unpublished MA thesis, University of Toronto (OISE).

Haig, K. 1967. 'E. Cora Hind'. In *The Clear Spirit: Twenty Canadian Women and Their Times*, edited by M.Q. Innis, 121–41. Toronto: University of Toronto Press.

Haines, M.R. 1990. 'Western Fertility in Mid-Transition: Fertility and Nuptiality in the United States and Selected Nations at the Turn of the Century'. *Journal of Family History* 15, no. 1:23–48.

Handl, J. 1984. 'Chancegleichheit and Segregation: Ein Vorschlag zur Messung ungleicher Chancenstrukturen und ihrer zeitlichen Entwicklung'. *Zeitschrift fuer Soziologie* 13, no. 4:328–45.

Hare, J. 1994. 'Concerns and Issues Faced by Families Headed by a Lesbian Couple'. *Journal of Contemporary Human Service* 75, no. 1:27–35.

Harman, L.D. 1995. 'Family Poverty and Economic Struggles'. In *Canadian Families: Diversity, Conflict and Change*, edited by N. Mandell and A. Duffy, 235–70. Toronto: Harcourt Brace.

Harris, K.M. 1991. 'Teenage Mothers and Welfare Dependency: Working Off Welfare'. *Journal of Family Issues* 12, no. 4:492–518.

Harrison, D., and L. Laliberté. 1994. *No Life Like It: Military Wives in Canada*. Toronto: James Lorimer and Co.

Harrison, M. 1991. 'The Reformed Australian Child Support Scheme: An International Policy Comment'. *Journal of Family Issues* 12, no. 4:439–49.

Harvey, E.B., et al. 1990. 'Toward an Index of Gender Equality'. *Social Indicators Research* 22:299–317.

Hathaway, J.C. 1994. 'Implementation of a Contextualized System of Family Class Immigration'. Discussion paper for the National Consultation on Family Class Immigration, convened by the Department of Citizenship and Immigration, Government of Canada, and the Refugee Law Research Unit, Centre for Refugee Studies, York University, Toronto.

Hawkins, A.J., and D.J. Eggebeen. 1993. 'Are Fathers Fungible? Patterns of Coresident Adult Men in Maritally Disrupted Families and Young Children's Well-being'. *Journal of Marriage and the Family* 53:958–72.

Health Canada. 1993. *Adult Survivors of Child Sexual Abuse*. Ottawa: Health Canada, Family Violence Prevention Division.

Herman, D. 1990. 'Are We Family? Lesbian Rights and Women's Liberation'. *Osgoode Hall Law Journal* 28, no. 4:789–815.

———. 1991. '"Sociologically Speaking": Law, Sexuality and Social Change'. *Journal of Human Justice* 2, no. 2:57–76.

———. 1994. 'A Jurisprudence of One's Own? Ruthann Robson's Lesbian

Legal Theory'. *Canadian Journal of Women and the Law* 7, no. 2:509–22.

Herman, J.L. 1981. *Father-Daughter Incest*. Cambridge: Harvard University Press.

_____. 1992. *Trauma and Recovery*. New York: Basic Books.

Hetherington, E.M., et al. 1978. 'The Aftermath of Divorce'. In *Mother-Child, Father-Child Relations*, edited by J.H. Stevens, Jr, and M. Mathews, 149–76. Washington: National Association for the Education of Young Children.

Hilton, J.M., and V.A. Haldeman. 1991. 'Gender Differences in the Performance of Household Tasks by Adults and Children in Single-Parent and Two-Parent, Two-Earner Families'. *Journal of Family Issues* 12, no. 4:114–30.

Hochschild, A. 1989. *The Second Shift*. New York: Viking.

Hofford, M., et al. 1995. 'Family Violence in Child Custody Statutes: An Analysis of State Codes and Legal Practice'. *Family Law Quarterly* 29, no. 2:197–219.

Holland, W.H., and B.E. Stalbecker-Poutney. 1990. *Cohabitation: The Law in Canada*. Toronto: Carswell.

Holter, H. 1970. *Sex Roles and Social Structure*. Oslo: Universitetsforlaget.

Hudson, J., and B. Galaway, eds. 1993. *Single-Parent Families*. Toronto: Thompson Educational Publishing, Inc.

Hughes, K.A., and H.T.G. Andrews. 1985. 'Children's and Family Rights and the Role of the State in Custody and Child Protection Matters'. In *Justice Beyond Orwell*, edited by R.S. Abella and M.L. Rothman, 365–83. Montreal: Les Editions Yvon Blais Inc.

Hughes, P. 1995. 'Domestic Legal Aid: A Claim to Equality'. *Review of Constitutional Studies* 2, no. 32:203–20.

Human Resources Development. 1994. *Inventory of Income Security Programs in Canada, January 1993*, cat. H75–16/1993E. Hull: Minister of Supply and Services.

Hyde, J.S., et al. 1993. 'Fathers and Parental Leave: Attitudes and Experiences' *Journal of Family Issues* 14, no. 4:616–41.

Inkeles, A. 1981. 1981. 'Modernization and Family Patterns: A Test of Convergence Theory'. In *Conspectus of History* 1, no. 6:31–63.

Institute of Law Research and Reform. 1984. 'Survey of Adult Living Arrangements: A Technical Report', Research Paper #15. Edmonton: Institute of Law Research and Reform.

Ishii-Kuntz, M., and S. Coltrane. 1992. 'Remarriage, Stepparenting, and Household Labor'. *Journal of Family Issues* 13, no. 2:215–33.

Jacobs, F.H., and M.W. Davies. 1991. 'Rhetoric or Reality? Child and

Family Policy in the United States'. *Social Policy Report* 5, no. 4:1–27.

Jaffe, A.J. 1972. 'Labour Force'. *International Encyclopedia of the Social Sciences*, vols 7 and 8, 469–73. New York: MacMillan.

Jenu, D., and M. Gazan. 1989. *Psychosocial Adjustment of Women Who Were Sexually Victimized in Childhood or Adolescence.* Ottawa: Health and Welfare Canada, Family Violence Prevention Division.

Johnston, P. 1983. *Native Children and the Child Welfare System.* Toronto: Canadian Council on Social Development in association with James Lorimer.

Jorgensen, S. 1995. 'Area Comparison Report, 1991 Census'. *Desktop Demographics, v2.51*, Compusearch.

Kaganas, F., and C. Murray. 1991. 'Law Reform and the Family: The New South African Rape-in-Marriage Legislation'. *Journal of Law and Society* 18, no. 3:287–302.

Keating, N., et al. 1994. 'Who's the Family in Family Caregiving?' *La revue canadienne du vieillissement* 13, no. 2:268–87.

Kelly, R.F., and S.H. Ramsey. 1991. 'Poverty, Children, and Public Policies: The Need for Diversity in Programs and Research'. *Journal of Family Issues* 12, no. 4:388–403.

Kertzer, D.I. 1992. 'Child Abandonment in European History: A Symposium'. *Journal of Family History* 17, no. 1:13–19.

Kingston, P.W. 1990. 'Illusions and Ignorance About the Family-Responsive Workplace'. *Journal of Family Issues* 11, no. 4:48–54.

Kitson, G.C., and L.A. Morgan. 1990. 'The Multiple Consequences of Divorce: A Decade Review'. *Journal of Marriage and the Family* 52:913–24.

Klein, T. 1993. 'Soziale Determinanten der Lebenserwartung'. *Kolner Zeitschrift fuer Soziologie und Sozialpsychologie* 45, no. 4:712–30.

Koel, A., et al. 1994. 'Patterns of Relitigation in the Postdivorce Family'. *Journal of Marriage and the Family* 56:265–77.

Kotkin, M. 1985. 'To Marry or Live Together?' *Lifestyles: A Journal of Changing Patterns* 7, no. 3:156–70.

Krane, J.E. 1994. 'The Transformation of Women into Mother Protectors: An Examination of Child Protection Practices in Cases of Child Sexual Abuse'. Unpublished Ph.D. thesis, Faculty of Social Work, University of Toronto.

Krashinsky, M. 1977. *Day Care and Public Policy in Ontario.* Toronto: University of Toronto Press.

Kroll, I.T., and L.B. Warneke. 1995. 'The Dynamics of Sexual Orientation and Adolescent Suicide: A Comprehensive Review and Developmental Perspective'. Unpublished paper, University of

Calgary and University of Alberta.

Kruk, E. 1993. *Divorce and Disengagement: Patterns of Fatherhood within and Beyond Marriage.* Halifax: Fernwood Publishing.

Kuhn, T.S. 1971. *The Structure of Scientific Revolutions*, 2nd ed. Chicago: University of Chicago Press.

Lalonde-Graton, M. 1985. *La p'tite histoire des garderies.* Saint-Lambert: Regroupement des garderies de la region Six C.

Lambda Legal Defense and Education Fund, Inc. 1992. *Domestic Partnership: Issues and Legislation.* New York and Los Angeles: Lambda Legal Defense and Education Fund.

LaNovara, P. 1993. *A Portrait of Families in Canada.* Ottawa: Statistics Canada.

LaRossa, R. 1977. *Conflict and Power in Marriage.* Beverly Hills: Sage.

_____, and D.C. Reitzes. 1993. 'Continuity and Change in Middle-Class Fatherhood, 1925–1939: The Culture-Conduct Connection'. *Journal of Marriage and the Family* 55:445–68.

Lesbian and Gay Immigration Task Force. 1992. 'Growing Old Together'. Brief to Bernard Valcourt, Minister of Employment and Immigration, May.

_____. 1993. *Regulations for Same-Sex Sponsorship: Looking at the Australian Model.* Vancouver: Lesbian and Gay Immigration Task Force.

Lesbian and Gay Legal Rights Service. 1993. 'The Bride Wore Pink: Legal Recognition of Our Relationships'. *Australian Gay and Lesbian Law Journal* 3:67–101.

Leslie, L.A., et al. 1991. 'Responsibility for Children: The Role of Gender and Employment'. *Journal of Family Issues* 12, no. 2:197–210.

Levasseur, K. 1995a. *Common-Law Relationships in Canada.* Ottawa: Department of Justice.

_____. 1995b. *Common-Law Relationships in Ontario: An Analysis of Statute and Case Law.* Ottawa: Department of Justice.

Lewis, J., and G. Åström. 1992. 'Equality, Difference, and State Welfare: Labor Market and Family Policy in Sweden'. *Feminist Studies* 18, no. 1:59–87.

L'Heureux-Dubé, C. 1993. 'Recent Developments in Family Law'. *Canadian Journal of Women and the Law* 6, no. 2:269–77.

Light, B., and R.R. Pierson. 1990. *No Easy Road: Women in Canada, 1920s to 1960s.* Toronto: New Hogtown Press.

Littleton, C.A. 1993. 'Reconstructing Sexual Equality'. In *Feminist Jurisprudence*, edited by P. Smith, 110–35. New York: Oxford University Press.

Loomis, L.S., and A. Booth. 1995. 'Multigenerational Caregiving and

Well-being: The Myth of the Beleaguered Sandwich Generation'. *Journal of Family Issues* 16:131–48.

Loscocco, K.A., and K.T. Leicht. 1993. 'Gender, Work-Family Linkages and Economic Success among Small-Business Owners'. *Journal of Marriage and the Family* 55:875–87.

Maccoby, E.E., C.E. Depner, and R.H. Mnookin. 1990. 'Coparenting in the Second Year after Divorce'. *Journal of Marriage and the Family* 52:141–55.

McConnachie, K. 1983. 'Methodology in the Study of Women in History: A Case Study of Helen MacMurchy, MD'. *Ontario History* 5, no. 1:61–70.

McDaniel, S.A. 1990. 'Towards Family Policy in Canada with Women in Mind'. *Feminist Perspectives* no. 17. Ottawa: Canadian Research Institute for the Advancement of Women.

McKie, C., and K. Thompson, eds. 1990. *Canadian Social Trends*. Toronto: Thompson Educational Publishing.

McKie, D., et al. 1983. *Divorce: Law and the Family in Canada*. Ottawa: Statistics Canada, Research and Analysis Division.

Mackie, M. 1995. 'Gender in the Family: Changing Patterns'. In *Canadian Families, Diversity, Conflict and Change*, edited by N. Mandell and A. Duffy, 45–76. Toronto: Harcourt Brace.

McKinney, J. 1966. *Constructive Typology and Social Theory*. New York: Appelton-Century-Crofts.

McLanahan, S., and I. Garfinkel. 1993. 'Single Motherhood in the United States: Growth, Problems and Policies'. In *Single-Parent Families*, edited by J. Hudson and B. Galaway, 15–30. Toronto: Thompson Educational Publishing.

McLeod, E.M. 1975. *A Study of Child Care Services at Canadian Universities*. Ottawa: Association of Universities and Colleges of Canada.

Majury, D. 1991. 'Equality and Discrimination According to the Supreme Court of Canada'. *Canadian Journal of Women and the Law* 4, no. 2:407–39.

_____. 1994. 'Refashioning the Unfashionable: Claiming Lesbian Identities in the Legal Context'. *Canadian Journal of Women and the Law* 7, no. 2:286–317.

Maloney, M. 1989. 'Women and the Income Tax Act: Marriage, Motherhood and Divorce'. *Canadian Journal of Women and the Law* 3, no. 1:182–210.

Maltz, W. 1992. *The Sexual Healing Journey: A Guide for Survivors of Sexual Abuse*. New York: Harper Perennial.

Manke, B., et al. 1994. 'The Three Corners of Domestic Labor: Mothers', Fathers', and Children's Weekday and Weekend Housework'. *Journal of Marriage and the Family* 56 (August):657–68.

Marks, N.F., and S.S. McLanahan. 1993. 'Gender, Family Structure, and Social Support among Parents'. *Journal of Marriage and the Family* 55:481–93.

Marx, K. 1961. *Selected Writings in Sociology and Social Philosophy*. Harmondsworth: Penguin.

Mayfield, M.I. 1990. *Work-Related Child Care in Canada*. Ottawa: Minister of Labour.

Melton, R.L. 1990–1. 'Legal Rights of Unmarried Heterosexual and Homosexual Couples and Evolving Definitions of "Family"'. *University of Louisville School of Law Journal of Family Law* 29, no. 2:497–517.

Meyer, D.R., and S. Garasky. 1993. 'Custodial Fathers: Myths, Realities, and Child Support Policy'. *Journal of Marriage and the Family* 55:73–89.

Meyer, D.R., E. Phillips, and N.L. Maritato. 1991. 'The Effects of Replacing Income Tax Deductions for Children with Children's Allowances: A Microsimulation'. *Journal of Family Issues* 12, no. 4:467–91.

Michelson, W. 1985. *From Sun to Sun: Daily Obligations and Community Structure in the Lives of Employed Women and Their Families*. Totowa: Rowman and Allanheld.

Miller, J. 1991. 'Child Welfare and Role of Women: A Feminist Perspective'. *American Journal of Orthopsychiatry* 61, no. 4:592–8.

Mitchell, L.M. 1993. 'The Routinization of the Other: Ultrasound, Women and the Fetus'. In *Misconceptions: The Social Construction of Choice and the New Reproductive and Genetic Technologies*, edited by G. Basen, M. Eichler, and A. Lippman, 146–60. Prescott: Voyageur.

Montagnes, A. 1967. 'Alice Wilson'. In *The Clear Spirit: Twenty Canadian Women and Their Times*, edited by M.Q. Innis, 260–78. Toronto: University of Toronto Press.

Montreal Day Nursery. 1960. *The Montreal Day Nursery*. Montreal: Montreal Day Nursery.

Monture, P.A. 1989. 'A Vicious Circle: Child Welfare and the First Nations'. *Canadian Journal of Women and the Law* 3, no. 1:1–17.

Morin, S. 1977. 'Heterosexual Bias in Psychological Research on Lesbianism and Male Homosexuality'. *American Psychologist* (August):629–37.

Muzzin, L., G. Brown, and R. Hornosty. 1995. 'Gender, Educational Credentials, Contributions and Career Advancement: Result of a Follow-up Study in Hospital Pharmacy'. *Canadian Review of Sociology and Anthropology* 32, no. 2:151–68.

National Council of Welfare. 1994. *A Blueprint for Social Security Reform.* Ottawa: National Council of Welfare.

_____. 1995a. *Poverty Profile 1993.* Ottawa: National Council of Welfare.

_____. 1995b. *The 1995 Budget and Block Funding.* Ottawa: National Council of Welfare.

National Forum on Family Security. 1993. *Family Security in Insecure Times.* Ottawa: Canadian Council on Social Development.

Nett, E.M. 1988. *Canadian Families Past and Present.* Toronto: Butterworths.

Newcomb, M.D. 1983. 'Relationship Qualities of Those Who Live Together'. *Alternative Lifestyles* 6, no. 2:78–102.

Newman, K. 1993. *Progress Postpone: Abortion in Europe in the 1990s.* London: International Planned Parenthood Federation (Europe Region).

Niemi, I., and B. Anachkova. 1992. 'Sharing of Housework'. In *Housework Time in Bulgaria and Finland,* edited by L.M. Kirjavainen, 12–40. Helsinki: Statistics Finland.

Niemi, I., et al. 1991. *Time Use in Finland, Latvia, Lithuania and Russia.* Helsinki: Central Statistical Office of Finland.

Nock, S.L. 1995. 'A Comparison of Marriages and Cohabiting Relationships'. *Journal of Family Issues* 16, no. 1:53–76.

Novac, S.I. 1994. 'Boundary Disputes: Sexual Harassment and the Gendered Relations of Residential Tenancy'. Unpublished Ph.D. thesis, Graduate Department of Education, University of Toronto.

O'Brien, C.A., and L. Weir. 1995. 'Lesbians and Gay Men Inside and Outside Families'. In *Canadian Families, Diversity, Conflict and Change,* edited by N. Mandell and A. Duffy, 111–40. Toronto: Harcourt Brace.

O'Connell, H. 1994. *Women and the Family.* London: Zed Books.

O'Hara, B. 1993. *Working Harder Isn't Working.* Vancouver: New Star Books.

Okin, S.M. 1989. *Justice, Gender and the Family.* New York: Basic Books.

Ontario Law Reform Commission. 1993. *Report on the Rights and Responsibilities of Cohabitants under the Family Law Act.* Toronto: Ontario Law Reform Commission.

Ontario Social Assistance Review Committee. 1988. *Transitions.* Toronto: Ministry of Community and Social Services.

Orton, M.J., and E. Rosenblatt. 1986. *Adolescent Pregnancy in Ontario: Progress in Prevention,* report 2. Toronto: Planned Parenthood Ontario.

_____. 1991. *Adolescent Pregnancy in Ontario 1976–1986: Extending Access to Prevention Reduces Abortions and Births to the Unmarried,* report 3.

Hamilton: School of Social Work, McMaster University.

_____. 1993. *Sexual Health for Youth: Creating a Three-Sector Network in Ontario*, report 4. Toronto: Ontario Study of Adolescent Pregnancy and Sexually Transmitted Diseases, Faculty of Social Work, University of Toronto.

Orwell, G. [1949] 1962. *Nineteen Eight-four*. Harmondsworth: Penguin.

Ostry, S. 1968. *The Female Worker in Canada*. Ottawa: Dominion Bureau of Statistics.

Pahl, J. 1989. *Money and Marriage*. New York: St Martin's Press.

Papanek, H. 1973. 'Men, Women and Work: Reflections on the Two-Person Career'. In *Changing Women in a Changing Society*, edited by J. Huber, 852–71. Chicago: University of Chicago Press.

Parliamentary Subcommittee on Equality Rights. 1985. *Equality for All*. Ottawa: Minister of Supply and Services Canada.

Parson, T. 1955. 'Family Structures and the Socialization of the Child'. In *Family, Socialization and Interaction Process*, edited by T. Parsons and R.F. Bales, 35–131. Glencoe: Free Press.

_____, E.A. Shils, and J. Olds. 1951. 'Values, Motives and Systems of Action'. In *Towards a General Theory of Action*, edited by T. Parsons and R.F. Bales, 47–278. Cambridge: Harvard University Press.

Parvikko, T. 1991. 'Conceptions of Gender Equality: Similarity and Difference'. In *Equality Politics and Gender*, edited by E. Meehan and S. Sevenhuijsen, 36–51. London: Sage.

Pask, D.E. 1989. 'The Effect on Maintenance of Custody Sharing'. *Canadian Journal of Women and the Law* 1, no. 2:155–81.

_____. 1993. 'Family Law and Policy in Canada: Economic Implications for Single Custodial Mothers and Their Children'. In *Single-Parent Families: Perspectives on Research and Policy*, edited by J. Hudson and B. Galaway, 185–202. Toronto: Thompson Educational Publishing.

_____, and M.L. McCall, eds. 1989. *How Much and Why? Economic Implications of Marriage Breakdown: Spousal and Child Support*. Calgary: Canadian Research Institute for Law and the Family.

Pateman, C. 1992. 'Equality, Difference, Subordination: The Politics of Motherhood and Women's Citizenship'. In *Beyond Equality and Difference: Citizenship, Feminist Politics and Female Subjectivity*, edited by G. Bock and S. James, 17–31. London: Routledge and Kegan Paul.

Pedersen, M.H. 1991–2. 'Denmark: Homosexual Marriages and New Rules Regarding Separation and Divorce'. *Journal of Family Law* 30:289–93.

Peplau, L.A. 1991. 'Lesbian and Gay Relationships'. In *Homosexuality: Research Implications for Public Policy*, edited by J.C. Gonsiorek and J.D. Weinrich, 177–96. Newbury Park, CA: Sage.

Phillips, L., and M. Young. 1995. 'Sex, Tax and the Charter: A Review of *Thibaudeau v. Canada*'. *Review of Constitutional Studies* 2, no. 2:221–304.

Pierson, R.R. 1986. *'They're Still Women After All': The Second World War and Canadian Womanhood*. Toronto: McClelland and Stewart.

Pike, R. 1975. 'Legal Access and the Incidence of Divorce in Canada: A Socio-historical Analysis'. *Canadian Review of Sociology and Anthropology* 12, no. 2:115–33.

Pilon, S. 1993. 'La pension aimentaire comme facteur d'appauvrissement des femmes et des enfants en droit quebecois'. *Canadian Journal of Women and the Law* 6, no. 2:349–70.

Polikoff, N. 1983. 'Gender and Child-Custody Determinations: Exploding the Myths'. In *Families, Politics, and Public Policy: A Feminist Dialogue on Women and the State*, edited by I. Diamond, 183–202. New York: Longman.

Popenoe, D. 1993. 'American Family Decline, 1960–1990: A Review and Appraisal'. *Journal of Marriage and the Family* 55:527–55.

_____. 1994. 'The Family Condition of America: Cultural Change and Public Policy'. In *Values and Public Policy*, edited by H.J. Aaron, T.E. Mann, and T. Taylor, 81–112. Washington: Brookings Institute.

Pulkingham, J. 1989. 'From Public Provision to Privatisation: The Crisis in Welfare Reassessed'. *Sociology* 23, no. 3:387–407.

Raabe, P.H. 1990. 'The Organizational Effects of Workplace Family Policies'. *Journal of Family Issues* 11, no. 4:477–91.

Rand, A. [1946] 1961. *Anthem*. New York: Signet Books.

Ransel, D. 1992. 'Child Abandonment in European History: A Symposium'. *Journal of Family History* 17, no. 1:19–22.

Richardson, J. 1988. *Court-Based Divorce Mediation in Four Canadian Cities: An Overview of Research Results*. Ottawa: Minister of Supply and Services.

Ridley, C.A., et al. 1978. 'Cohabitation: Does It Make for a Better Marriage'. *The Family Coordinator* (April):129–36.

Rindfuss, R., and E.H. Stephen. 1990. 'Marital Noncohabitation: Separation Does Not Make the Heart Grow Fonder'. *Journal of Marriage and the Family* 52:259–70.

Ristock, J.L. 1991. 'Beyond Ideologies: Understanding Violence in Lesbian Relationships'. *Canadian Women's Studies* 12, no. 1:74–9.

_____. 1994. '"And Justice for All?" ... The Social Context of Legal Responses to Abuse in Lesbian Relationships'. *Canadian Journal of Women and the Law* 7, no. 2:415–30.

Roberts, J.V. 1994. 'Criminal Justice Processing of Sexual Assault Cases'. *Juristat Service Bulletin* 14, no. 7 (March):1–20.

Robinson, I., et al. 1991. 'Twenty Years of the Sexual Revolution, 1965–1985: An Update'. *Journal of Marriage and the Family* 53:216–20.

Robles, A., and S.C. Watkins. 1993. 'Immigration and Family Separation in the US at the Turn of the Twentieth Century'. *Journal of Family History* 18, no. 3:191–211.

Robson, R. 1994. 'Resisting the Family: Repositioning Lesbians in Legal Theory'. *Signs* 19, no. 4:975–96.

Rodgers, K. 1994. 'Wife Assault: The Findings of a National Survey'. *Juristat Service Bulletin* 14, no. 9 (March):1–21.

Rothman, B.K. 1989. 'Women as Fathers: Motherhood and Childcare under a Modified Patriarchy'. *Gender and Society* 3:89–104.

Royal Commission on New Reproductive Technologies. 1993. *Proceed with Care*, 2 vols. Ottawa: Minister of Government Services.

Rubin, L.B. 1985. *Just Friends: The Role of Friendship in Our Lives*. New York: Harper and Row.

Rudd, N.M., et al. 1990. 'Welfare Receipt among Black and White Adolescent Mothers: A Longitudinal Perspective'. *Journal of Family Issues* 11, no. 3:334–52.

Rusk, P. 1993. 'Same-Sex Spousal Benefits and the Evolving Conception of Family'. *University of Toronto Law Review* 53:170–85.

Russell, D.E.H. 1982. *Rape in Marriage*. New York: Collier Books.

_____. 1986. *The Secret Trauma: Incest in the Lives of Girls and Women*. New York: Basic Books.

Ryder, B. 1990. 'Equality Rights and Sexual Orientation: Confronting Heterosexual Family Privilege'. *Canadian Journal of Family Law* 9:39–97.

Sachdev, P. 1988. *International Handbook on Abortion*. New York: Greenwood Press.

Samuelsson, G., and O. Dehlin. 1993. 'Family Network and Mortality: Survival Changes through the Lifespan of an Entire Age Cohort'. *International Journal of Aging and Human Development* 37, no. 4:277–95.

Sanchez, L. 1994. 'Material Resources, Family Structure Resources, and Husbands' Housework Participation: A Cross-National Comparison'. *Journal of Family Issues* 15, no. 3:379–402.

Saraceno, C. 1990. 'Women, Family, and the Law, 1750–1942. *Journal of Family History* 15, no. 4:427–42.

Schmitz, C. 1995. 'Custodial Parent Can Move, Despite Joint Custody'. *Lawyer's Weekly* 15:08 (23 June):4.

Schneider, M.S. 1986. 'The Relationships of Cohabiting Lesbian and Heterosexual Couples: A Comparison'. *Psychology of Women Quarterly*

10:234–9.

Seccombe, W. 1993. *Weathering the Storm: Working-Class Families from the Industrial Revolution to the Fertility Decline*. London: Verso.

Sevenhuijsen, S. 1991. 'Justice, Moral Reasoning and the Politics of Child Custody'. In *Equality Politics and Gender*, edited by E. Meehan and S. Sevenhuijsen, 88–103. London: Sage.

Sev'er, A. 1992. *Women and Divorce in Canada: A Sociological Analysis*. Toronto: Canadian Scholars Press.

Shelton, B.A., and D. John. 1993. 'Does Marital Status Make a Difference? Housework among Married and Cohabiting Men and Women'. *Journal of Family Issues* 14:401–20.

Siim, B. 1991. 'Welfare State, Gender Politics and Equality Politics: Women's Citizenship in the Scandinavian Welfare States'. In *Equality Politics and Gender*, edited by E. Meehan and S. Sevenhuijsen, 175–92. London: Sage.

Skrypnek, B.J., and J.E. Fast. Forthcoming. 'Balancing Work and Family in Canada: Family Needs, Collective Solutions'.

Sleeth, P., and J. Barnsley. 1989. *Recollecting Our Lives: Women's Experience of Childhood Sexual Abuse*. Vancouver: Press Gang.

Snell, J.G. 1991. *In the Shadow of the Law: Divorce in Canada, 1900–1939*. Toronto: University of Toronto Press.

Stacey, J. 1993. 'Good Riddance to "The Family": A Response to David Popenoe'. *Journal of Marriage and the Family* 55, no. 3:545–7.

Stafford, R., et al. 1977. 'The Division of Labour among Cohabiting and Married Couples'. *Journal of Marriage and the Family* 43–55.

Starrels, M.E. 1992. 'The Evolution of Workplace Family Policy Research'. *Journal of Family Issues* 13, no. 3:259–78.

Statistics Canada. 1992. *Divorce 1990*, cat. 82-003S17. Ottawa: Minister of Industry, Science and Technology.

_____. 1993a. *Births, 1991*, cat. 84-210. Ottawa: Minister of Industry, Science and Technology.

_____. 1993b. *A Portrait of Families in Canada*, cat. 89-523E. Ottawa: Minister of Industry, Science and Technology.

_____. 1993c. *The Daily*, cat. 11–001E (18 November).

_____. 1994a. *Characteristics of Dual-Earner Families*, cat. 13-215. Ottawa: Minister of Industry, Science and Technology.

_____. 1994b. *National Income and Expenditure Accounts* (quarterly estimates, fourth quarter, 1993), cat. 13-001, vol. 41, no. 4. Ottawa: Minister of Industry, Science and Technology.

_____. 1995. *Women in Canada: A Statistical Report*, cat. 89-503E. Ottawa: Minister Responsible for Statistics Canada.

Stets, J.E. 1991. 'Cohabiting and Marital Aggression: The Role of Social Isolation'. *Journal of Marriage and the Family* 53:669–80.

Straver, C.J. 1981. 'Unmarried Couples, Different from Marriage?' *Alternative Lifestyles* 4, no. 1:430–74.

Symons, E. 1991. 'Under Fire: Canadian Women in Combat'. *Canadian Journal of Women and the Law* 4, no. 2:477–511.

Tatchell, P. 1992. *Europe in the Pink: Lesbian and Gay Equality in the New Europe*. London: GMP Publishing.

Thomlison, R.J., and C.E. Foote. 1991. 'Children and the Law in Canada: The Shifting Balance of Children's, Parents', and the State's Rights'. In *Continuity & Change in Marriage & Family*, edited by J.E. Veevers, 439–49. Toronto: Holt, Rinehart and Winston of Canada.

Thompson, L. 1991. 'Family Work: Women's Sense of Fairness'. *Journal of Family Issues* 12, no. 2:181–96.

_____. 1993. 'Conceptualizing Gender in Marriage: The Case of Marital Care'. *Journal of Marriage and the Family* 55:557–69.

Tilly, L.A. 1992. 'Child Abandonment in European History: A Symposium'. *Journal of Family History* 17, no. 1:1–7.

Traustadottir, R. 1991. 'Mothers Who Care: Gender, Disability, and Family Life'. *Journal of Family Issues* 12, no. 2:211–28.

Trovato, F. 1991. 'Sex, Marital Status, and Suicide in Canada: 1951–1981'. *Sociological Perspectives* 34, no. 4:427–45.

_____, and G. Lauris. 1989. 'Marital Status and Mortality in Canada: 1951–1981'. *Journal of Marriage and the Family* 51:907–22.

Tuttle, R.C. 1994. 'Determinants of Fathers' Participation in Child Care'. *International Journal of Sociology of the Family* 24:113–25.

United Nations. 1971. *Demographic Yearbook*. New York: United Nations.

_____. 1983. *Demographic Yearbook*. New York: United Nations.

_____. 1992. *Demographic Yearbook*. New York: United Nations.

_____. 1993. *Human Development Report 1993*. New York: Oxford University Press.

Urquhart, M.C., and K.A.H. Buckley, eds. 1983. *Historical Statistics of Canada*, 2nd ed., edited by F.H. Leacy, cat. CS11–516E. Ottawa: Minister of Supply and Services.

Valpy, M. 1995. 'Creepy Genetics Unchecked'. *Globe and Mail* (28 July):A15.

Vanier Institute of the Family. 1993. *Inventory of Family-Supportive Policies and Programs in Federal, Provincial and Territorial Jurisdictions*. Ottawa: Vanier Institute of the Family.

_____. 1994. *Profiling Canada's Families*. Ottawa: Vanier Institute of the Family.

Van Kirk, S. 1992. '"The Custom of the Country": An Examination of Fur Trade Marriage Practices'. In *Canadian Family History*, edited by B. Bradbury, 67–92. Toronto: Copp Clark Pitman.

van Wel, F. 1994. '"I Count My Parents among My Best Friends": Youths' Bonds with Parents and Friends in the Netherlands'. *Journal of Marriage and the Family* 56:835–43.

Veevers, J.E., ed. 1991. *Continuity & Change in Marriage & Family*. Toronto: Holt, Rinehart and Winston of Canada.

Vicinus, M., ed. 1973. *Suffer and Be Still: Women in the Victorian Age*. Bloomington: Indiana University Press.

Waaldijk, K. 1993. 'The Legal Situation in the Member States'. In *Homosexuality, a European Community Issue: Essays on Lesbian and Gay Rights in European Law and Policy*, edited by K. Waaldijk and A. Clapham, 71–130. Dordrecht: Martinus Nijhoff.

Wachtel, A. 1988. *The Impact of Child Sexual Abuse in Developmental Perspective: A Model and Literature Review*. Ottawa: Health and Welfare Canada, Family Violence Prevention Division.

Ward, D. 1990. 'Gender, Time, and Money in Caregiving'. In *Scholarly Inquiry for Nursing Practice: An International Journal* 4, no. 3:223–35.

Ward, R.A. 1993. 'Marital Happiness and Household Equity in Later Life'. *Journal of Marriage and the Family* 55:427–38.

Warde, A., and K. Hetherington. 1993. 'A Changing Domestic Division of Labour: Issues of Measurement and Interpretation'. *Work, Employment & Society* 7, no. 31:23–45.

Waring, M. 1988. *If Women Counted: A New Feminist Economics*. New York: Harper and Row.

Warneke, L. 1995. 'Sexual Orientation: A Reconsideration of Issues'. Unpublished paper.

Weitzman, L.J. 1985. *The Divorce Revolution: The Unexpected Social and Economic Consequences for Women and Children in America*. New York: Free Press.

Weston, K. 1991. *Families We Choose: Lesbians, Gays, Kinship*. New York: Columbia University Press.

Whyte, W.H. 1956. *The Organization Man*. New York: Simon and Schuster.

Wilson, B. 1985. 'State Intervention in the Family'. In *Justice Beyond Orwell*, edited by R.S. Abella and M.L. Rothman, 353–63. Montreal: Les Editions Yvon Blais Inc.

Wilson, B.F., and S.C. Clarke. 1992. 'Remarriages: A Demographic Profile'. *Journal of Family Issues* 13, no. 2:123–41.

Wilson, M., and M. Daly. 1994. 'Spousal Homicide'. *Juristat Service*

Bulletin 14, no. 8:1–14.

Wolf, D.A., and F.A. Sonenstein. 1991. 'Child-Care Use among Welfare Mothers'. *Journal of Family Issues* 12, no. 4:519–36.

Yeager, K.E., and M.H. Strober. 1992. 'Financing Child Care through Local Taxes: One City's Bold Attempt'. *Journal of Family Issues* 13, no. 3:279–96.

Young, C.F.L. 1994. 'Taxing Times for Lesbians and Gay Men: Equality at What Cost?' *Dalhousie Law Journal* 17, no. 32:534–59.

Zamyatin, Y. [1972] 1983. *We.* New York: Avon Books.

Zelditch, M., Jr. 1955. 'Role Differentiation in the Nuclear Family: A Comparative Study'. In *Family, Socialization and Interaction Process,* edited by T. Parsons and R.F. Bale, 307–52. Glencoe: Free Press.

Zielinski, S. 1995. 'Access over Excess: Transcending Captivity and Transportation Disadvantage'. In *Change of Plans: Towards a Non-sexist Sustainable City,* edited by M. Eichler, 131–56. Toronto: Garamond.

Zuckerman, W. 1991. *End of the Road: The World Car Crisis and How We Can Solve It.* Cambridge: Lutterworth Press.

Zweibel, E.B. 1993a. 'Canadian Income Tax Policy on Child Support Payments: Old Rationales Applied to New Realities'. In *Single-Parent Families: Perspectives on Research and Policy,* edited by J. Hudson and B. Galaway, 157–84. Toronto: Thompson Educational Publishing.

———. 1993b. 'Child Support Policy and Child Support Guidelines: Broadening the Agenda'. *Canadian Journal of Women and the Law* 6, no. 32:371–401.

———. 1994. 'Why Family Support Guidelines Are on the Family Law Reform Agenda'. In *Child Support: The Guideline Options,* edited by R. Finnie et al., 157–71. Montreal: Institute for Research on Public Policy.

Index

Note:
*IR refers to the individual responsibility model of the family,
P to the patriarchal model, SR to the social responsibility model.
Notes (pages 194 to 244) are not indexed.*

DATE DUE